WORD ON THE STREET

"If you consistently build and strengthen a business' culture, that culture will consistently build and strengthen your business. Jim Knight's book, Culture That Rocks, aims square at the many challenges surrounding this quest, and provides insight for any leader looking for ways to build stronger, happier and more productive teams."

- Jim Sullivan
CEO, Sullivision & Author of *Multiunit Leadership* and *Fundamentals*

"Jim Knight is THE true Rock Star! In today's hyper-fast and competitive business environment the one true competitive advantage for a company is their culture. Jim captures the best of the best in culture and presents the blueprint for any company to create a 'culture that rocks.' He has given every leader in business the gift of understanding what it takes to build, lead and grow cultures that make a difference. This is the one book with the perfect lyrics for creating cultural success!"

- Kathleen Wood
Founder & CEO, Suzy's Swirl and Author of *The Best Shift of Your Life*

"In a world where hype often eclipses substance, you have found 'true north.' Jim Knight pours out wisdom and practical advice culled from decades in the trenches at Hard Rock and interlaces it with broad industry experiences as a consultant and trainer in hospitality. Despite the rich content in Culture That Rocks, Jim finds a way to transfix, entertain and transform. If this book were a rock concert, I would be clamoring for a 5th encore. Thanks, Jim for translating the mysteries of 'culture,' 'employee engagement,' and 'branding' into a memorable, inspiring, and essential tool. Culture That Rocks holds a revered place on my bookshelf."

- Joseph Michelli, Ph.D.
Chief Experience Officer, The Michelli Experience & NY Times #1 Best-Selling Author of *Leading the Starbucks Way, The Zappos Experience* and *The New Gold Standard*

"The sea of sameness that floods the industry workplace and marketplace is the single biggest competitive obstacle to both established and fledgling brands. Culture That Rocks is the antidote. Jim Knight has the experience, passion, vision and heart to tap into the emotional side of service, and knows how to leverage the employees who think and act like 'rock stars.' I cannot imagine a more relevant book for any service sector leader to make a well thumbed, annotated and, most of all, implemented template for elevating or renewing your business."

- Joni Thomas Doolin
Founder & CEO, People Report

"Finding, defining and living your personal or brand culture all the time is rarely an easy journey. Culture That Rocks provides a great roadmap that has the potential to change your personal and brand culture forever."

- Louis Basille
Founder & CEO, Wildflower Bread Company

"Culture That Rocks is the most original and unique addition to a very over crowded field of leadership and culture books written over the past ten years. It brings a very useable, easily read set of stories combined with facts and work templates that provide action ideas to any organization that must rely on PEOPLE to deliver their products through exceptional culture and service! If your organization needs engaged, effective people, then you need this book."

- Harry Bond
Chairman, Monical's Pizza Corporation

"Culture That Rocks is an excellent, practical guide that provides a roadmap for long-term success. This book changes attitudes and reminds us what is really important—OUR PEOPLE. In our crazy, hectic world, it's easy to forget that nothing inspires results and high-level commitment more than an engaged team of cultural ambassadors. Jim Knight challenges you to evaluate your own organization, ask yourself the tough questions and figure out how you can make a positive impact. Engaging and Transformative—everyone can learn something from this great book!"

- Paul Hineman
Executive VP, National Restaurant Association

"Right from the introduction, you can get the sense that you're about to peer into the inner workings of a business that is special. Culture That Rocks does not disappoint. Jim Knight's illuminating exploration of what made the Hard Rock Cafe one of this generation's most successful brands is not only fascinating, but offers practical guidance for both current and emerging leaders. With organizational culture becoming THE differentiator in a competitive global marketplace, this book should be at the top of your reading list."

- Paul Meshanko
Founder, Legacy Business Cultures & Author of *The Respect Effect*

"Culture That Rocks is an eclectic mix of storytelling and practical advice. This how-to business book is full of examples, philosophies and best practices designed to inspire leaders to amp up their company's culture in every area. Like Hard Rock's brand attributes, Jim's approach in this book is authentic, passionate, irreverent and unpredictable...all vital differentiators in today's social media driven world where all players have access to competitive data and insights. Jim was truly our culture guru and people development rock star. His passion for excellence is woven into every page of this book. Enjoy the ride...!"

- Hamish Dodds
President & CEO, Hard Rock International

"There are people that were meant to be the front man of a band. They command the audience, inspire minds and can move people. Jim is the front man for creating a Culture That Rocks. He was born for this and this book is him, in print: awesome, intelligent and authentic. He's done it, written it and you need to get it. Rock on!"

- Scott Stratten
Wannabe Rock Star & Best-Selling Author of *UnMarketing*

"Jim Knight's approach to service and hospitality is not just a series of best practices for any company where he has demonstrated years of successes—it's a way of living, building a culture and running a business that everyone can and should follow and practice. Jim has lived it, implemented it and taught it for decades. On being the best at creating a culture of service, Culture That Rocks will inspire you and show you the way."

- Kat Cole
President, Cinnabon

"Culture That Rocks is a book that truly rocks! It gets to the core of what is needed to make cultural shifts in organizations to becoming highly engaged and well branded. As a musician, software developer and creator of teams and organizations, I have a deep respect for Jim Knight and this new book, because it celebrates the creative, extraordinary individual and organization. It raises up those who want to go above and beyond, challenge the status quo, and become the very best in the world. Buy this book and allow it to spread like wildfire in your organization—let it ignite sparks in those who are dampened by the malaise of corporate America and build a fire for all to perform at their highest and best."

- Louis Carter
Founder & CEO, Best Practice Institute

"Fostering a culture that truly engages frontline workers with paying customers is critical to orchestrating compelling experiences. For two decades, Jim Knight has worked tirelessly in the trenches of training and development—the mosh pit of 'human resources'—for one of the most recognizable and memorable brands on the planet. His guidance in Culture That Rocks is sure to help wake up any organization in need of energizing its soul."

- Jim Gilmore
CEO, Strategic Horizons LLP, Speaker &
Co-Author of *The Experience Economy* and *Authenticity: What Consumers Really Want*

CULTURE THAT ROCKS
How to Revolutionize Your Company's Culture

JIM KNIGHT

CULTURE THAT ROCKS
How to Revolutionize Your Company's Culture

Published by:
Knight Speaker LLC
1527 Hawkesbury Ct.
Winter Garden, FL 34787

CultureThatRocks.com
KnightSpeaker.com
@KnightSpeaker

First Edition: October 2014

Jacket Design by Chris Reed/Heidi Brown
Photography by Jill Harper (Digital Brand Makeover) and Kelly Canova

ISBN 978-0-9903386-0-4

Printed in the United States of America

Text printed utilizing lead free soy ink, on recycled stock from the New Page Corporation mill, which is certified in accordance with the leading sustainable forest chain of custody certification bodies.

This book is dedicated to Alec & Sydney –
who revolutionized my culture and rocked my world.

Special thanks to the following, who each directly supported me in some way along the journey to craft *Culture That Rocks*: Troy, my Mom & Dad, Clinton Anderson, Brianna Barrick, Peter Beaudrault, Harry Bond, Hamish Dodds, Monique Donahue, Molly Fletcher, Alie Gaffan, Jim Gilmore, Donna Goldwasser, Brandon Hill, Paul Hineman, Amanda Hite, Matt & Maxine Kelly, Michael Kneidinger, Beth Mahoney, Alison McCue, Rob Paterkiewicz, Chris Reed, Nick Sarillo, Jennifer Swan, Steve Routhier, TJ Schier, Mike & Carol Shipley, Teresa Siriani, Jim Sullivan, Ari Weinzweig, Axum Coffee and Hard Rock International.

Early-in-life thank yous go to Carole Sims, Marvel Comics and Tom Peters. As an English teacher, a printed visual fantasy land and a service business guru, respectively, each of these influences established the platform for my love of writing and impacting cultures.

An extra nod goes to Kathleen Wood, who became a dear friend and career mentor for me during my transition into author and entrepreneurship. Channeling her words, Kathleen helped me to "aspire higher."

Much appreciation goes to Heidi Brown, who patiently brought the book to life with her fantastic layout & design skills.

Finally, big time thanks goes to Justin Spizman, my editor, who challenged me, kept me on the straight & narrow and patiently helped me organize my thoughts into more coherent language. Justin made me a better storyteller.

TABLE OF CONTENTS

	Forward	1
Sound Check		3
Chapter 1	For Those About to Rock	5
Chapter 2	Become the Catalyst	11
Chapter 3	Bands & Brands Alike	21
Chapter 4	The Leadership Effect	31
Chapter 5	The True Differentiator	45
Chapter 6	Be the Chocolate	57
Chapter 7	Culture Warriors	67
Chapter 8	Funerals, Healthcare & Hospitality	83
Chapter 9	Rock Stars vs. Lip-synchers	101
Chapter 10	In Search of…3C Employees	117
Chapter 11	The Island of Misfit Toys	131
Chapter 12	Experiences & Individuality as Weapons	141
Chapter 13	Comic Book Communication	157
Chapter 14	The Rise of the Machines	175
Chapter 15	Purpose is Instrumental	187
Chapter 16	Communicate Like Crazy	209
Chapter 17	Profitable Growth, Promotable People	229
Encore	Cultural Nirvana	251
	Index	255

FORWARD

I never worked for Hard Rock Cafe. As the CEO of TGI Friday's and President of Applebee's, I competed with Hard Rock literally around the globe. In the early 90's, as casual dining was exploding in the US, it was in its infancy in the global market place.

Just as quick service competitors looked for McDonald's in each country they entered, at Friday's we looked, and often found, Hard Rock. Repeatedly, I would discover these successful restaurants that would be popular to not only Yanks and Brits, but the local clientele as well. As I would learn, this is not easy to do. This requires defining culture within cultures that stand for something relevant to locals and travelers alike. I became curious about how they could prosper in so many cultures and countries.

Along the way, I met Jim Knight, with his legendary spikey haircut, always dressed cool and energetic beyond most people I know. At the time, he ran global training and development for the Hard Rock brand. What I came to learn about Jim over time, is that not only was he one of the most passionate brand ambassadors I had ever met, but he was also uniquely different as a professional Human Resource executive.

Jim, as you will learn in this information-packed, inspiring and entertaining book, is an organizational strategist. He defines culture as a broader, more strategic component of organizational success, better than anyone I know. At the heart of Jim's skill set he is a strategic thinker that has a passion for teaching. His background and experience is exceptional, but how he transforms the purpose of an organization into the hearts, minds and actions of the employees is the proof of the magic.

I believe this book will challenge leaders to consider the implications of a greater focus on culture as a strategic imperative in improving or maintaining results. As I have often stated, none of us work for a logo or buy from a logo. Engaged employees and raving customer fans are looking for something more.

Culture That Rocks presents the timeless truth…that leadership and culture do indeed make a difference!

Wallace B. Doolin
Chairman & Founder, TDn2K
(People Report, Black Box Intelligence, White Box Social Intelligence)

Former President & CEO, TGI Friday's
Former President & CEO, Carlson Restaurants Worldwide
Former President, Applebee's
Former Chairman, President & CEO, Buca Di Beppo
Former President & CEO, La Madeleine
Former President & CEO, Flakey Jake's

Board Member: Share Our Strength, Famous Dave's, Splick-It, Phasenext Hospitality and Livelenz

Board Member Emertitus: National Restaurant Association and Past Chairman of the National Restaurant Association's Educational Foundation

SOUND CHECK

"Either I just interviewed for the last time in my life or I just made a horrible mistake."

That's exactly what I thought in April of '91 as I sat in my "New Hire Orientation" on the mezzanine floor of the Hard Rock Cafe in Orlando, Florida.

I was in awe—mouth open, eyes bugged, mind racing and heart pounding. Across from me was a manager who had hair below his shoulders and delivered the company information with his sunglasses on. Beside me hung Eddie Van Halen's 'Frankenstein' guitar, close enough to touch. Ninety decibels of classic Zeppelin were ringing in my ears. Buzzing about was without a doubt the most interesting collection of humans I'd ever seen in one place— every one of them moving at blazing speed. The place was a sensory mosh-pit. It was a rush. And I was immediately hooked.

If Rock 'n' Roll were a tangible thing, this is what I imagined it would look and feel like. The energy, the attitude, the diversity, the sex appeal…wow! What a culture! It was both exhilarating and frightening at the same time. In fact, I wasn't even completely sure if this environment was going to be for me. But as the manager wove through the unbelievable story of the Hard Rock brand, this became much bigger than a new job for me…it ballooned into a cultural lifestyle. And this was just Day 1.

Unbeknownst to me at the time, I would become a part of pop culture. What started out as a summer gig eventually turned into a 21-year love affair with a single brand—and unquestionably the career of a lifetime. A career that hailed from "joining the band" as a staff-level host and evolved through various management positions and corporate training levels until I ultimately landed my final role as an executive for one of the most recognized and respected cultural brands in the world.

My responsibilities as Senior Director of Training & Development for this incredible, global brand ran the gambit of creating, implementing and overseeing every facet of organizational training. This included creating staff-level print manuals, implementing manager-in-training programs, facilitating the instructor-led corporate university, certifying worldwide training locations, producing training videos, directing company e-Learning initiatives, executing leadership transitions and traveling to property locations around the world to deliver on-site classes and measure operational and training standards. During that time, my team received several prestigious awards in various categories, and we were eventually recognized by Training Magazine as one of the Top 125 training departments in the world.

I'm sure luck played a part in my success at Hard Rock, and certainly the backdrop of working in a music-inspired environment provided liberties I might not have had elsewhere. I am convinced, however, the quality of my work, my tenure in the position and the industry recognition I received were all clear results of my hard work, passion and commitment to growing the brand and bettering my skills as a developer of people.

Sometimes I get giddy thinking about the magnitude of my cultural transition. I started out as a restaurant host in a single location, unsure if I could even "hang with the band," and eventually reached a level of responsibility that allowed me to affect and protect one of the world's greatest cultures. That job-of-a-lifetime absolutely rocked my world. And yet now I think it was just the opening act to my headlining career.

Throughout my time as a training professional for Hard Rock and a cultural catalyst for other companies, I've travelled the planet utilizing both persuasion and proven teaching methods to influence cultures in markets that seemed unchangeable. I have networked with thousands of professionals across multiple industries in my quest to learn and teach others to be more effective in their personal lives and professional careers.

While a firestorm ignited in my soul that first day at Hard Rock, the life-changing personal moment during my orientation to the brand was quickly amplified into an evolutionary journey of discovery—and I learned how bold ideas and daring risks can alter the course of an organization's culture.

Are you on a quest to strengthen your company's culture? Then you have in your hands all you will need to start your journey. Among the best practices I've shared in the following pages, I hope you'll find one that becomes the unforgettable hook every great song needs.

Trust me, revolutions are started by a single person with a great idea.

Let's find yours.

1
FOR THOSE ABOUT TO ROCK

"Music is always a reflection of what's going on in the hearts and minds of the culture."
- Tori Amos

Most companies ignore organizational culture. It's not important to them. Business leaders have been conditioned to focus exclusively on strategy and operations, with the hope that a strong culture will eventually be developed once they attain some success. It's totally understandable… and completely wrong.

The reason great brands focus on organizational culture first and foremost is so it will drive the ultimate business success. Focusing exclusively on tactical nuts and bolts will forever keep the company from cultural nirvana— and companies that succumb to this small-time thinking will continue to wallow around in a malaise, constantly pushing the program or strategy-of-the-day to attain any financial success.

Rock star brands understand the difference between the two approaches and seek a higher purpose. They constantly opt for the long-term sustainability of culture versus the limited focus of an annual strategy. As iconic management consultant and writer Peter Drucker once famously put it:

"Culture eats strategy for breakfast."

Drucker was so right. Unlike processes, tool, products and strategies, all of which can be easily copied, culture is unique. So unique, in some cases, that replicating it is too hard for a competitor to even attempt. And that's the advantage. A great organizational culture provides differentiation for consumers and employees alike. And it *should* be hard to copy. But it shouldn't be hard to understand. Therein lies the reason so many businesses ignore culture—they don't understand it.

So, that's where we need to start…understanding what culture is.

I define an organization's culture as simply "a collection of individual behaviors." That's the purest and easiest definition I can think of to really communicate how a brand's culture can be affected.

Some will say that culture is *everything*, while others will insist it is only the outwardly-visible characteristics that truly define the company culture. Claiming that organizational culture is too broad to narrowly define, many won't even try, but then they wonder why their ability to explain it to others—

and it's very existence—tends to be fuzzy. Although I'm in the "culture is everything" camp and do indeed see proof of its existence in every facet of a brand, I have come to believe that all roads lead back to human behavior. Essentially, culture is inherent in the behaviors of a company's employees. Some would like to believe that the culture is defined by a set of behaviors that remain unchanged over time, but they do change because individuals change—they come and go in a brand all the time. Culture change is inevitable. What we want is the *right* culture change.

Surround yourself with the right people, and you'll have the right culture.

I'll share a lot of different elements when it comes to creating a "culture that rocks," many of which may be low-level programs or best practice-driven initiatives that can easily be implemented. But all organizational practices—positive *and* negative—only exist because individuals *make* them happen. Therefore employee behavior will always be home base for us as we journey together toward creating, maintaining, enhancing or even revolutionizing your company's culture.

Remember: culture is only as strong or weak as the employees that collectively make up the heart and soul of the organization.

THE STORY AND THE STEPS

Like you, I know that, to be effective, any new concept on "culture" must be more than some unproven, lofty, warm and fuzzy philosophy. But it also must be more than a shotgun list of examples you can try. The best approach is one that has a symbiotic relationship between the emotional hook of the "why" to do something and the technical practicalities of the "what" and "how" it actually gets done. You need both the story and the steps. I will provide both.

As we weave through bold philosophies like "becoming a culture catalyst," I will provide specific suggestions on how to do that, such as "become great at one or two things first and get some credibility."

I can only provide a singular, personal perspective on where to begin and what to expect in your quest to create or improve your organization's culture, but the steps I outline here are based on a variety of solid observations and experiences accumulated over the last thirty years. Countless business books, years of conferences and sought-after networking opportunities have surely shaped my approach, but many of the key suggestions I will give are based on my personal experiences working for one of the strongest company cultures that exist today.

The power of the Hard Rock brand and its business practices has helped shape many of the ideas I plan to share with you. My passion and commitment for this company and its values runs deep within me and has molded the type of person that I am today. It has certainly influenced the concepts I, and others on my team and in the leadership ranks, have created. No doubt, you will experience some brand-inspired currents and eddies that will carry some of the cultural points I make.

That said, I believe the recommendations I share will apply to you, regardless of your business. Whether you are looking to establish an initial guest service approach for a new company or to re-invigorate and better develop your existing internal or external culture, the concepts here will put you on the right path. Read on to discover the proven best practices that can help you create a blue print for your own "culture that rocks."

This might be one of the hardest things you will ever do. But when it happens, it's euphoric.

Like being at your first rock concert—it's unforgettable.

ORGANIZATIONAL GOALS

When you purchased this book, you invested in the future. The future of your career, the future of your business and the future of an integral piece of your company's identity—its culture. Through thick and thin, good times and bad, a business thrives and flourishes based on the strength and authenticity of its culture. Companies with strong and anchored cultures will grow and prosper while those with weak and frail cultures will wilt and eventually die. *Culture That Rocks* is a one-stop guide to help you build a rock-solid and powerful culture.

As I started to put my thoughts into words back in 2008, I reflected on what was going on in the world at the time. It seemed to me that in the global economic downturn, the focus of many companies (other than the obvious of staying in business) was on meeting three goals:

- Differentiated Value Proposition
- Unparalleled Customer Loyalty
- Strong Employee Engagement

I will delve deeper into these broad observations throughout the book. In the meantime, the following is a brief explanation of these desired organizational outcomes prevalent at the time:

Differentiated Value Proposition

Every organization has competitors—the ultimate goal is to be distinctively different, in a positive way, than the rest. Your company's value proposition is an amalgamation of many factors, but is rooted in how great the product is, how uniquely the service is delivered or how favorable the price seems to the customer. There is value in uniqueness and this is a high priority for rock star brands looking to separate themselves from the "wannabes."

Unparalleled Customer Loyalty

During moments of uncertain financial environments, people make deliberate and conservative purchasing decisions. Companies that separate themselves from the rest are the ones delivering something so memorable it creates enhanced value and consumer loyalty. When brand affinity is created, you have a better shot at getting repeat business.

Strong Employee Engagement

In every organization, the way the product is sold and/or the service is de-livered will determine its ultimate success…and this is predicated upon people. Therefore, to achieve the *Differentiated Value Proposition* and *Unparalleled Customer Loyalty* discussed above, your employees have to consistently make the right decisions. And *that* will only occur if those employ-ees are fully engaged, happy and committed to the organization's mission.

The need to achieve these three organizational outcomes was certainly magnified by the global turmoil at the time, but these desired results are also required to strengthen a brand's overall culture in any environment. I am fortunate to have great experience and some expertise in each area.

GETTING THE BAND TO #1

As jazzed as I was to be immersed in an organizational culture like Hard Rock that excelled in these areas and many others, my quest has always been to share my philosophies and learnings with other brands so that they too can attain "rock star" status. The mission of *Culture That Rocks* is to help organiza-tions create, maintain and even revolutionize their corporate cultures.

During those tough economic years, when uncertainty and fear ran ram-pant throughout the business community, everyone scrambled to be seen as the best choice in their competitive set. Some brands were singularly focused on only one of the goals listed above, while others desperately attacked all three, in order to survive or better distance themselves from the rest. But everyone sought the limelight.

Even today, this is still the drive of most leaders. They're on a perpetual quest to get their band to #1. But to do that, in many cases, they're going to have to change some things about the company. They are going to have to make a commitment to enhancing their company's culture. This might mean subtle changes for some organizations; others may require a drastic overhaul. Why invest in these changes? Because at the end of the day, a company's culture contributes an enormous amount to its success.

CORE FOCAL POINTS

To accomplish those three broad outcomes with excellence, I discovered specific touch points that are crucial to a rockin' corporate culture. These cross-industry "core focal points" have to be addressed and nurtured if there is to be any hope of getting your organization to the place you want it to be.

The cultural ideals and stories I'll share are grounded in service delivery, organizational change, hiring practices, training philosophies, retention strategies and practically every area of the Employee Life Cycle. Through studying these crucial pieces of a company's cultural makeup, I have learned valuable lessons that you can implement into your own business strategies to reshape and ignite the culture of your company.

Each and every company has core focal points—places where the rubber meets the road. These non-negotiable, high-priority areas require enormous time and attention as well as laser-like focus and nourishment to facilitate the growth of a business.

Culture That Rocks will offer you concentrated advice and guidance to improve the following areas of your business:

- **Service** – creating a consumer-obsessed service mentality
- **People** – hiring only right-fit talent that reflects your brand
- **Infrastructure** – departing from the status quo and implementing proven best practices
- **Purpose** – creating an inspiring mission for the business
- **Leadership** – doing the things you say you will do, creating followers through commitment vs. compliance

I will address each of these concepts throughout the book, providing you with real solutions and proven methods. Whether it's an evolution or a revolution that you seek, each chapter is chock-full of ideas for changing how your brand looks, feels, behaves and is perceived by others.

ROCK AND ROLL

Because I share both broad philosophy and detailed, tactical recommendations, the end of each chapter includes review sections titled "Greatest Hits

That Rock" and "This is How You Roll."

"Greatest Hits That Rock" offers readers an at-a-glance review of each chapter's main messages and most impactful points. These can be considered the main lyrics of the overall tune, so that you won't get lost in the melody and the beat. Like any great sustainable song, lyrics matter.

"This is How You Roll" takes these main thoughts even further, providing direct questions or discussion points that can be used as a "gut-check" for your organization and prepare you for the cultural change you hope to influence. Make a note of the ideas that immediately resonate with you and take them back to your team as thought-starters. Discuss them collectively to determine how they can be applied to your organization.

Look for something like this at the conclusion of each chapter:

GREATEST HITS THAT ROCK   **THIS IS HOW YOU ROLL**

Key Learning:
Detailed takeaway description

- Direct question/discussion point
- Additional question/discussion point

Key Learning:
Detailed takeaway description

- Direct question/discussion point
- Additional question/discussion point

In the end, this book is meant to be a blue print for fostering the type of organizational environment you've always imagined possible.

I sincerely hope you take the learnings shared here and implement the ones that make sense for you, so that your company culture eventually feels more like what you remember in the past or desire for the future.

Be warned, however: Building an organization that "rocks" is not easy. It's flat-out hard and requires a lot of strength, patience and commitment… but it's an absolutely worthwhile endeavor. Like anything that matters, the journey is a tough one, but it makes the encore that much sweeter.

In the immortal words of AC/DC…

"For those about to rock, I salute you."

2

BECOME THE CATALYST

"I'm not saying I'm gonna change the world,
but I guarantee that I will spark the brain that will change the world."

- Tupac Shakur

I've always admired people who are loyal to an organization for a long period of time—individuals who have watched their ideas come to life, take flight and even grow into organizational norms. These are the people who move mountains and shift cultural identities in a positive way; I call them "culture catalysts." They don't just ride the back of the brand for their own interests; they earn the right to represent the organizational culture with the passion and commitment they put into the company's success. Partly because of tenure, but mostly because of dedication and fearlessness, they attain culture catalyst status and the right to influence the organization.

Still, why would anyone like myself stay at a single job or with a single employer for so long? Let's be honest, in this day and age most people's resumes consist of numerous jobs and experiences. Sure, my parents and grandparents stuck to one or two main careers during their lifetimes, but that doesn't seem to be the norm anymore. What was it, then, that created this loyalty in me? Without question, it was the culture.

Part of my loyalty surely stemmed from the organization's mission, vision, mottos and values, but the collection of individual behaviors assembled in a specific company is what sealed the deal for me. More than anything else, the *people* represented the brand culture. In the case of Hard Rock, the individuals were pretty unique. Radical, in fact to most. That just made the organization's personality stronger and more appealing to me. Hard Rockers are the reason I stuck around for as long as I did.

AN ARMY OF DIVERSITY

I believe surrounding yourself with different yet like-minded people with a passionate mission is one of the ways to positively affect company culture. Perhaps your company's employee base is not as unique as other brands, but certainly this belief in an "army of diversity" permeates most organizations. It must. The value of a diverse workgroup has been long-touted by Human Resources professionals and organizational psychologists alike. They maintain that a more inclusive workforce fosters better, more creative solutions to problems, thereby leading to sustainable growth. And when people join an organization that is inclusive of others, they are more likely to stay longer and commit to the organization's mission. When that happens, the culture becomes even stronger. This was the case for me at Hard Rock. The unbelievable mix of diversity and individuality embodied a company culture like none other.

If your business is dependent on people for its results, hiring the same type of people will almost inevitably yield the same results you've been getting. The results might not be bad, but they could be better with some fresh thinking thrown into the mix. To avoid this "sea of sameness," it's better to surround yourself with different personalities, all galvanized to achieve their collective mission.

Hiring a diverse workforce is only one way to enhance your company's culture—and one that I will spend more time on in later chapters. But before I get too deep into specific tactics, let me share an individual viewpoint.

PERSONAL CULTURE SHIFT

Going all the way back to when I was a young boy, I can point to specific moments when I was on a clear path of my choosing, only to have my world rocked, hurling me in a different direction. At one point I thought I wanted to be a fireman or a paramedic like my father—until we rolled up to a traffic accident and I witnessed what a horror it was. He saved lives, but the trauma was too much for me. That one moment steered me away from that profession. I also spent most of my childhood wanting to play organized football…until the day in high school that I put on the uniform and went to practice. I was hit so hard the first time that the air was knocked out of me. That moment certainly changed my mind, and my body, about playing football. Another life-changing moment occurred in college, where I studied music and hoped to become a professional musician. I soon discovered that to make a living in that field, you actually had to be really good. I was adequate, but not great. This key realization again altered my professional direction in life.

I call these moments "personal culture shifts." They are the defining moments in a person's life, each contributing to that individual's identity. Those personal life changes may have been uncomfortable and full of uncertainty at the time, but they also helped shape my internal, personal culture and made me who I am today. As a member of the Hard Rock team for more than twenty years—and an individual who both reinvented his personal culture and positively influenced a company's character—I am confident the experiences that shaped my personality will help to shape yours.

We all go through personal culture shifts. Whether or not these events are considered positive at the time, they all become learning experiences. Some will look at these moments as things that happen *to* them, while others will look at them as things that happen *for* them. It's a mindset, really. Some people just look at life positively and think that every experience happens for a reason and that those moments are, in fact part of life's discovery. They are open to the journey and where life takes them. Other people have more of a victim mentality and look at these personal inflection points as negative. They believe life's experiences just happen, randomly imposing changes on their life's plan. These people are rarely prepared for the change; they tend to feel as though their world is caving in around them, rather than opening up to new possibilities.

Regardless of the viewpoint, we all have these moments. They are what make us unique and allow us to bring different perspectives to the party. I chose the first approach—to look at my experiences as opportunities to learn. Whether it was shifting away from a career as a paramedic or realizing that becoming a professional musician wasn't in the cards for me, I was cool with taking the lessons that stuck with me and applying them to my future decisions. Those critical moments in life helped me distinguish between my real strengths, which could be utilized further, and those things that were probably never going to be strengths for me, which deserved less attention and energy. Looking at life's experiences like this can be incredibly empowering.

The same will be true as you navigate the path toward your own shift in culture. The long and winding road may not lead you to where you initially thought it would, but you should celebrate the journey just the same. You may get lost, you may even change the route a few times, but if you stay focused with laser-like precision, your desired result will be there for the taking. You can still reach your goals; you just have to pick the right vehicle to get there.

When it comes down to it, changing both your inner-culture and the culture of your organization will be among the most challenging responsibilities you have in life. It takes time, persistence, effort, know-how, and passion. But it's not impossible. And it's completely worthwhile.

MY LIFE WAS ROCKED, LITERALLY

My cultural identity shifted again when I applied at a new Hard Rock Cafe that had just opened in town. I figured I could use my past experience and newfound passion for the industry to work at a restaurant built around music—and make some good money at the same time. Little did I know my life was about to be rocked. I soon discovered that I loved my night job with this music brand a lot more than my day job as a middle school teacher. Soon my personality began to change. The more stoic and professional life of a public educator was being replaced with the freedom and irreverence that comes with Rock 'n' Roll. It was crystal clear: My cultural identity was drastically shifting.

It wasn't long before I quit teaching to focus my energy on Hard Rock. Within months I became a trainer and began traveling around the world for the company, helping to open new locations in places like Nashville, Mexico City and Madrid, among others. It was the perfect job for me: I worked in a high-energy industry, listened to music all day and traveled the globe, all while teaching and training others to become brand ambassadors.

And yet, as much as I loved the overall experience, what really attracted me to Hard Rock was the people who worked there. These real-life "rockers" were my heroes and made me feel like a founding member of the band. They went out of their way to include me in their world and only asked that I do the same in return: contribute to, rather than take from, the brand's mission. They never judged me. Instead, they allowed me to be myself, discover my true identity and help others do the same along the way. I also appreciated the fact that we were all different from the rest of world and all of the "normal" people in it; attitudinally and aesthetically. Being welcomed into a family of outcasts, having felt like one myself, made me realize that I was home, that this was the place for me. In fact, everything I'd done up to that point in my life only prepared me for my true calling with Hard Rock.

No doubt, I had fallen in love with a company's culture—or to be more precise, I fell in love with a collection of individual personalities which *made up* the culture. It was a culture that matched my own. My personal values were in complete alignment with those of the company. I had found a home and I planned to stay.

Two decades later, applying for an entry-level host position at Hard Rock now seems like a distant memory. I can hardly believe it was the last time I would have to interview with a company, nor imagine what my life would be like without this emotional connection to an organization.

This amazing bond can occur within all of us. As an independent cultural catalyst, you have the opportunity to build a striking relationship with your company and become a fire-starter for great change. This is why the old adage, "do what you love and love what you do" is so relevant today. Perhaps the first few jobs you have are simply to serve some basic needs: shopping at the mall, going to the movies, downloading music. But when you start turning your attention to a career, you really want to make sure that your job, where you spend the majority of your waking life, is the type of work that is both rewarding and contributes to your personal mission.

You may have already found that role—or you may still be on a quest to find the right organization. Either way, developing an emotional connection to a company is key to your personal fulfillment and your ability to participate in a brand's culture. If organizational culture change is important to you, you'll need to be in alignment with the company's identity *before* you can be "invited to the party" of affecting culture. So, if you love your organization but acknowledge that it needs a bit of a cultural revolution, having a deep emotional connection with the brand will help you become a catalyst for that change.

WANT CHANGE?

My initial goal after "joining the band" was to prove I deserved to wear the Hard Rock logo and belong to that unique tribe. But to be fair, I was pretty lucky. I had joined an organization that already oozed culture. Others are not so fortunate. Some people have inherited a company culture that is in decline, while others were there during the "good ole days" and have watched it slowly slip way. Whatever situation you find yourself in, different cultural concerns will require different responses.

Want to change things, but don't know how?

While this may be a simple question with an equally simple answer, wanting change is one thing; making it happen isn't so easy. Whether you have joined a company that needs a shot of Adrenaline or you've been hanging out for years in an organization that requires major surgery to resuscitate its failing heart, any company's culture can be enhanced for the better. And sometimes that can start with one brave person.

For years, people have been charged with creating, maintaining or re-inventing an organization's culture, often with little guidance about how to do it or where to start. In fact, you may suddenly find yourself as the "lucky" one asked to take on this daunting responsibility. But whether you are running point on this initiative, holding the purse strings, part of a support team tasked with making changes, or simply an innocent bystander who longs for the company to resurrect its golden years once again, you will no doubt feel the growing-pains of change as it occurs to and around you.

Your first challenge is convincing the masses that it's time to amp up the culture. Unfortunately, change isn't received well by most. People hate it. If you are indeed the catalyst responsible for creating and delivering organizational change, even in the spirit of building up the culture, you can expect some resistance from others in the company.

To rattle the thinking of staunch resisters, I have actually used sobering language like this:

"If you hate change, then you're really going to hate extinction. Because that is what will happen to the brand if a company never alters course to stay fresh, relevant or at the pace of society."

Organizational change has to happen in every brand at some point to ensure its survival. It's inevitable. But if the change is sufficiently discussed, meticulously plotted out and clearly communicated to all levels, then buy-in is possible—and so are results. It can be done. It must be done.

To shift the cultural pillars of a company, someone's got to be the catalyst.

WALK FIRST, THEN RUN

There may be many people who would love to see cultural change in their company, but they do not personally make hiring decisions or have any direct reports. They don't have the ability to surround themselves with talent. What then? Does the analogy still work? I can assure you it does. In fact, that's the exact predicament I found myself in twenty-one years prior to joining Hard Rock.

Early in my career, when I went from working as a host in a single cafe to working in the brand's worldwide headquarters, I wanted to immediately make a huge impression on the company culture. I had big ideas and plenty of drive. After some good advice and serious soul-searching, however, I decided to start small and affect only those few things I could directly control. I started with my own attitude: I focused on being positive and controlling my emotions. The next "baby steps" in my career evolution involved focusing on just a few staff-level training initiatives. I meticulously attacked the Employee Handbook and the New Hire Orientation process. By going after these entry-level, field-based products and programs and overhauling them to match the culture and address fundamental learning principles, I earned enough clout within the organization to move on to other company initiatives.

With a little guidance from my boss, Mike, and a whole lot of earned trust with him, I made enough headway to eventually grow my circle of influence and take on more responsibilities in the organization. By validating the use rate of the programs I launched and securing positive feedback on their value to frontline workers, I generated enough "wins" to be trusted with even bigger responsibilities.

Eventually, Mike allowed me to take over all staff-level training programs; a few years later, I assumed all management-level training responsibilities, as well. Ultimately, my "job" developed into a full-blown career managing the learning and development culture of the entire organization…including Mike's responsibilities after he left the company.

All of that was only possible because of my boss' direction to start small and do a few things really well. I had to walk first, before I was able to run. Because of this approach, I was able to progress from creating training manuals and videos in those early days to producing e-Learning courseware, facilitating a corporate university and opening new properties around the world. By the time I "retired" from corporate life, I had the ability to influence the company's culture in nearly every facet of the people side of the business.

START THE REVOLUTION

With the right passion, drive and commitment to your craft, you too can take on the role of catalyst and create a culture that rocks. It may take some time and a different path, but if you are determined and stay focused on crushing your current responsibilities, it will lead to bigger things. Trust me on this. I've known many people—in my industry and other businesses—who have taken this approach and attained the same level of success in their own companies.

When I joined Hard Rock, it wasn't a culture that needed to be revolutionized, but a historic one that needed to be protected and perpetuated for the foreseeable future. And this is absolutely just as important. In a sense, my team became the face and voice of the company culture. We had our hands in almost every internal staff communication and learning program, and, via the employees, many guest-facing initiatives, as well. Like most organizational training departments, we represented and trained the brand culture with the hope that the employees would parlay it to the guests. It was a tremendous responsibility, but one we relished. By producing materials and concepts that exemplified the culture and "spoke" to the employees, our department garnered high praise over the years. We were known for producing only high quality work and our initiatives were always well received and even anticipated. Because of this positive track record, we quickly became culture catalysts and champions for the brand. We certainly weren't the only ones in the organization with this critical responsibility, but our team had developed wide-reaching influence over the company's culture.

That's how cultural revolutions start at companies: A single person or department running with a great idea.

Culture catalysts are people who protect the company heritage, yet aren't afraid to create new sparks within the brand to stoke the cultural flames.

Every company needs them, and you can be one of those fire starters. For real change to occur, someone's got to be the heroic individual who takes the first steps toward thinking differently, applying new ideas and then fearlessly defending those decisions later.

> *"If we all thought the same all the time, nothing would ever change. Every company needs mavericks."*
>
> - Richard Branson, Founder & CEO, Virgin Airlines

I couldn't agree more.

And you can be one of these mavericks…a culture catalyst.

To help you, I'll share some very direct and clear concepts you can implement into the fabric of your company to begin this crucial transformation. However, before embarking on *changing* an organization's culture, let's better define exactly what culture *is*.

GREATEST HITS THAT ROCK

THIS IS HOW YOU ROLL

Avoid a Sea of Sameness:
It's better to surround yourself with different personalities, yet all of whom are passionate and like-minded in their collective mission.

- Is your company dependent on people for its results?
  o If yes, debate whether your brand does/does not have an extremely diverse workforce—in age, race, gender, belief system, aesthetic look.

Embrace Personal Culture Shifts:
The long and winding road may not lead you to where you initially thought it would. Celebrate the journey. Every personal experience is a part of your cultural identity.

- Even though your desired life path may not have taken you where you initially thought, are you happy with the journey?
- Can you think back to specific life experiences (even the negative memories) and mentally tag those as positive shifts for you in your ultimate career destination?
  o Explain.
- Are you happy with the direction of your life's legacy, both personally and professionally?
  o Share these.

Walk First, Then Run:
Make small changes that are within your direct control—and do them well; these "wins" will lead to greater cultural influence.

- In your current role, what decision-making authority do you have over your organization's systems, processes or direction?
- Discuss the initiatives within your direct control that you can immediately affect for the better.
- Discuss the pathway to grow your circle of influence in the brand's culture.
- What results could be anticipated if you crushed some small change initiatives?

Be a Cultural Catalyst:
Being a catalyst for change is hard work, but well worth the endeavor if you're truly passionate. Cultural revolutions are started with a single person running with a great idea.

- Do you feel as though you could be a catalyst for cultural change in your organization?
- Would you feel comfortable in this role, even if it means challenging the status quo?
  o Explain how you would deal with this.
- Discuss whether others would accept you or your team taking on the catalyst role and, if not, how they might be convinced.

3

BANDS & BRANDS ALIKE

"Destiny is a feeling you have that you know something about yourself nobody else does. The picture you have in your own mind of what you're about will come true."

- Bob Dylan

The phrase "company culture" can be a difficult one to define. Ask any five people what corporate culture is and you are likely to get five completely different answers, some specific, some vague. And it's possible that all of them would be right.

Here's the dilemma: If some people in the organization have a positive, definitive view of the culture while others are clueless or even shrug it off as a "nice-to-have," there will be widespread confusion about the company's direction and possibly even its desired business outcomes. We need a universal definition of culture.

To further complicate the issue, "culture" is a nebulous, unseen principle, hard to prove and harder still to measure, yet people know it exists and is part of everything the company does. But if we can't nail this esoteric notion down to a coherent definition, it cannot be easily shared with others. Before you can shift a company's culture, we need to define it.

So, what is it? What exactly is company culture?

Most organizational experts will say that a company's mission, vision, values, rituals, traditions, beliefs, customs, standards, methodology and jargon all combine to create an environment over time. This environment, commonly understood by all, impacts how team members interact with one another and their customers—and, ultimately, the overall performance of the business. This collective soup of characteristics creates an almost human-like personality: a culture.

Rock bands are like that, too. Fans of live performance-based artists will swear a quantifiable personality exists in their favorite band, even if they are unable to adequately define the individual characteristics that make up that personality.

Consider the "cultures" of three generational touring artists:

The Grateful Dead

This '60s group was known for its unique, half-day concert events that included customized set lists for every performance, depending on the moment and vibe of the crowd. The Dead allowed fans to actually record and share their live concerts for free—taboo at a time when other artists sought to capitalize on any available revenue. Their approachable, communal philosophy of organically sharing their art with listeners inspired the hardcore fans to dub themselves Dead Heads. Fans of the band will swear that the Dead Head culture is real and alive.

Jimmy Buffet

Like the 'Dead before him, this artist creates a unique, cultural experience at his live concert events. His songs and performances represent and reflect the carefree Key West lifestyle that his listeners crave. Affectionately called Parrot Heads, loyal fans live vicariously through Buffet's music in the only way they can: over a beer, dreaming of life in the sun and water. They often enjoy his music in large groups, via pre-concert tailgate parties that have become both famous and synonymous with Jimmy Buffet.

The Dave Matthews Band

Perfecting the live music tour experience in wildly-popular summer concerts, this group has become today's Grateful Dead. Following in the footsteps of the cultural rock icons who preceded them, band members—all monster musicians in their own right—have created a laid back sound that connotes a worry-free lifestyle. It is the band's fan obsession, however, that has created its culture. The band utilizes technology in various ways to facilitate direct communication with loyal listeners, building a cult-like following for Dave Matthews. By releasing advanced copies of music and pre-selling concert tickets to members of the fan club, the group has created a massive network of built-in fans, further solidifying loyalty to the band. I have several friends who will gladly pay for and follow DMB along its entire summer tour—just for the cultural experience.

Ask any Dead Head, Parrot Head or Dave Matthews fan if these bands have a culture and the resounding answer will be "yes." Perhaps they won't point to the exact characteristics I've described here—although some fans will certainly list even more—but people know a thriving culture when they experience it.

A COLLECTION OF BEHAVIORS

A company's culture then, is the brand's personality. It's like a living organism—literally a culture in a petri dish. In fact, that's where the word comes from and why the analogy is critical to my definition. The brand's personality changes as different "micro-organisms" affect it. See where I'm going here? People are the microorganisms in an organization's culture. They each come to the table with their own personal culture shifts and their own learned behaviors.

Whether you agree with the organizational experts I mentioned earlier—that culture is an amalgam of a company's mission, vision, values, mores and practices—or believe that a company's culture is defined solely by its outwardly-seen environment, the culture of any organization can only exist because of the people embodying it.

As a company both succeeds and struggles through the years, its culture—this collective personality—becomes more profound for all stakeholders. That, in turn, wields greater influence on those within to conform to organizational norms. In this perpetual cycle, those influenced employees then continue to strengthen the brand's culture in a mutually inclusive manner, making the personality more defined. Consumers experience and come to know a company's culture because of the consistent, widely-shared, collective behaviors of the internal team.

Take note: This doesn't just apply to a desired or positive organizational culture; it is simply how a company's "personality" is established and thrives. An organization's founders and leadership may hope that their culture is positive and that it won't change over time…but it does. People are coming and going all the time. Just like a rock band, the culture is only as strong or weak as the people that are currently employed and collectively make up the heart and soul of the organization.

Southwest Airlines' President Emeritus, Colleen Barrett co-authored a book in 2010 with business icon Ken Blanchard called, *Lead with LUV: a different way to create real success,* in which she explained why it would be so hard for another company to completely copy the airline's well-documented, rock star culture—the secret sauce. She put it this way:

"I don't dictate our Culture; none of our Officers do. Rather, it stems from the collective personality of our People. And they are what makes us the provider of choice in the airline industry."

Southwest Airlines is widely known for its unbelievably great culture—internally and externally. So much so, *Fortune Magazine* has recognized the carrier in its annual survey of corporate reputations, where it has landed consistently near the top amongst America's Top Ten most admired corporations in the world…every year since 1994. That doesn't happen by accident. The airline's executives and the general public know results like that are predicated on a collection of committed brand ambassadors.

There are many adjustments that can be made to an organization's processes and infrastructure in order to enhance the perceived culture. Like any system, however, these changes are only as effective as the human beings making them. So, while I will discuss tactical, process-driven best practices that produce results, remember that *people* are at the core of any cultural shift. *People* ultimately create and drive change. *People* make the culture.

HERITAGE VS. CULTURE

People often equate an organization's culture with its history. But while we all love nostalgia, it's not the same as culture, nor can the words "culture" with "heritage" be used interchangeably. Because culture can be a difficult concept to prove, however, it's just easier for people to wrap their company culture up in its storied history.

A company's heritage is rooted in the past. Companies like Nike, Google and Virgin Airlines have a rich heritage complete with founding values, traditions, customs and success stories. These are the storytelling opportunities that must be captured and shared, so that the lineage can thrive and the entrepreneurial spirit can continue to inspire the new leaders that come on board. This storytelling is part of the role of a culture catalyst. He or she must become a "keeper of the cultural flame," helping the knowledge capital of the brand to flourish.

Certainly, a company's history will influence a person's perception of its culture, but you cannot just rely on the cool stories of how the brand got started, its meteoric rise or even its length of existence to define the culture. Heritage is about the past.

Culture, on the other hand, is about the present. If the culture of a brand is the collective employee behaviors that exist in the company, that culture is unique at any given time, depending on who is in the organization at that moment.

Where would The Who be in our mental musical soundtrack if guitarist Pete Townshend were not in the band? Would Rush still be in the Rock 'n' Roll Hall of Fame if drum god Neil Peart were never a part of that Canadian Prog-Rock trio? Would KISS have had such an influence on other musicians if the fire-breathing, tongue-lashing, demon child Gene Simmons had never picked up the bass? Would The Black Eyed Peas still be "The Peas" without front gal Fergie?

Every member of the band is critical. Lose a member, add a member or replace a member and the band is forever changed. Perhaps for the better, perhaps not. The hope, of course, is that the group's evolution is positive, rewarding, successful and sustainable…but it is completely dependent on the collective mix of the band's roster.

Businesses are exactly like that.

Every company, therefore, is in constant flux as people come and go. The culture is ever-evolving…never stagnant. It is either getting stronger or weaker depending on who's employed at that time. As someone leaves the company, the organizational culture changes. It may be a small shift, but it is a shift nonetheless. As a new team member joins the company, the culture morphs again. This ever-changing push and pull creates a fluid environment for a business' culture as it continues to move and make its way downstream.

Think of culture change from this systemic standpoint: As one piece of the culture leaves and another one joins, the individuals that make up the culture of an organization will begin to replace one another and eventually reinvent company culture entirely. Sometimes the change happens dramatically, as when someone in a key leadership role leaves and is replaced by a new executive. Other times, change results from small shift after small shift, until it becomes blatantly apparent to everyone. Regardless of how quickly a company's culture changes, the revolving door of new hires guarantees that it will, inevitably, change.

Heritage is important and should be captured and effectively shared, but the here-and-now is what most people seek to address. The present state of things—ultimately defined by individual behavior—is the actual company culture. Employ the right brand ambassadors and you create a culture that rocks.

CULTURE IS LIKE O$_2$

Regardless of the industry, an organization's culture is its lifeblood. That culture, when strong and vibrant, can seem to pump through the veins of the masses and guide, inspire and motivate each person to rise to the challenges required.

When the culture is unknown, uncertain or even unbearable, the company's lifeblood may be so tainted that the organization becomes anemic. As a result, poor decisions become common. People lose interest. Results become skewed. The culture inevitably dies and employees become paralyzed. They lack the desire to do even the most basic tasks that could help the company perform better. It becomes a downward spiral in which the business relies on individuals to survive, but those same valuable assets cannot personally identify with the current state of the company's culture, and are therefore not motivated to help.

Ignoring the health of the culture is like failing to clean a fish tank and allowing the water to get dirty and the green algae to take over, leaving the fish gasping for air.

It should be clear by now that culture is everything. It's like Oxygen to you and me. In fact, I actually use that specific analogy to identify those companies that have strong organizational cultures. Strong cultures are life-breathing Oxygen to the body, while weak ones are like poisonous Carbon Monoxide.

Strong Culture = Oxygen (O_2)
Weak Culture = Carbon Monoxide (CO_2)

See if you agree with the following list of brands that, in my opinion, are pumping Oxygen through their organizational veins:

- Nike
- Southwest Airlines
- Apple
- Starbucks
- The Container Store
- Walt Disney World
- Chick-fil-A
- Zappos.com
- Coca-Cola
- Oprah Winfrey
- Amazon
- Publix Supermarkets
- LEGO
- Cinnabon
- Harley-Davidson
- In-N-Out Burger
- Pixar
- Victoria Secret
- FedEx
- Ritz-Carlton
- IKEA
- First Watch
- Home Depot
- Red Bull
- Google
- Geek Squad
- Virgin Airlines
- Whole Foods Market

We are all familiar with most of these companies—and for good reason. They are all wildly successful. Many of them are Fortune 500 businesses or recipients of awards like "Most Admired Place to Work"—and each of their leaders could be my co-authors on how to create a strong, positive culture. They have a track record (a heritage, if you will) of building culture that resonates not only with their employees, but also with the public, on a wide-spread, even global, level.

Imagine walking into the headquarters of Google, Zappos, Starbucks or any of these great companies. What would it look like? What would it feel like? What would you hear? What would you observe about the employees? My guess is that you already have a preconceived, positive idea about such an experience. You have these preconceptions, in part, because of the culture these companies have created in the public domain. They want you to identify their names and products with strong culture because it will eventually help to sell their products or use their services. Their focus on ethos is remarkable, and they've continued to fine-tune and perfect it throughout their existence.

The evidence is clear in the totality of a company's business outcomes and eventual lifespan.

Culture matters. Just ask Steve Jobs, Phil Knight, Howard Schultz or Richard Branson.

THE CULT OF PERSONALITY

Once you have a fundamental understanding of what culture is, the next step is identifying the exact type of culture with which your company identifies. Before you can improve your culture, you have to understand the fabric of which it is made.

We do the same thing in our personal lives. As we discover who we are and how we want to live our lives, our personality and internal culture become more apparent.

When I was 14, we took a type of personality test in middle school. Like many of today's psychometric hiring assessments and competency-based profiles that help determine "right fit" hiring for businesses, this test was supposed to provide an early indication of the careers we might choose in the future. I always thought it was so cool you could answer a series of test questions and, based on your responses, find out what you were most-likely destined to be—or at least be pointed toward a specific career to match your perceived talents. My friends and I loved this novelty test and we talked about it all the time.

Based on how I answered those test questions, my report stated that I was most likely to be an airplane pilot. Airplane pilot, huh? At that point in my life, "pilot" wasn't even on my radar screen. In fact, I remember pining for the usual careers kids my age dreamed of: policeman, fireman, veterinarian and doctor.

Some people go through their whole lives without knowing what they want to be or do for a living, but as a result of that test, I had direction. I felt like I had an inside track—a secret compass pointing me toward True North. Having a grounded sense of purpose in life affected me. So that's where I started directing my career path—toward airline pilot.

Like many professionals, however, my career choice underwent a bit of a cultural shift along the way. My long and winding road took me somewhere completely "off the grid." My professional indicator turned out to be just what I initially thought it was: a novelty. It wasn't until later in life that I understood and developed my real talents, and they were pretty far from my childhood dreams and that long-ago test.

The same is true when it comes to identifying company culture. Both internally and externally, it is vital to discover and acknowledge the type of culture that envelops your organization. Just like a young middle-schooler taking a personality test, your first step in creating a cultural shift is giving your brand a thorough assessment. Not to define the company, but to create a starting point for a change in direction, if needed.

THE CULTURE TEST

Although it's a bit less formal than the psychometric test I took as a teenager, it can be just as enlightening to ask the following questions of yourself and others in your organization:

- What would you say are the observable characteristics that make up the company culture?
- How is your company's culture taught (video, instructor-led classroom, wallet cards, posters, print manuals, storytelling social media, etc.)?
- What examples of positive business results can you point to as resulting from your company's strong brand culture?
- What do you think your *employees* would say are characteristics that make up the culture?
- What do you think your *customers* would say are the characteristics that make up the culture?
- Does your company's executive team refer to the brand's culture in discussions and important decisions?

These questions can help you "climb under the hood of the car" and discover whether your organization is in a good place—perhaps just needing a little protection to keep it sustainable—or if it is in serious need of a cultural overhaul. When you and others answer questions like these, the brand's personality becomes glaringly apparent.

The listed above are only thought-starters; they are, in fact, just a partial list of the questions included in my Cultural Self-Awareness Survey, which you can access for free at www.CultureThatRocks.com. Feel free to download, distribute and discuss the questions with your teams to develop an organic, collaborative assessment of your business. At the very least, it will give you a baseline from which you can plan a process for creating, maintaining or altering your company's culture.

LEARNED BEHAVIORS = PERSONAL CULTURE

Once you understand your company's personality, you can begin to study the character and qualities of the individuals that form it. On a micro-scale, each individual person actually has an internal culture, and just like an organization's culture, it is made up of all the attitudes, beliefs, life experiences and associated values the individual has internalized as a result of those experiences. This is a person's unique personal culture—his or her identity.

Additionally, behavioral scientists tell us that all human behaviors are *learned* behaviors and choices (I gleaned this information from a combination of high school Psychology and Stephen Covey's *The Seven Habits of Highly Effective People*). In other words, people learn or decide to retain the portions of their life experiences that matter to them. These experiences become a part of them forever. Some are deeply buried; others are displayed on the surface for all the world to see. Either way, people are who they are because of what and how they have learned.

It is critical to acknowledge that employees join your organization with behaviors they have learned over time from their parents, school, religion, community groups, friends, television, social media sites, and the playground. By the time an individual gets to your company, the behaviors that make up his or her internal culture are well-engrained—and they may be a benefit or a hindrance to your brand. Your awareness of this will help you make better hiring and management decisions.

Regardless of the industry or the business model, if you focus on the individual—in hiring, teaching or cultivating—you can create a "culture that rocks" for your company. After all, people are the living embodiment of culture. Who you employ and how they interact with each other and the customer is in the foundation of delivering positive, sustainable business results.

The Power of Individual Behavior:
An organization's culture is the collection of individual behaviors that exist in the company at any given time—and those individuals are constantly changing.

- What individual behaviors impact your company's current culture?
- Discuss whether you think the people who collectively make up the current company culture represent the brand well.
- When you think of your organization's culture and the individuals who represent the brand well, do only a few come to mind or are there too many to single out?
  o Name the employees who stand out and explain why.

Heritage v. Culture:
Celebrate the past (heritage), but focus primarily on the present and the future (culture).

- When you think of your company's heritage (past reputation), what characteristics come to mind?
  o Which of these characteristics still exist today?
  o How do you know they exist?
- Describe what the current company culture "feels" like to you.

Culture is Life:
Great brands pump cultural Oxygen through their organizational veins, while weak ones exude Carbon Monoxide.

- To which of the successful, strong brands listed in this chapter can you hold your company's culture up as just as strong?
  o Specifically, in what ways?
- After answering the sample Cultural Self-Awareness Survey questions in this chapter, could you validate your organization's personality as strong or anemic?

4

THE LEADERSHIP EFFECT

*"You cannot exploit culture. You have to earn the right to represent it
and you have to do it every bloody day."*

- Isaac Tigrett, Co-Founder, Hard Rock Cafe

A company's culture starts at the top with strong, directed leadership. This is true whether the culture is to be created, maintained, adjusted or completely reimagined.

When I discuss "culture" with business leaders, most of our conversations center around the desire to enhance their company's culture, even get back to the "good ole days." But a fortunate few get to experience a brand during its inception, when it comes blazing out of the starting gate with a strong culture. I can assure you, this type of an environment does not happen by accident. It develops because a careful founder fuels the initial cultural flame of the organization.

By definition, a person who starts his or her own organization should be considered a catalyst—at least of a business—but to create a culture so crystal clear that the company's "personality" is blatantly apparent to all requires deliberate thought, strategy and action. Business leaders who rise to this challenge take on the added mantel of *culture* catalyst. Culture catalysts do more than ensure the long-term viability of a company's financial health; they also recognize the staying power of a strong brand personality. They aspire to positively ingrain the brand's culture into the end user's psyche.

Other top executives have *inherited*, rather than created, their company's culture—strong or weak—from a previous leader or even the organization's founder, and are then empowered to *become* catalysts. This can be quite daunting for the new leader and, again, requires deliberate thought, strategy and action. Like the entrepreneur who started the brand in the first place, the new leader must take great care to ensure the business' viability, both financial *and* cultural.

Harkening back to my earlier definition, a company culture is initially created by an individual's methods and behavior. So whether or not they purposefully seek to affect the organization's culture, leaders, by nature of their position, will do so with their actions or inactions. This leadership effect can have positive or negative consequences for the brand's culture.

Leaders have the power to light up or extinguish the cultural flame of a company. Those that "get it" bring the flamethrower and indeed know how to light it up.

I'm a big fan of the cultural catalyst.

CULTURAL TRAILBLAZERS

Let me tell you about a couple of my hospitality heroes—cultural trailblazers who understand that company culture means everything to the success of a business. Even in their previous lives—when they worked for other successful brands instead of running them—each of these leaders were considered catalysts. They understood the importance of a strong culture and the results it could generate, and their experience solidified their vision of how their own companies would look, feel and operate one day.

Kat Cole - Cinnabon

Nobody epitomizes a culture catalyst more than Kat Cole, President of Cinnabon. Her story is amazing. From her job as a part-time Hooters waitress in high school, Kat rose through the ranks to become a Vice President at that chicken wings and beer company within just 7 years. By the age of 32, she was running the multi-channel Cinnabon brand. Kat is the poster child for what hard work, dedication and positive energy can achieve.

It certainly wasn't an easy journey; Kat went through several personal culture shifts growing up. Living with 2 sisters and a single mother on $10 per week for the entire family, Kat moved into "responsibility" mode pretty early in life. She began working to help provide for her family as early as she could, eventually dropping out of college to support the greater cause of "family survival." Kat's plans for becoming an engineer or lawyer were derailed further when she was offered the unique opportunity to open Hooters restaurants in international markets. I have always known Kat Cole to be a student of life and learning, so you can imagine how hard it was for her to put her studies and career dreams on hold. However, this opportunity became the inflection point—the personal culture shift—that put her on an accelerated path to greatness.

Kat's sky-rocketing trajectory through the business world has been well-documented in magazines, videos and television interviews, especially when she pushed the cinnamon bun brand into the $1 billion club while simultaneously earning her MBA in her spare time. In my opinion, however, she's never received enough media attention for her love of people and commitment to the success of others. No doubt, Kat Cole is accomplished, talented and smart, but her positive approach toward people—and life in general—is infectious. She has a way of making everyone around her feel great...a cherished mark of an inspiring leader.

I have personally seen Kat in some frustrating life situations: when things were not going according to plan at work, or when a cancelled connecting flight forced her to miss an important event, or when she was eaten up by bed bugs in Ethiopia…even when she ripped a leg tendon in a snow-skiing accident that required surgery and months of physical therapy. Yet I have never seen her lose her cool or fall into a negative slump. She is the embodiment of the power of positive thinking. Kat Cole inspires everyone around her, especially her employees.

One of the proudest moments of Kat's career was when she was featured on the U.S. television show *Undercover Boss*. That show allowed her, even as President of a well-known brand, to go "undercover" in her own company to better understand the inner workings of the organization. Because of the show's format, the leader is able to get to the hearts of employees and discover their very personal hidden needs and desires. During the course of the Cinnabon episode, we saw Kat's interactions with four employees, all of whom were very competent, passionate and committed in their own roles, but who each revealed personal strife or grandiose dreams while they worked beside their president in disguise. Kat admits that she was emotionally moved by how her brand ambassadors were making a positive difference in people's lives, yet struggled in some way on their own.

When Kat divulged her identity in the "big reveal" at the end of the show, she showed the world what type of leader she was by taking the unique opportunity to affect these four employees—providing both the opportunities and financial support necessary for each to fulfill their dreams. She completely rocked their world and, in the process, became a rock star herself.

Kat was already one of our industry's emerging leaders before *Undercover Boss*, and I can tell you with confidence that she lives her life like this with everyone, every day. All the television show did was spotlight the type of leader she has always been. Cinnabon's product is fantastic, but the leadership of Kat Cole is what amplified a "culture that rocks."

Nick Sarillo – Nick's Pizza & Pub

A newfound cultural hero of mine is Nick Sarillo, Founder & CEO of Nick's Pizza & Pub, a 2-unit pizza brand in Illinois. Although Nick's has enjoyed wide notoriety in the pizza world and among Chicago's growing community of experiential brand-seekers, I was oblivious to this company's story and culture until recently. As soon as I was exposed to the brand, however, I knew that Nick and I were members of the same tribe.

I was "virtually" introduced to Nick by email, via a mutual friend at a networking conference who thought we shared some similar business ideas around culture and insisted we should know each other. I studied up on the company and eventually joined Nick at his Crystal Lake, Illinois restaurant location. What I discovered blew my mind. But it wasn't the monster-sized, multi-floored, custom-designed and built, 350-person capacity restaurant that drew me in, nor was it the stellar quality of the menu itself. The mind-searing brand differentiator in this company was the pervasive culture of the employees and their leader.

Founded with the purpose-driven mission of "providing the community an unforgettable place where families could relax and have fun," the cultural nuances and results are blatantly clear…validated by every employee discussion and customer interaction I observed. It was so refreshing to see a top executive go "all in" when it came to making his organization's culture the lynchpin of its success.

Check out some of the processes Nick has put into place:

- **Purpose & Values** – well-defined, understood, discussed daily and fully embodied by all employees
- **Self-Managed Job Duties** – a wall-mounted, color card-based task list of all opening, closing and running duties, utilizing peer-to-peer accountability, for each position
- **Learning Environment** – a detailed certification process for every team member to determine pay increases, plus a clear, identified path of personal and career development that team members complete at their own pace and desire
- **Open Book Finance** – ongoing education on financial acumen and the health of the business for team members at all levels
- **Trust-and-Track Leadership** – manager education on how to be a coach instead of a cop
- **3-step Feedback Process** – non-threatening, structured communication to provide all employees with clarity on their performance
- **Community Involvement** – authentic, community-based philanthropic initiatives, including the donation of five percent of all sales to charitable causes
- **Nick's University** – an instructor-led seminar allowing the outside world to "look under the hood" and experience the brand's proven best practices

Remember, this is a pizza joint.

The processes Nick Sarillo put into place are the same types of organizational initiatives you might find in a big, hierarchal enterprise. There's a reason this brand enjoys less than 20 percent annual team member turnover—unprecedented in the restaurant industry. There's a reason servers have been known to receive a $1,000 tip on a $25 check—not once, but several times. There's a reason a customer paid in full for one employee to go back to Ireland and visit family, knowing the team member could not have afforded it otherwise. There's a reason the parents of some of Nick's employees have singled out the brand as the catalyst for positive behavior changes and improved communication skills in their kids.

These things do not happen by accident. They are a result of leadership.

The results are undeniable. The metrics are quantifiable.

In his book, *A Slice of the Pie: How to Build a Big Little Business*, Nick Sarillo shares many of his beliefs and management practices revolving around organizational culture. He openly discusses his own personal culture shifts during his previously life in construction, his early-in-life authoritative and harsh leadership style and the many mistakes he made before he got it right. But he *did* ultimately get it right, and now he clearly believes in, embodies and teaches the relevance and power of a great culture in business.

At Nick's Pizza & Pub, culture is everything. It strengthens the entire organization, even in tough times. Especially in tough times.

One of the book's more compelling stories shared in the book, is about a situation that landed Nick on the cover of *Inc. Magazine* and in an *NBC Nightly News* interview with Brian Williams. In 2001, in the wake of a global economic crisis, it was revealed that Nick's Pizza & Pub could no longer financially sustain itself and the business was literally within days of total financial collapse. Nick disregarded traditional marketing and investor advice; instead, he engaged the community in an honest, risky, completely unorthodox plea to rally around him—and it worked. The culture of this brand was so strong that its loyal fans could not fathom their lives without it. The 105 percent sales increase that week didn't just rescue the company; it became the springboard for the year-on-year increased sales results that Nick's has enjoyed ever since.

Culture matters.

In an August 2012 article titled "Culture Drives Every Decision, Every Action," posted on www.talentminded.com, Nick Sarillo put it this way:

"What we've proven at Nick's is that you don't need to be a large, sexy, headline-grabbing company to have a great culture. You can reap all the benefits of a world class culture—including more enthusiastic teams, lower attrition, more innovation, better customer service and, ultimately, better financial performance—by disciplining yourself and your organization to make the company's culture a high-priority consideration in every decision you make and every action you take. It may be counterintuitive, but I know that unique, inspiring, transformative cultures are latent within even the smallest, most ordinary, most commoditized and most poorly performing of organizations. Even the humble pizza parlor or corner grocery has the potential to change the world. What's required is for leaders to define the desired culture and work single-mindedly to nurture it and make it real."

With only 2 locations in the far-flung suburbs of Chicago, is there any doubt as to why Nick's Pizza & Pub is one of the nation's Top 10 busiest independent pizza companies in terms of per-store sales?

Kat Cole and Nick Sarillo are cultural trailblazers. And they rock my world.

THE QUEST FOR CHANGE

Knowing that organizational cultures can only be affected by people and their behaviors, it should be clear the change process starts with a leader.

A single person, regardless of position, can make a difference in enhancing a company's culture, but that impact will be limited and relative to your level within the organization—at least until a cultural change movement can gain momentum. When it comes down to it, executive leadership has the biggest influence, both positive and negative, on a brand's culture. Movements are powerful and there is great value in making your voice heard, so never stop playing your part to drive the culture. However, the reality is that culture catalysts are often the ones up top.

The beauty of an executive's quest to change a company's culture and ensure a sustainable future is the speed of change that's possible. An individual in a leadership position can make big things happen quickly.

The flip side of that scenario occurs when a company's leader demands results at the expense of the culture. This person is either dismissive of the value of culture or just doesn't understand the concept in the first place. Company results can still be achieved in these organizations, but the culture will take a hit, many times an unrecoverable one. A leader's influence is swift and broad and can be monumentally rewarding or damaging to the overall health of the brand's culture.

CONCEPTUAL CONFUSION

The reason you should *define* culture before you begin to discuss *changing* it is that some leaders still see the overall notion of company culture as a nebulous, touchy-feely concept. To them, culture is the "softer side" of the business and warrants little attention or respect. These executives have either not worked in an environment in which the culture was nurtured or they simply do not acknowledge those things that cannot be easily seen or measured. They may even relegate management of the company's "personality" to the Human Resources department and never fully get their own arms around the concept.

For some, culture is actually considered non-essential and even a hindrance to achieving top-notch business results. I'm not sure how that belief exists in the face of contrary examples like Nick Sarillo's, which prove culture's critical role in sustained success, but it does. And most often, this belief stems from culture's lack of definition in the business world.

For decades, corporate employees have hidden behind the esoteric label of "culture," touting the importance of it without assigning any measurable value to it for the leader. The value of clearly identifying a company's culture and its tangible characteristics cannot be understated, as it will provide a foundation from which to orchestrate change. If the top executive requires that quantifiable, even financial results be tied to all initiatives, then throwing down the "culture card" to make a point or justify a need will just lead to its dismissal by that executive. Fortunately, culture catalysts have gotten much better at making their points for change by connecting cultural objectives to the company's performance results.

Let that serve as a guidepost for Human Resources and Learning/Development professionals when they seek executive support or financial resources for initiatives that would enhance or galvanize the brand's culture. Results-oriented executives need to see an ROI (Return on Investment)…or as I like to say, a Return on Culture (ROC). It's okay to be passionate about the brand's culture, but you must also think carefully about how you will deliver your proposal—backed up with facts, not just feelings. You will encounter less resistance and your cultural influence will grow.

CULTURE DOES INDEED MATTER

Remember, shifting a culture to one that rocks is a massive undertaking, but it garners epic, long-term results. Performance-oriented cultures possess statistically better financial results.

When you hear about culturally strong brands like Whole Foods, In-N-Out Burger, LEGO or Walt Disney World, there is no doubt about the validity of their results in almost every area. Employee morale is higher and turnover is lower than their industry norms. People are passionately and actively engaged in the business. And because of these internal factors, there is organizational alignment across the entire brand, all focused on collectively achieving the company's goals, including the all-important financial ones. What starts out as an internal approach magnifies itself into external, profitable and sustainable results.

As brilliant business guru Seth Godin once stated:

> *"Powerful organizations and great brands got there by aligning with and accelerating tectonic cultural shifts, not by tweaking sales one at a time."*

Culture matters.

And yet there are still some leaders who just don't get it. They do not study or celebrate the financial successes of such vibrant cultures as Nordstrom, Coca-Cola, Five Guys or Virgin Airlines. Instead, they harbor a minimalist's view of culture and rely solely on muscling the results through standard processes and procedures. If this pervasive mindset exists at the top, confusion will spread throughout the organization.

If the masses see their company's culture a certain way and the leader perceives it in another (or not at all), the organization will not be aligned and company results could be at risk. Too often, a company's staff and managers internalize a crystal clear vision of their brand's culture, while its leaders simultaneously maintain a blurred or unfavorable perception of it.

Ironically, these same leaders often attribute their negative business results to an unhealthy organizational culture. They might not use those words, but they talk about the lack of will from the team or a flawed process or clashing visions of the overall goal. Whether they look at these issues as part of the brand's personality or just some broken tactic, they are indeed cultural in nature. Fix the culture and you fix the company.

Whether someone believes in culture or not, it does exist and has a monumental effect on both internal employee behaviors and external company performance.

Just to be clear, I'm not putting all of the responsibility for culture on the backs of company leaders, but they definitely have a greater ability to change the culture than anyone else in a company. As the wise Uncle Ben advised a young Peter Parker in *Spider-Man*, "With great power comes great responsibility." The responsibility in the corporate world isn't just for short-term financial results, but also for long-term growth. The brand's image, which includes its culture, is the most critical component of that company's competitive differentiation over time. The culture must be effectively nurtured by the people entrusted to keep it vibrant and sustainable. When the leader of the band is not supportive, it makes for frustration, conflict and ultimately long-term destruction.

THE OASIS SYNDROME

Noel Gallagher, of the rock group Oasis, attests to this frustration when he recalls his vision of the band's direction compared to that of his brother and lead singer, Liam. Their well-documented on-stage arguments and differing opinions were legendary. Liam, the band's founder and leader, constantly cursed and yelled at his brother and the other musicians and crew on stage, often during the middle of performances over even the smallest of issues.

I love Oasis. But I remember paying good money to see the band, only to have Liam go into one of his tirades and walk off stage before the show ended. The audience never got to hear the group's biggest hits, "Wonderwall" and "Champagne Supernova." What a disappointment. For the band that, in its early years, promised the world that it would be the next Beatles, this culture conflict between the leader and the rest of the band was like poison. The disruptive internal personality conflict within Oasis ultimately led to the group's break-up in 2009.

It took eighteen long years for the band to go from record-breaking phenom to disbandment, but even through all its successes, Oasis was dying a slow death due to the unhealthy internal culture. It was death by a thousand cuts.

The same can and does happen all the time, in organizations where the leader and the rest of the company are not singing off the same sheet of music. Just because your company is experiencing good times right now, the business will eventually be at risk if the leadership culture is not strong.

THERE'S PLENTY TO BLAME

When things are good, morale is great. If a company spends the time and resources to build a pond full of positive culture for its employees to swim in, everyone is happy. However, when the culture becomes noticeably weak, people begin blaming one another.

Partners in Leadership, the strategic team that produced the *The Oz Principle*, call it "The Blame Game." When things go awry, we refuse personal accountability—and that's when the mud-slinging begins. We start assigning blame to all those that influenced or allowed the culture to change for the worse. Even if the cultural change occurred slowly and over the course of several years, there's always someone, or some department, to blame. You know these people well. They may sit in the corner office…they may lurk in the cube beside you…they may have even left the company years before… or they may very well be staring back at you in the mirror. Whatever the case may be, the finger-pointers simply throw gas on an already rampantly burning fire.

While there is certainly plenty of blame to go around when the culture goes astray, that attitude ultimately poisons both the mind and the spirit. We would be fools not to acknowledge what got the company into its current state, but we must also realize it's in the past.

The better attitude is one that looks toward the future and focuses energy on the big picture of what you're trying to accomplish with your organization. This positive, confident, forward-looking approach will both help you avoid the blame mentality and prepare your team for dealing with obstacles as they rear their ugly heads. With that positive and present approach, you can better defend against negativity from others and avoid getting sidetracked by the need to assign fault for past circumstances. Nothing can be gained from blaming others, but everything can be accomplished by staying in the present and forging forward on your quest to enhance the culture. Just be prepared to deal with those that will still resort to the blame-game when the culture is anemic.

You may be one of the fortunate few who have never experienced this type of organizational frustration, but most of us have been there before. Even the best companies go through some periods of cultural flux. Once you realize there are actionable steps you can take to get the company back on track—overhauling some brand collateral, making better hiring decisions, implementing a customer-focused service philosophy, getting your work group more involved in the community, etc.—you will be both empowered and better positioned to implement change.

ALL THINGS ARE CREATED TWICE

In many organizations, regardless of the current leadership, the culture has been so stagnant for so long that changing it seems like too big of an initiative to undertake. But great brands, even ones that have lost their way, can be reignited. It has to start with change.

So how do you deal with cultural paralysis when you are the one challenged with creating or changing the overall attitude of a company? Since all things are created twice—first mentally and then physically—you start the process of cultural change by first making a mental decision.

In everything a person does, there is a gap of time between thought and action. It might be a fraction of a second between deciding to go right and actually turning, or it could be months of planning before going on a vacation. Mental decision first, then physical action. For bigger initiatives, you really need to have a well-developed, studied strategy. It's probably best to have a plan when you go to get a new haircut or build a house. The same is true of making organizational enhancements to your brand's culture. Before you jump in and start making radical changes, you must first mentally decide you can make a difference in the culture. Think it through, get feedback and input from others, secure some champions of your plan within the organization…then go for it.

Can you clearly identify the areas of your company that need to be amped up or revolutionized?

Take another look at the organizational focal points I identified earlier and decide whether you have a clear focus on which areas of the brand need a little love:

- **Service** – creating a consumer-obsessed service mentality
- **People** – hiring only right-fit talent that reflect your brand
- **Infrastructure** – departing from status quo and implementing proven best practices
- **Purpose** – creating an inspiring mission for the business
- **Leadership** – doing the things you say you will do and creating followers through commitment vs. compliance

The company may need some real care and attention in each of these areas, but you can't do everything all at once. Which areas are the most critical? Which actions will generate the highest impact? Those are the ones you should focus on first.

OLD RESOURCES – NEW IDEAS

The first step in any cultural shift is to identify and evaluate which part of the company's culture you hope to change. This will help you develop a course of action to begin the actual modification. It could be the service approach—the way your product is delivered to the consumer. It could be you want to focus on your performance management—the way you manage and lead others. Perhaps you want better storytelling to reinforce your company's heritage. Or it could be your charitable side that yearns for change, when you realize social-conscious consumers are looking for more philanthropic places to spend their money. Whether it's an individual slice of the company that needs addressing or an entire overhaul of the organization is in order, you can position yourself to be a change agent for the brand by identifying the sub-section of the company that most needs a cultural makeover.

There is no shortage of resources to assist us in improving a company's performance in several of these areas, whether your goals are service-oriented, leadership-focused or results-driven. Go to any bookstore—or simply do an Internet search for these words—and you'll discover a world of support. There are already hundreds of books, articles and collateral on these topics, not to mention a countless number of public speakers, DVDs and dedicated websites focused on each subject. Yet I have not found a resource to date that cobbles these elements together into a single format—and certainly not one that is wrapped in a brand-defining cultural case study. Even with all the resources available, we still find ourselves yearning for the "next big thing" that will raise the bar on our own performance or the products we produce.

That's the whole purpose of *Culture That Rocks*. Now that we have defined company culture, highlighted the importance of it and singled-out the key role that leadership plays in its continued health, we need to consider the actual ways we can enhance it.

In the remaining chapters, I'll dive into each of the core focal points and provide you with examples and best practices that you can discuss, debate and implement into your own company—and get your brand back to rock icon status.

Leadership Dramatically Affects Culture:

When the leader of the band is not supportive of or does not understand a company's culture, the result is organizational frustration, conflict and long-term destruction.

- Do you feel that your company's leadership is singing off the same sheet of music as the rest of the organization?
  o If yes, point to specific instances where there is conflict in the brand's mission or direction.
- Debate whether the misaligned culture is a result of poor leadership or a weak and unwilling employee base.
- When making a point for organizational change, do you and your team connect cultural objectives to the company's performance results?
  o If not, how could this be accomplished going forward?
- Are the company's results due to leadership "muscling" the business or the nurturing of a positive culture?

The Blame Game:

Even if the company culture is weak, you still must avoid the blame mentality.

- Discuss whether a "blame mentality"—people complaining about the way things are and pointing out who is at fault—exists in your organization.
- Debate whether most in the organization are focused on looking positively toward the future or blaming others for the past.

Think, Then Act:

All things are created twice—first mentally and then physically. Decide that you can make a difference…then act!

- Clearly identify what areas of the company need to be revolutionized, based on organizational core focal points.
- Discuss the parts of the company culture that you can immediately affect for the better.
- Before you start making organizational changes, have you formulated a solid plan based on feedback from others?
  o Have you secured your champions?
  o Discuss the steps and processes associated with these initiatives.

5

THE TRUE DIFFERENTIATOR

"If you are lucky enough to be different, don't ever change."

- Taylor Swift

I've defined company culture as a collection of individual behaviors, but you may still have a preconceived notion of exactly what "culture" is. Perhaps you see culture as external—the way others see your brand. Or you might equate culture with your internal environment—the way the employees feel and act. Of course, culture is actually a combination of both, but it always starts internally.

An organization's public "personality" doesn't just occur and thrive on its own; it is predicated upon the internal micro-culture of human beings making it come to life. In the land of affecting organizational culture change, these really are pre-requisites of each other.

Changing internal employee behaviors therefore directly affects the end-user's view of the brand's culture. If you seek to change the image projected to the general public, you have to change the way your organization behaves and operates internally.

I'm going to make a flying leap and assume that many of you are looking to improve your company's execution in a specific area. Regardless of your industry, you either sell a product or provide a service, and you think that improving the way your product or service is delivered to others can help create the cultural overhaul you seek.

I've therefore dedicated this chapter to the topic of "service," as this is a key element in the orchestration of cultural change in many companies.

What's the point of working on all the tactical initiatives required for running the business if the overall crux of the business is in providing a service to others—and *that's* the part of the brand that is broken? Addressing everything but the main function of the organization is like rearranging the deck chairs on the Titanic. There may be additional organizational issues to address, but for these specific service-oriented companies, hope for success in other areas of the business only exists when it's anchored with phenomenal customer service at the core.

Fix this and, in many companies, the culture will flourish.

FROM ABUNDANCE TO SCARCITY

Hospitality experts realize the one true differentiator—the one characteristic that separates the average from the best, especially in a strained economic environment—is service, pure and simple.

Industry professionals are reminded of this every day by an onslaught of readily-available competitor data and various industry-tracking tools that correlate customer service metrics with financial growth. But never was it more apparent, to restaurant and hotel experts and the non-industry public alike, than during the global economic crisis in 2008-2009.

In a front-page story during the summer of '09, *USA Today* highlighted the hospitality industry as one of the business segments suffering the most during that tough economic time. As part of that story, the writer noted that when you strip away all the "bells and whistles" of any two competing foodservice or hotel businesses, families will choose one brand over the other because of the known service provided.

As the general public shifted from economic abundance to scarcity, people began assigning more value to the things they bought and did. They became much more cognizant of where they were going to spend their money, especially when it came to the non-essentials purchased with disposable income. Eating at a restaurant, staying at a hotel, going on a cruise, gaming at a casino— these are not day-to-day basic needs; they're luxury items. And yet even more financially stable households began to think more carefully before spending on those services.

Of course many people still travelled and dined out, but the businesses that continued to succeed during those tough times were the ones that focused on exceeding guests' expectations, thereby providing enhanced value. During this time, many hospitality brands were able to leapfrog over their competitors, fueled predominantly by their guest service approach.

TAKE A BITE OF THE APPLE

The delivery of an experience is more critical to overall guest perception than anything else. In fact, the rest of the experience is purely "bricks and mortar" and will never be enough to separate the mediocre companies from the great ones.

For example, consider Steve Jobs and his company, Apple Computers. As a revolutionary, Jobs focused just as much energy on the design and packaging of his products as he did on their performance. He understood that when it comes to marketing and successfully selling technology, the experience—even before the package is opened—can actually make a difference in a consumer's relationship with the company. From the sleek rounded corner design of the hardware itself, to the feeling of the actual packaging, to the act of removing it from its parcel—somehow, Steve Jobs made computers sexy. But it doesn't stop there.

As much of a marketing icon as Steve Jobs was, he knew that the product itself wouldn't be enough. To truly differentiate his product from the competition, he needed to wrap it in a blanket of world-class service. Jobs' intention was to create a love affair between the consumer and his products; accomplishing that would require a symbiotic relationship between the product and the service.

In his quest to make the purchasing experience positive and hassle-free, Jobs created the Apple store—a place saturated with knowledgeable and caring employees. Although the stores are usually packed with customers, it's not uncommon to see as many staff as guests. While many retailers, particularly technology companies, would look to reduce labor costs by reducing the ratio of staff members to store sales, Apple ignores the industry norm and instead goes big, practically posting an employee within arm's length of every customer. And it pays off. The monumental amount of product sold and the glowing customer reviews far outweigh the extra profit the company might generate by reducing staff. In fact, most experts think the change would be detrimental to sales. I'm sure the brand follows a specific staff-to-customer formula or guideline, but you wouldn't know it by walking in to an Apple store. One thing is clear: Labor cost does not seem to be a priority at Apple; the service experience does.

Steve Jobs took this philosophy a step further when he created the *Genius Bar*, a group of knowledgeable problem solvers stationed in the back of every Apple store. Customers can schedule time to meet with these "geniuses" and troubleshoot technological difficulties—or sign up for person-to-person tutorials to get familiar with and maximize the potential of their new toys. This added another layer to the Apple experience, making it that much more memorable.

No doubt Apple makes a great product, but it's the consumer service experience—in each and every Apple venue or telephone conversation with a brand employee—that is legendary and revolutionary. Apple is definitely an example of the connection between service and overall product experience. And because of this approach, Apple has become one of the most successful companies in the world. At the time of this book's writing, stock prices have reached a high of $700 per share, second only to Google, with its annual earnings outperforming the Gross Domestic Product of most countries.

This does not happen by accident. Service is a big part of culture.

GUEST-OBSESSED MENTALITY

As you compare companies within a competitive set, the value of service becomes even more apparent. There are many examples of companies with products nearly indistinguishable from their competitors, yet one flourishes while the other flounders. In these cases, history will often prove the single differentiator between success and failure was the service each company provided to consumers—not the physical product being sold.

U.S. technology retail giants Best Buy and Circuit City are prime examples. Virtually identical in their inceptions and basic product offerings, these competitors couldn't have been further apart in their approach to the market. Best Buy prides itself on fostering a guest-obsessed mentality that has become the standard to which most other retailers aspire—and that single-handedly rendered Circuit City, which relied solely on the products it sold, obsolete. Many of us have shopped in one or both of these companies' stores. Think about your experience when you walk into a Best Buy and compare it to shopping at Circuit City. It is quickly apparent that, while these stores swim in the same pond, they are oceans apart in consumer service. I should say "were"... Circuit City went out of business.

Although Best Buy has experienced some organizational issues of late, the company took a preferably different path than Circuit City—and the public is better off because of it. Brand advocates of Best Buy can only hope that the company does not fall into the same trap as its competitors and lose sight of the thing that made it great in the first place: a customer-centric service philosophy.

THE DELIVERER MATTERS MOST

When it comes down to it, the true differentiator in sustainable business is service.

Using the backdrop of the Hard Rock brand and its service practices, I will present a differentiated take on "guest service" that is both unique and memorable, yet helps bring fundamental, business-critical concepts to the top of your mind—such as developing customer loyalty by creating memories, and understanding that the product itself is not enough for today's consumer. But I'll tell you one thing in advance: The unforgettable service experience you want your customers to have will not come from a product or initiative; it will happen because of a person.

Creating memorable experiences is the ultimate goal in service-oriented businesses, but that's just the desired by-product. *How* you actually get to the point of competitor domination is what separates the good from the great. And this is again going to rely on human beings. Becoming a rock icon, rather than a "one hit wonder" starts with ensuring that you have the right talent delivering the right service—a concept we will explore in upcoming chapters.

The common theme is simple: The deliverer matters most.

LOOK OUT: FISH!

No company better exemplifies the idea that the "deliverer matters most" than the world famous Pike Place Fish Market in Seattle, Washington. Most American business professionals are by now well aware of the famed "fish throwers," whose unique delivery system started organically as a fun way for the fishmonger employees to sell fish.

Imagine working long, grueling shifts in a stinky environment, performing the same mundane tasks of stocking, selling and packing fish day after day. Not the usual place one would expect memorable service, but the employees did indeed create such an environment. It started with an attitude the brand calls its *FISH!* Philosophy: Employees were empowered to go beyond just filling orders and instead create an unforgettable experience for customers—not to mention an unparalleled work environment for each other, now envied by companies around the world.

The FISHmongers started by showcasing products for passersby with attentive service and witty banter, but then they took it to the next level by passionately and loudly announcing a customer's order before tossing the fish to another employee from across the market display. This unique experience was then perpetuated by being captured and shared with the business world through popular and inspiring educational *FISH!* videos, workbooks and seminars.

News of this unique culture at a local fish market was quickly spread by word of mouth. Businesses everywhere began to see the immediate, applicable value of delivering memorable service in their own organizations, regardless of the industry or business type. The appeal was simple: If fishmongers could create a culture that rocks, then we can certainly figure out a way to create better experiences for *our* consumers.

This unexpected showmanship performed by a unique cast of characters is now legendary. In fact, Pike Place Fish Market is the #1 tourist destination in the city. Think about that: a fish market as the ultimate attraction. Sounds unbelievable, but it's true.

These employees made the art of selling fish cool and relevant to the average customer.

The deliverer matters most. Employees are the reason *FISH!* is so popular...not the product itself.

THE KEY TO CONSUMER LOYALTY

If my definition of company culture rings true—that it is, at the core, a collection of individual human behaviors—then, logically, a great guest service culture is only possible with great service-minded individuals.

The person empowered to provide unparalleled customer service is the key to creating consumer loyalty. Consumer loyalty ensures repeat business, which in turn ensures ongoing, profitable growth for the company. As a believer in this "service-profit chain," you have to start with employees to put this domino effect to go into motion.

So how do you get employees to deliver the type of memory-making service that will get your brand to the top of the charts? There are actually many factors to consider, from how employees are trained, to how they are treated by management, to how they are rewarded for positive performance. Before any of that, however, employees need to connect to something bigger than the work itself. They need purpose and a sense of belonging to a worthwhile community. And that requires a little storytelling.

THE COOLEST STORY IN THE HISTORY OF STORIES

Storytelling is a critical part of employee branding and therefore a crucial component of a company's culture.

Employees yearn to be part of a great story. If people can connect to something important to them—or even something bigger than themselves—then asking them to deliver world-class service or create a premium product will be a much easier task. They will do it out of commitment to the brand, versus compliance with a boss. People will do things on behalf of the company not because they *have* to, but because they *want* to. They see the bigger picture and are emotionally involved. Compelling stories motivate people to provide amazing service to consumers. If your employees identify with your company's story and wholeheartedly believe in it, they will work hard to be positive and meaningful representations of it. That's the power of great brands.

Hard Rock International is just such a brand. In fact, Hard Rock's iconic heritage is one of the coolest stories in the history of stories, and it constantly inspires employees to work hard representing that story. The company's remarkable success—it's ability to stand out among its competitive set—is legendary. And it is predominantly due to the brand's dedication to world-class service.

People familiar with Hard Rock will usually acknowledge that its service approach is worthy of high praise. Sure, the irreverent Rock 'n' Roll environment is a great backdrop, but the heart of the brand is its guest service delivery, a performance indicator that regularly earns high marks on guest surveys. It's one of the things that people like the most about the company, and that's not by coincidence. The brand prides itself on being a revolutionary when it comes to offering "service that rocks." The company views every consumer's visit to its hotels, casinos and restaurants as an opportunity to change that person's expectations about exactly what top-notch service should look and feel like. Simply put, Hard Rock strives to become the measuring stick for all other companies.

Just as I hope to share some of Hard Rock's fascinating lore and solid business practices, the company does the same for the thousands of new hires drawn to this legendary brand. Facilitated New Hire Orientations, delivered around the world, are designed to inspire, motivate and even emotionally hook a person to the brand, with the understanding that these "rockers" will then deliver a spectacular and memorable service experience to its guests.

When Hard Rock International came into the world in the early 1970s, it made its mark on pop culture as a restaurant. But the strength of this brand's culture allowed it to thrive in multiple countries and across several businesses, including cafes, hotels, casinos and live music venues. Stacking *that* hospitality brand against the same global organizational goals I observed in '08—differentiated value proposition, unparalleled customer loyalty and strong employee engagement—sets the stage for the rest of my message around enhancing a service culture. After all, Hard Rock is beloved around the world and has become a relevant culture in dozens of International markets.

Irreverent and unpredictable in many of its business practices, Hard Rock boasts a very *intentional* service approach that can serve as a guide for any organization looking to change its culture. Like that brand, any company that can find a service niche and be remarkably great at it will enhance its culture. Hard Rock therefore provides a great case study for organizations looking to differentiate themselves from their competitive set and ultimately become positively positioned at the top of the public's mind. The undisputed cultural phenomenon of the Hard Rock brand is part of the palate with which I continue to paint to this day.

THE FOUNDERS

When Hard Rock Cafe founders Isaac Tigrett and Peter Morton originally set out to create a Tennessee truck stop diner in the United Kingdom, their goal was to introduce the British to American comfort food like hamburgers, milkshakes, BBQ ribs and apple pie, but they also hoped to open a restaurant where everyone would be welcomed and treated the same, regardless of social status. They went to great lengths to ensure the delivery of premium quality products the likes of which the English had never seen *and* to develop a business model that would change the world: great American fare, flavored with a heavy dose of Rock 'n' Roll, yet operating with a social conscience.

Still, it wouldn't be enough.

Even during Hard Rock's inception, Tigrett and Morton knew that "unique service delivery" would be the sustainable x-factor in their business—the thing that would differentiate their product from all the others. So their focus was on delivering unparalleled customer service and cutting edge, but authentic, experiences. Still prevalent today, service is clearly the undisputed key to success for any experience-delivering company.

RECREATE "MOM"

Isaac and Peter's desire to create a place where everyone would be welcomed equally, but serviced individually, could only be fulfilled by the employees they hoped to hire. So although the Founders put tremendous thought, care and attention into every physical guest touch point in the restaurant, their greatest achievement was in hiring the right staff to deliver these unforgettable experiences. You might think they would have gone after a youthful employee base, but instead they hired only 30+-year-old women as their original servers. Of course, you couldn't possibly get away with marketing for and hiring this narrow and select group today, but things were different in the '70s.

Their approach sparks an interesting question: What was it about a 30-year-old woman in the 1970's that, in the Founders' eyes, made her uniquely capable of delivering experiences that would resonate with customers? For starters, she was exactly the type of waitress you would actually find in a road-side diner or truck stop in the American South, which was the themed business model of the first cafe. But their rationale transcended even that notion.

Their idea was simple: Let's recreate "mom."

It certainly didn't hurt that a more experienced service employee came with none of the perceived baggage of a 19-year-old—but that was just a small part of their reasoning when they selected the original staff.

Most of the London Hard Rock Cafe's original servers were plucked from local hotel restaurants and private clubs, but their technical expertise was also not the sole driving force behind the Founders' decision. No doubt it helped in areas like attention-to-detail, sense of urgency and an impeccable work ethic, but Peter and Isaac determined right away that dining customers wanted to be treated as special, as if they were having dinner at their mother's house …where they would be constantly coddled.

The personalized, organic and unpredictable experiences delivered by "mom," the Founders believed, would create unforgettable memories for their customers. This approach was quite forward-thinking at the time, but it wound up being the lynchpin of the cafe's long-term success.

All of that happened more than four decades ago. Fast-forward to today: The guests and employees are a bit different, aren't they? The out-of-the-box thinking employed by Hard Rock's Founders worked for them for a long time, but the world has continued to change. In the '70s, '80s and '90s, you could create magic just by pairing great people with great service-oriented companies. Today, that perfect marriage between employers and potential employees is rare.

Today's consumers are aware of this all too well. The general public knows great customer service has sadly been whittled away over the years. People say it to me personally, they validate it in focus groups and it's blatantly clear in industry-wide surveys. You may have come to the same conclusion based on your own experiences; I'm sure you don't need a detailed report to prove it. It's a pretty transparent problem in service industries everywhere.

You could even do your own impromptu guest survey by asking ten random people what they think about customer service today; it wouldn't be shocking if the responses mostly landed in the "mediocre" to "poor" range. It's equally possible that none of the responses would fall into the "good" to "great" categories. People just know. And they yearn for the "good ole days" of being treated as special when they go out to eat, stay in hotels or shop in their favorite stores.

The average consumer may blame this service decline on lack of employee training or the "way kids are brought up today," but in any case, they are smart enough to realize that the problem isn't with a process, it's with the human beings who fulfill it.

Creating memorable experiences is still the ultimate goal for lifestyle brands like Hard Rock, but now it has become everyone's sacred mantra. And in today's environment, it's the one that really matters.

WHAT WOULD MOM DO?

So what does the type of server Hard Rock chose to hire more than forty years ago have to do with a company's inner-culture today?

Remember, this type of careful employee selection was revolutionary in the hospitality industry at the time. Nobody was doing it. And therein lies the point: Hard Rock managed to find a novel and unique way to transform the way it offered its product, and that became the defining element of the brand's success.

When you consider shifting your company's culture through the way it presents products and services, you should be looking for the same type of defining element—something unique compared to your direct competitors. In other words, you have to find your own way to recreate "mom." Clearly, I don't mean that you should channel your inner mother. But to be a culture catalyst you have to identify the best route for providing your service—and then figure out how to implement it into the inner-workings of your organization.

To make the connection in your own company, here are a few "What Would Mom Do?" suggestions for you to consider:

- **Allow employees to be unique, even different than everyone else**—Mom loved you exactly the way you were
- **Make customers feel special, like they are guests in your home**—the way Mom made you feel every time you walked into her house
- **Authentically connect with others, not as a technique, but with genuine interest**—just as Mom listened and paid attention to your every word

Mom was right about a lot of things, and we could all learn a thing or two about making others feel special from her. In the next few pages, we'll review these basic, motherly tenets as we go deeper into enhancing your company's execution of a product or service.

GREATEST HITS THAT ROCK	THIS IS HOW YOU ROLL
Service Breeds Success: Hope for success in other areas of the business only exists with phenomenal service anchored at the core. There should be a symbiotic connection between the overall service and product experience.	• If you are in an organization that sells a product or a service, is your *service* culture strong? 　o How do you know for sure? • Does your brand dominate the rest of your competitive set in service delivery? 　o Explain why or why not. • Do you feel like your company has the right staff-to-guest ratio to ensure great customer service? • Debate what the right ratio should be.
The Deliverer Matters Most: Unforgettable service experiences do not happen because of an initiative or a product, but because of a person.	• Do your employees connect with the brand's story and seek out passionate, committed ways to represent the company? • List out your brand's clear staffing differentiators that separates you from your closest competitors. • Discuss whether your brand focuses too much on sales staff labor costs, when there should be more employees to provide great service.
Be A Storyteller: Employees need to belong to a great community with a great purpose. Great storytelling is a critical part of employee branding, which leads to commitment vs. compliance.	• Does your company heritage have a compelling story to be told? • How is the story captured and shared in your company? • Is the story of your brand's beginnings and philosophies told in an inspiring way when new employees join your company? • Debate whether or not you even have the right collateral and/or storytellers to properly relate the message.
Recreate Mom: Make strong authentic connections between the employee and the consumer—the way your mother made you feel every time you walked into her house.	• How do you think your guests feel when interacting with your brand? • Debate whether or not your customers feel as though they are treated as special. • Discuss your brand's customer survey scores—specifically the ratings regarding service delivery.

6
BE THE CHOCOLATE

"I don't ever want to do anything mediocre."

- Amy Winehouse

Aren't you flabbergasted when you actually experience great service? I know I am. Most consumers simply do not regularly receive fantastic service, so they are generally not used to it. It is clear, however, that when great service exists, it fuels the fire of success. Sure, there's something to be said for being loyal to a local joint or even sticking to what we know based on consistency and familiarity, but most of us crave a different type of service experience. One that takes us aback, pleasantly surprises us, and exceeds expectations…the type of experience that's different than what everyone else is offering. We all want to feel special and be catered to as individuals.

Unfortunately, very few companies have actually capitalized on this "make me feel special" approach. The businesses that focus on this concept know that it's key to their sustainable success and work diligently to build it into their organizational culture. Great guest experiences are not the result of a one-time program or annual initiative with these companies; they are generated through authentic guest-obsessed tendencies and have always been a central part of the brand's day-to-day behaviors.

For example, Hard Rock is the physical manifestation of Rock 'n' Roll for many fans of the brand. In a sense, it is as close to raw music and rock icons as the average person will ever get. Every time you walk into one of the branded venues, it's as though you've just entered a concert arena and have front row seats to see your favorite band. That's the experience the brand tries to create for each and every customer.

The real connection, however, occurs with the staff. Hard Rockers are the bridge between the guests and the spirit of Rock 'n' Roll, the cultural backbone for the company. The way Rock was borne into the world—with an authentic, irreverent and unpredictable attitude—has become the philosophy by which the company operates. You might be shocked to discover that Hard Rock's service model does indeed include irreverence and unpredictability, but that's exactly the tight rope the brand walks to deliver high-quality standards with an attitudinal flair. Great service, pumped through an amplifier. Employees are taught to always be respectful, but also to help their guests take a walk on the wild side; that combination provides a better chance of creating a memorable experience. It's also a combination that few other brands would dare attempt, keeping them firmly mired in the word of mediocrity.

> *"To be Rock...I can't see us being vanilla ice cream.*
> *There's nothing wrong with vanilla, but people need a little chocolate in their lives...*
> *and I think that's what we provide. We get to be the chocolate."*
>
> - Mike Kneidinger, former VP of Company Cafes, Hard Rock International

That's the analogy this former company executive used in training classes when he talked about the brand representing Rock 'n' Roll and battling against mediocrity. In the land of ice cream, creating a unique service experience is about being the chocolate in a world full of vanilla.

Sometimes reinventing culture through service is about being different. It is about finding the societal norm and then going against the grain, swimming upstream while everyone else takes the path of least resistance.

SERVICE UNIQUENESS GETS REWARDED

Unique and unforgettable guest-employee interactions separate Hard Rock from its competitors. They are internally celebrated by the brand and externally recognized in the public domain.

Internally, collectible service pins are awarded regularly to those employees who exceeded specific guest satisfaction scores on a customer survey or a Mystery Shopper's report. The company pin culture at Hard Rock is unbelievable. So when, during a pre-shift team meeting for example, an employee is recognized with a pin for great service, that desired behavior is more likely to be duplicated by his or her peers. As an added benefit, the best service-oriented Hard Rockers also get scheduled for their preferred shifts, allowing them to make more money or establish their own work/life balance.

Externally, the unique service provided is what guests like most about the brand. Guest surveys and consumer brand health studies validate this. Loyal fans certainly love the music and memorabilia environment, but the overall experience provided by the employees is what lures people back time and time again. Everyone wins with repeat business, which is a key component in the organization's sustainability.

Being different has its benefits.

This unique approach translates into a tremendous responsibility for the thousands of global team members who wear the Hard Rock logo, and one they collectively take very seriously. Front-line employees know that they cannot simply deliver on basic service standards. That's the bare minimum for staying in the game. It's what they do *additionally* that creates memorable experiences. If staff members were content with only delivering basic service, the brand would fall into the same forgettable malaise that so many others deliver. Mediocre. Middle-of-the-road. Boring. Nothing special.

The notion that uncompromising service delivered by an authentic employee is the way to the customers' hearts permeates the overall attitude of the Hard Rock brand. You too can channel this attitude to create your own culture that rocks.

WALK THE LINE

Here are a just a few ways in which employees can provide guest service that's different than the norm:

- Rather than delivering a memorized script, greet guests authentically, using generational-speak appropriate for the specific customer
- Actually interact with people while you ride together in the guest elevator—something that a few in the hotel industry see as taboo
- Make genuine eye contact with shoppers standing in line to purchase something; give them the look, head nod or verbal confirmation of "I'll be right with you."
- Move at lightening speed in response to every guest's request, even if they are the only patrons around
- Kneel down at the table when taking a customer's food order, immediately creating a more intimate and stronger connection between the guest, the employee and the brand

Would any of these actions contradict your brand image? Are some of them too over-the-top for you? Do you wonder how your customers will react or worry about the types of guest interactions your staff might initiate? Only *you* can answer, based on how open you are to change and how receptive you believe your brand would be to walking the line of unpredictability.

By the way, the suggestions above are extremely "safe" recommendations by Hard Rock standards—they're practically baseline "givens" for the brand. But if these are not the irreverent liberties that Hard Rock employees are empowered to take in their quest to rock people's worlds, they could certainly be a start for your organization. You may not be able to implement all or even any of these ideas—but be aware that your risk-taking competitors may.

More and more, people today want uniqueness in their service experience. The baseline for service has been raised. Average is no longer good enough. Excellence is the new Average.

In other words, if you want to improve culture through service… be the chocolate, not the vanilla.

FOUR-LETTER WORDS

When it comes to service, it's easy for some companies to succeed these days because so many others aren't even trying. The bar is set extremely low. Most organizations offer consumers very little and yet expect to receive an enormous return on it. Too many companies wallow around in Pleasantville—where everything is "shades of grey" safe—offering completely *forgettable* service to their consumers.

This may be because there are fewer role models to emulate. Looking around, there are only a select few companies that really ooze fantastic customer service. The truly standout service companies have seemingly all but disappeared. Sadly, we live in an era where great guest service is no longer the norm, but rather the exception. Companies talk about it and executives are aware of it, yet few actually address it—even those that are supposed to be running service-oriented companies.

This societal shift did not occur overnight. The downward spiral began more than two decades ago, and there seems to be no end in sight. It's as though all of the restaurants, hotels and retailers gathered in a massive conference and collectively agreed to be mediocre, just to see what would happen. Because it *actually* happened.

Now here we are with the dinosaur-like notion that customer service is an afterthought, that there's little added incentive to be a true service provider. This simply *has* to change. And it can. In fact, once it does, the culture and success of your company will mirror this transformation.

It's easy to tell when a guest interaction is stuck in this mediocre quagmire; just listen to the verbal cues customers give when they're asked about their experience. Look for the predictable "four-letter words" which I believe will eventually put a company out of business (no, not *those* four-letter words). Ask a guest, "How is everything?" and if the experience is pretty forgettable, you'll hear one of the following four-letter words:

- Fine
- Good
- Okay

These words scream mediocrity. At the very least, the customers are not getting great service. The interaction doesn't have to be poor, just forgettable. A guest does not have to be venomous and blatantly upset with the service provided for it to make a negative difference in your brand's success. In fact, being forgettable can be worse than being just plain bad. When service is actually *bad*, you often have a chance to salvage the experience and even blow away the guests' initial expectations with some service recovery techniques. However, if your company is *forgettable*, it leaves no lasting impression and little reason to ever return. You are run of the mill, average, typical and ordinary. This mediocre strategy leaves little hope for any brand's sustainability.

AVOIDING THE FORGETTABLE

To avoid four-letter words, your company may have to change some of its service practices.

You might start by adjusting the way you ask people about their experience. When you ask "How is everything?" in a very casual and uninterested way, then you can expect a canned, unconscious four-letter response that matches the tone of your question: "Fine." Consumers are so used to this question that they have developed automatic responses that connote as much emotion and care as the person who asked "Everything okay?"

One way to avoid this type of a response is to ask specifically about the food item, the hotel stay or the theme park ride. That specificity will provide you with the type of realistic feedback you want, but also will most likely influence the customer to engage with you a bit more. Everybody wins here, as an authentic moment is created for the guest.

Another way to minimize these four-letter word responses is to alter the customer environment. If you create an environment that supports the mission of having a guest-obsessed service mentality, the end-user will respond differently when asked how their *experience* is going. In brands that have hired and trained individuals to make solid eye contact, authentically smile at people, move as if they can't move fast enough for the guests and cater to customers' every need to their surprise and delight, it's doubtful that, when prompted, customers will respond with a simple, unemotional "Good" or "Okay." It's more likely you'll hear "It's awesome!" or "This place rocks!"

ACCEPTABLE MEDIOCRITY

Unfortunately, lukewarm service is so prevalent in our society that most people no longer even recognize it as such. It's simply the norm. In fact, service that doesn't verge on being poor is not only accepted; it's actually expected. This revealing quote from Ken Blanchard's book, *Raving Fans* says it all:

"People expect bad goods and rude service.
If the abuse isn't worse than they expected, they'll be back for more."

This mindset has created what I call "acceptable mediocrity." And we have all contributed to its creation.

I'm sure that at one time or another, you have experienced a mediocre interaction with a person or a company, only to shrug it off because you like the product, the price point or the convenient store location. Other times, however, you let it go simply because you're used to tepid service. By allowing this totally forgettable interaction to go unaddressed, we endorse its continuation. This is "acceptable mediocrity."

VOTE NOW!

Every once in a while, the combination of mediocre service and an uncaring attitude creates enough of a perfect storm or bad experience that someone decides to act. The customer either points out the poor experience to a supervisor, takes the time to call or write a letter to the corporate office, leaves a negative online review, or simply leaves, vowing never to return to the establishment because of the poor experience. The latter is the ultimate stance on one's principles, hitting the business where it hurts the most—in its financial pockets.

Brave people vote with their feet. Deciding to not shop, eat, drink or stay somewhere based on a consistently uncaring or poor experience says a lot about one's personal integrity. But most of the time, we don't stand on principle, eventually crawling back to the establishment again and again because of the product, the price or the convenience. As consumers, we give these notions far greater value than the actual service provided. Customer service is now an artifact, rarely considered by the business and hardly cared for by the consumer. This cyclical relationship *has* to come to an end. We *have* to break the chain and reinvigorate companies with pure, uncut, quality service. This is a critical part of creating and maintaining a strong culture.

I am not immune to "acceptable mediocrity." Although I talk about it all the time, am constantly cognizant of its existence and am now writing about it in this book—I am, sadly, a part of this reality. I tend to be one of those consumers who votes with his feet. When an experience is blatantly middle-of-the-road or slightly poor, my response is to just not go back. My family and close friends know this is how I am wired, and they've seen me take a harsh stance on lackluster or bad service experiences. But even I would have a hard time adding some businesses to my "no go" list…simply because I am running out of places where I can go. So like many others, I've come to accept mediocrity, because at least it's not *bad* service. I have learned to deal with the tepid.

As part of your brand's desire to enhance its organizational culture, mediocrity must be avoided at all costs. Becoming forgettable is the fastest way to help your competition become the headlining act.

We'll continue to explore some of these concepts in upcoming chapters, but here are a few suggestions to specifically help you avoid mediocrity:

- Hire employees who naturally do battle against the mundane because it's in their nature
- Recommit and retrain every employee to become guest-obsessed
- Enhance your recognition and rewards for those employees who go above and beyond in providing customer service
- Convene with your staff regularly and discuss how to differentiate your brand from others
- Take risks in delivering a product or service with an approach that is fresh and unpredictable
- Join networking associations to understand what your competitors are doing, then do something unique

UNINTENTIONAL CONSEQUENCES

Sometimes, the customer's experience is affected negatively by a single moment. It may be unintentional, but nevertheless enough to derail the entire experience.

There are literally hundreds of details we have to get right for customers to feel they've had a positive, even memorable, experience. Yet it only takes a single moment for it to go sideways. One misstep can ruin an entire experience. This is especially true in hospitality, mostly because there are so many other, similar places a consumer can choose. The hospitality customer has many options, so the service experience is *that* much more important for sustainable health.

I can't tell you the number of times I have visited a restaurant where everything was perfect, from the time I parked my car to the moment I asked for the check, only to find myself stuck in the last phase of the experience, emphatically scanning the room for my server, waiting interminably to pay the bill.

That single lack-of-awareness moment, even at the very end of the experience, negated all the perfect practices that came before it. Was it intentional? Absolutely not. But this part of the experience is a fundamental part of any restaurant's service model. A key tenet in the restaurant world is that we should never let the guests wait to pay. What was looking to be a memorable and successful experience turned into a below average, forgettable one…and it happened at "the drop of a hat." Just *that* quick to go from great to poor, because of a single person's behavior. The worst part is most poor service examples like these are absolutely avoidable.

If the unfavorable service is unintentional, and the overall product, price and experience is still favorable, it's much easier to forgive the weak service once and simply hope the behavior isn't the norm. Personally, a scenario like that would result in a return trip from me. I would give the business another shot. However, if the service is flat-out poor or consistently lackadaisical, then that business becomes one of the places forever etched onto my "no go" list, banished for all time, with zero hope of a future visit.

In many cases, apathy is the ultimate culprit. The employee or employees simply didn't care—or at least didn't appear to care. And apathy contributes to "acceptable mediocrity."

To recap: A great service approach is critical to a brand's culture. Great service—not mediocre service—creates lifelong customers. Even in companies with weaker perceived cultures than their competitors can, with just a few shifts in their service approach, make a huge difference in their overall cultures. And those that aspire to change their service culture need only spend a little energy and focus on their staff-to-guest interactions to truly become memorable and separate themselves from the rest.

Find Your Chocolate:
Find a novel and unique way to deliver your product. In a vanilla world, people need a little chocolate in their lives—be the chocolate!

- Do you feel as though your service approach is a differentiator for you among your competitors?
  o Explain why or why not.
- If not, what could you start doing—or stop doing—that would get your consumers to acknowledge service as a cherished benefit?
- Discuss possible service initiatives that would allow your team members to be "unpredictable" with customers.

Avoid the Forgettable:
Four-letter words like "fine," "good" and "okay" should be avoided at all costs—they will eventually put you out of business.

- Are you confident that these four-letter words are not used by your customers when they're asked about their experience with your brand?
- What systems do you have in place to eliminate these words from your consumers' feedback?

Un-Acceptable Mediocrity:
Don't engage in "acceptable mediocrity." Vote with your feet—your guests do.

- Are you the type of person who takes a stand on mediocre (or poor) service by vowing to not return to a business?
  o Explain why you would or would not do this.
- Debate whether your brand experience currently falls into the middle-of-the-road category, where customers are aware of the mediocrity but continue to come back.
- How positive are your year-on-year guest counts?
  o Discuss the reasons for your results.
- Debate whether "feet voters" are voting *for* you or *against* you because of mediocrity.

7
CULTURE WARRIORS

"The best subjects are always people; who never fail to amaze me by their unpredictability."
- Ronnie James Dio

The Rolling Stones, arguably one of the greatest Rock 'n' Roll bands of all time, was the highest grossing concert act every time the band went on the road—especially in the latter stages of its career. It wouldn't matter if the band produced or sold a new record ever again, the group would still sell out each and every show, even while commanding a premium price. And people would pay it—just to watch Mick Jagger and Keith Richards do their thing on stage. Fans lucky enough to get tickets to a Stones show were willing to pay the price *for* the show, *because of* the show. And they did this time and time again. It did not matter how many times these "lifers" saw The Rolling Stones, if the band was in town, its dedicated and determined followers would find a way to see the show.

People only repeat what they like.

The same is true in the service industry. If a business provides service that exceeds the consumer's expectations, that consumer's return is almost guaranteed. And it will be early and often. So it's no coincidence that many of the great service stories you hear reference the same few companies—companies that continue to produce consistent and healthy results.

SERVICE CULTURE VETERANS

In this chapter, you will find numerous examples of world-class, service-oriented companies, each of which I consider "monsters of rock." They are The Rolling Stones of the service industry. Many of them will not be the "usual suspects" you think of—you may not have even heard of some of them. But when it comes to great service, storytelling is one of the best ways to become personally inspired and ultimately motivated to act on the change you desire. Perhaps, within this collection of my service culture faves, you will find the spark you need to change your company's internal culture.

Here are a few of the well-known brands that have always stood out to me.

Nordstrom

Department store giant Nordstrom is one of those companies with a decades-long run of providing great experiences directly to its consumers. Surely by now you've heard the infamous story of how a customer returned an unsatisfactory set of tires and received a refund from the store. This story helped define Nordstrom's service culture—largely because of the fact that the brand doesn't sell tires.

That single story-heard-round-the-world is the stuff of legends. The in-the-moment decision from a single employee to accommodate a person who was not even a Nordstrom customer—does not happen instinctively. Without a doubt, the environment in which this salesperson felt empowered to take such bold action was already present at Nordstrom.

Are you bold enough as a business to take back an item without a receipt or proof of purchase...or even an item not sold by your brand? Because cultures like Nordstrom's do this without fear. And those organizational cultures are creating new fans every day.

Disney

The Walt Disney World organization is also a master at culture. When founder Walt Disney sought to create the "happiest place on Earth," he purposefully focused on every detail of the guest's theme park visit so he could better control the overall experience. A swarm of human street sweepers are let loose in the park daily to keep immaculate order. Hedges are clipped and grass is mowed at night to keep up the illusion of perfection in guests' eyes. Buildings, rides and natural landscape are all designed to keep you from catching even a remote "behind the curtain" view of the park's inner machinery. Mickey Mouse's face is even imprinted in the bowls of cigarette ashtrays strewn throughout the park. Yes, everything is purposefully themed—but all of that only sets the stage for the real magic: guest interactions with employees.

In the company's initial on-boarding program, *Traditions*, all Disney cast members are taught fundamental service principles that include the art of creating "magical memories." In a nutshell, Disney teaches each of its 60,000+ employees that they are empowered to take moments out of their scheduled shifts to create experiences so memorable the guests involved will not forget the interaction for the rest of their lives. These unforgettable moments are called "magical memories." This simple concept has helped align an entire workforce with Disney's culture.

Starbucks

And let's not forget about Starbucks. For a variety of reasons, this company is solely responsible for making coffee cool. But it's not just about the coffee, is it? Loyal fans of the company love just about everything Starbucks does: its quality product, the trendy artwork on the walls, a mix of overstuffed and ergonomic furniture and a leading-edge approach to fair trade practices and socially-conscious initiatives. But it's the personalized service provided by quick and knowledgeable "baristas" that make this brand a daily routine for millions. You get in, out and caffeinated quickly and efficiently with the help of a pleasant and professional employee who probably looks and behaves just a little bit differently than coffee shop employees looked and behaved before Starbucks entered our lives.

While Starbucks' unforgettable service practices may not perform on as grand of a stage as those of Disney or Nordstrom, the coffee company still leaves its mark on our society with the way each of us have been treated while in one of its stores: special. Whether it's the unique language they've created for our coffee, the fact that the baristas write our names on the cups or that they commit our customized drink orders to memory, it all works for them.

I actually refer to the company as "Fourbucks," because that's what I'm willing to spend for every single cup of the Starbucks experience—four dollars. I could go elsewhere, pay less or wait in a shorter line, but when it comes down to it, Starbucks has earned my business with the service experience it offers. This experience is worth my four bucks, two times a day, five days a week. Do the math. I spend $2,000 a year at Starbucks when I could just drink the free coffee at work or spend 10 percent of that cost by brewing it at home.

It is not a single story that defines these organizations, but a definitive service culture, rich in a heritage of customer obsession. And for that, I am a fan of each.

LESSONS FROM THE GIANTS

Culture doesn't happen by accident. It has to be developed and fostered. As much as Starbucks' leader, Howard Schultz, focuses on the product, he knows that the environment and the way in which it is delivered matters just as much. Perhaps culture was not deemed critical—or even considered—at the company's inception, but as the brand began to scale beyond selling bulk coffee and eventually just a single store in Seattle, it garnered a heightened focus as one of the company's key value offerings.

This is something to consider if you are a small business on the cusp of expanding your brand. It's certainly not easy to come out of the gate with a phenomenal culture as a small company or single-location start-up, but it is definitely *easier* than being a massive organization trying to hold onto or maintain a great culture.

When you are a small company, you have better control over all the nuances that go into making up the culture, especially the individual behaviors that are hired and developed. Once you cross the threshold of having multiple, geographically wide-spread locations and must rely on other company leaders to make local decisions about talent, systems and processes, the task of maintaining culture becomes much more difficult.

Great brands continue to painstakingly develop and foster their organizational cultures because they understand how critical their reputations are. Culture is everything to them. And it should be for you.

Here are just a few lessons we can learn about fostering culture from these well-known brands:

- Take great care when thinking through what you want your culture to be—before it gets too big to effectively maintain
- Surround yourself with competent decision-makers that act in the best interest of the brand, especially when leadership is not around
- Empower your employees to create "magical memories" with their guests
- Never stop developing the culture—regardless of the company's size

SMALL BUT LEGENDARY

These three venerable legends—Nordstrom, Disney and Starbucks—may already be etched in your brain as cultural icons, but there are many other entrepreneurial companies, some big and some small, that "get it." These companies have taken great care and attention to separate themselves from the rest. They have found ways to differentiate themselves from their competitors and have avoided mediocrity with their memorable service cultures.

Remember, *USA Today* reported in 2009 that "service," above all else, was the ultimate deciding factor for families choosing where to eat. It really is the one true differentiator when it comes to similar businesses. This is not exclusive to hospitality. Part of creating a "culture that rocks" is ensuring that you have a *service* culture that rocks. The service delivery is more important than the product itself. To grab more market share, even as a small company, your brand has to win the war of differentiation with your competition. Unparalleled service is the way to do it.

Let me share just a few personal, memory-searing experiences with some lesser-known brands whose cultures would rival the giants. Each of these culture warriors has figured out that customized, personalized service is the secret to avoiding mediocrity and creating a successful brand. Borrowing a phrase from my friend Michael Rawls, these less-public companies and stealth individuals use "service as their weapon-of-choice to do battle against the mundane."

Yellow Dog Eats

Twenty minutes from my home, in the Central Florida township of Gotha, lives one of the greatest restaurant "finds" around. Overshadowed by the unlimited amount of casual dining available in the greater Orlando area, Yellow Dog Eats was once only known to the locals. But as its reputation began to spread, even tourists discovered the small restaurant's website and eventually flocked to the restaurant to experience the legendary service and fantastic food.

In a restaurant named after his beloved yellow Labrador Retriever, throwback chef and entrepreneur Fish Morgan has carved out one of the trendiest places in the area. While the restaurant hangs its hat on serving mouth-watering classic sandwiches, soups and desserts with an eclectic twist, *that* is only a small fraction of the experience. The two-story house-turned-café is adorned with a potpourri of items: photos of yellow Labs, a handful of signed celebrity black & white photos, jars of homemade jams, jellies, condiments and sauces. Most would consider this a pretty odd array of knick-knacks, but that's just part of the overall charm.

Yellow Dog Eats is located across the street from a church in the heart of a conservative community, and for many years zoning restrictions meant Fish could only sell wine by the bottle. This would be a monumental handicap for many restaurants, as alcohol sales provide the largest profit potential—sometimes as much as 50 to 75 percent of the business' earnings. This challenge did not seem to phase Fish. In fact, it gave him an excuse to create an experiential window craved by the locals: free wine tastings in the evening to generate buzz and product demand. Still, this is but a backdrop to the overall experience. Without a doubt, the real secret ingredient to the business' success is its owner, Chef Fish Morgan.

After visiting the establishment dozens of times on my own, I began singing its praises and bringing friends to eat…all because of the owner. There was never a time when I brought a friend to Yellow Dog Eats that Fish did not come out of the kitchen or from behind the register to shake the new customer's hand, give him a huge embrace or even kiss her on the cheek. Not a common practice with complete strangers, but Fish pulls it off with a warm and welcoming disposition.

Chef Morgan certainly has an insatiable desire to talk. And he makes the most honest, off-the-cuff comments—usually the first thing that comes to his mind. At first contact, you would think his communication filter was removed at birth, but Fish's personality and approach is all by design. He "gets it." He knows exactly what it takes to stand out in the consumer's mind, and his authenticity and attention to service is unparalleled in the area. He may talk about his ongoing battle with the city commission over serving wine by the glass or he may slide into describing the time and preparation it took to make his unique pulled pork, but every conversation with Fish is a breath of fresh air compared to your usual meal-time conversation with a restaurant manager. Along with fantastic food, the culture this one person creates is the reason I continue to go back—and bring others with me—to Yellow Dog Eats.

You don't have to have an eclectic business or be the company's owner to create the same type of environment. You and the people you surround yourself with just need to be as passionate and committed as Fish is to rocking people's worlds. Approach every single customer as if he or she is a VIP or your best friend. Treat people like they're special and their positive experience is practically guaranteed.

Make people feel special and the culture will thrive.

Jellyfish

I had another fantastic service experience while I was helping to open a restaurant in the Dominican Republic. On one of our free nights, the new management team took the Director of Operations and me to dinner at a local outdoor restaurant called Jellyfish. The fresh seafood was spectacular, the scenery was picturesque and the conversations were great—but it was the music that really made it a memorable evening.

When we first walked in, typical Caribbean music was playing in the background for the six to eight different parties already seated. About halfway through our meal, however, I noticed a switch from local Reggae, Merengue and Pacheta music to the more-familiar Classic Rock tunes I love—now playing prominently in the foreground. At the end of our table, my friend Tom Perez and I lost ourselves in the journey back to the '60s and '70s, singing along to every tune. When I asked the restaurant manager what radio station was playing so I could tune into it during my stay on the island, his response took me aback. He said it was not a traditional Dominican radio station, but rather came through the satellite radio he installed a few months earlier, just for an occasion like this.

He apparently noticed that I was an American when I walked in, so he perfectly selected the right time to switch the station, making the music an organic part of the experience—specifically for me. Wow. Talk about someone who is motivated to customize an experience to his clientele. Too cool. Of course, the enjoyable environment compelled us to stay longer than we planned for desserts and coffee, which didn't hurt his business either. That was an experience I will never forget and a memory I often share with friends and colleagues.

This is a subtle yet phenomenal way to enhance your organization's culture. Regardless of your business, look for a way that you can personalize or customize the experience for your consumers, like this restaurant owner did for me—and don't be afraid to go for it. When the service experience moves from a traditional business process to one that is thoughtfully catered to the individual, the customer will remember it forever. You can expect the guest to not only come back, but also tell everyone he or she knows about you. And those are the two most important metrics in any business.

Independence Airlines

Another company that created a "culture that rocks" was the low-cost airline Independence Air based out of Washington, DC. As an independent travel provider, the airline took a refreshing approach to their service model, which followed in the successful footsteps of Southwest Airlines.

There were many things I loved about Independence Air—some obviously resulted from planned initiatives, while others were impromptu moments created by the staff. My first impression came with the food offering. The first time I experienced food-for-purchase on an airplane, with brand-name snack choices like Doritos and Oreos, was on my inaugural flight with Independence. Sure, you still had to pay for the items, but this was pretty cool, especially when you were used to the generic bag of pretzels or peanuts. The decision was made at this airline to provide premium products to its passengers, albeit at a premium price, to create an upgraded experience. Everything matters when it comes to creating a memorable environment—airline snacks included.

Another of Independence Air's outstanding initiatives was a program called Happy Bag. The airline's overall goal was to change the common traveler's perception of flying by revolutionizing the baggage retrieval process—the part most expert fliers consider to be the worst part of the experience. The program had two basic components. First, Independence Air guaranteed that by the time you arrived at Baggage Claim, your luggage would be available. I confirmed this personally on each of my flights from Orlando to Washington, D.C. How they did this when other airlines couldn't is still beyond me. Even more amazing, the carrier immediately offered passengers a free, one-way flight if their checked baggage was lost. Rather than fighting customers for hours on the phone or in person, Independence Air simply took responsibility and made it right.

The second part of the Happy Bag program was the mind-blowing encore for me. During check-in, Independence Air attached its signature, bright blue luggage tag to every piece of checked luggage. Unbeknownst to the customers, one of these tags contained a travel certificate good for a free round-trip on any of the airline's routes. To everyone's surprise and delight, this was broadcast to passengers during the final arrival announcements as the aircraft landed. No one knew who would win, but the excitement of everyone standing around the conveyor belt at Baggage Claim—smiling at each other as we checked our tags—was priceless.

These loyalty initiatives created positive experiences out of what are traditionally hassles, and they certainly made an impression on me. Still, these initiatives don't hold a candle to what I recall the most about the air-line. It was the pervasive culture—the collection of individuals—that made the difference.

Every person at the airline with whom I came into contact was genuinely pleasant; the employees had an aura about them that implied they wanted to be around other human beings. They enjoyed their jobs and brought that enjoyment into the overall company culture. Whether they had been trained to appear like this or they were hired already embedded with this genetic coding, it was refreshing.

From check-in, to boarding, to departure, every interaction was spectacu-lar. Like Southwest Airlines, Independence Air allowed its flight attendants to dress casually and instill some humor into their safety announcements. They also occasionally replaced flight attendant safety announcements with pre-recorded versions of the announcements by local celebrities and political pundits, like James Carville and Mary Matalin. After landing, the pilots even came out and joined the flight attendants in handing breath mints to pas-sengers as they departed the plane. Nice, huh?

According to the Gallup Organization, an airline's customer service im-pacts brand loyalty four times more than its advertising. Apparently, this fact did not escape the founders of Independence Air. At the airline's inception, they formed an affiliate company of Human Resources experts, trainers and Marketing professionals called the Tribe Culture. This group's sole function was to create, instill and manage an internal brand culture at the airline. Employees were meticulously taught to live the company's brand promise, to "challenge the status quo to make travel faster, easier, and more interesting." Through employee training, intense leadership sessions and the development of a truly branded workplace environment, the carrier's employees were soon delivering a positive, energetic and on-brand experience—unlike anything else in the industry to their customers.

In just one year, those experiences made Independence Air the nation's number one airline in customer service, according to mystery shop expert Market Metrix. It was clearly apparent to me. It wasn't a single initiative that made the experience of flying with this airline great, but rather an overarching culture that rocked my world.

Your brand's culture can be like this. Consider creating or suggesting the formation of a "tribe culture" of some sort in your organization—consisting of representatives from all areas of the business. I'm sure many of Independence Airlines' ideas came from this core group of employees, including the ones to revolutionize mundane tasks like safety announcements and baggage retrieval. They seemed to put a twist on almost every customer touch point. You may not want or be able to go as far as making sweeping process changes in your company, but organizing a group of committed brand ambassadors like this will certainly challenge the status quo. And that's a good thing. This is one way to keep your culture fresh and unique.

Portofino Hotel

A friend of mine came to Orlando for a family vacation and stayed at the Portofino, a local themed resort hotel modeled after the famed bay resort in Italy and located at Universal Studios' Citywalk. After a long day of playing at the theme parks, the family dropped their merchandise and gifts in their room and went out for dinner. Upon returning to the room, his kids were amazed at what they discovered. The stuffed theme park characters they had bought during the day were now sitting in the bed, under the covers, sheets turned back, remote control "in hand"…watching the Cartoon Network on television.

Can you just picture what the kids' faces looked like at that moment? Sheer astonishment and pure joy. Obviously, an attentive housekeeper had set this up as part of the hotel's "turn down" service.

Whether this was part of the training that all housekeepers receive at a Loews-managed hotel property or an isolated individual who was quietly creating stealth experiences on his or her own, I don't know. But I continue to talk about that experience because of the unbelievable and thoughtful gesture by an individual.

Can you recall any unforgettable moments your brand has delivered as a result of an employee's self-driven initiative to create an experience? I'm sure there are a few. These stories need to be shared with everyone and celebrated in public. This will create an environment in which other team members will seize a moment to surprise the guest. Your employees need more choices in the "song book" than just the same ole Standards—the traditional content taught in their training manuals. This is the perfect opportunity where "heritage" and "culture" should meet. By capturing this housekeeper's out-of-the-box initiative as part of your ongoing service story, your company's culture becomes stronger and more defined. It's these unique moments, generated by an individual, that differentiate your brand from the mediocre. Share the stories. Foster their continuance. Enhance the culture.

Punta Cana Hard Rock Hotel & Casino

Another housekeeping "wow" moment came via my work colleague, Kate Podmore, who travelled to some meetings held at the company's hotel & casino in Punta Cana in the Dominican Republic. Upon arriving to her hotel room and unpacking her luggage, she noticed that one of her bottles of shampoo had exploded in its Ziploc plastic bag during her flight. The liquid mess was still contained in the bag, but shampoo now covered all of her other bottled amenities that were also inside the Ziploc. Kate had to leave immediately for an on-site meeting and did not have time to deal with the clean up, so she figured she would get to it later.

When she returned to her room later that afternoon, she was blown away by what she discovered. She had completely forgotten about the mess and the impending clean up until she went into the bathroom—and discovered all of her amenities had been completely cleaned and lined up as if there never were a mess in the first place.

What a moment in customer service.

Once again, an aware housekeeper recognized what happened during the flight and realized this hotel guest was going to have to deal with the mess once she returned to her room. Wanting to spare the guest from any activity that would take her away from a hassle-free Caribbean vacation, this employee took the time to clean up the spill. She didn't know Kate and she wouldn't be around when she walked back into the hotel room, but I bet there was pure joy in her heart and a smile on her face as she thought about what the guest's reaction would be when she returned.

Housekeeping is one of the hardest jobs in the hotel industry, especially since these employees are evaluated based on the number of rooms they can clean in a day. As Kate often states, among all the tasks listed in the job responsibilities of a housekeeper, you certainly won't find "clean up a guest's shampoo-filled plastic bag mess." And yet this person took the time. This faithful employee named Brenda took it upon herself to create an unforgettable experience my colleague will remember and share forever. And now I do, as well.

Do you have stealth individuals like these housekeepers working for your brand? Employees who are on the hunt to create memorable moments for customers, even though they will not be present to witness the magic? It may be something that should be taught, but I am a bigger believer that it would be easier and better if just hired—a point I'll address further in the next few chapters. If you have any influence in your organization's selection process, you need to develop a system for identifying people who have a natural, insatiable desire to surprise and delight your guests—and then get those people on board as soon as possible. These unpredictable moments from attentive brand ambassadors are the legendary stories people will talk about for the rest of their lives.

Cultures live off of these organic experiences.

Island Bay Resort

Cradled just south of Florida's southern mainland tip is Tavernier, an extension of Key Largo in the upper Florida Keys. Mike Shipley, my former boss at Hard Rock, and his wife Carol took over a flailing 10-room hotel called Island Bay Resort in December of 2000. Almost everything about the property, except for the spectacular Gulf of Mexico ocean view, was a travesty when they purchased it.

This was certainly a labor of love for the Shipley's, who attacked every physical guest touch-point. They painted everything (inside and out), hung customized photography & artwork on the room walls, installed new roofing throughout the property, completely swapped out the room furniture, upgraded the amenities, planted all-new native landscaping, created custom-built room decks & beach furniture and overhauled gravel and brick parking spots. Even the beach had to be completely re-imagined to provide the escapist oasis people had come to expect of the Florida Keys. Yet none of this came close to what the guests loved the most about their stay: the service.

No doubt having a background in hospitality influenced Mike and Carol in their approach to service, but they made a cognizant decision to raise the bar and truly blow people away with an authentic service-oriented experience guests would not find elsewhere. Their focused approach included laser-like attention to the smallest of details, a sense of urgency in responding to requests and personalized attention to every guest, all of which combined to reap monumental reward; to the tune of increased double-digit top line sales since they acquired the resort. Since the Shipley's took over this stagnant property, they have delivered year-on-year positive sales every year except 2001, when all travel-related businesses took a significant hit after 9/11. That kind of success doesn't happen because of a paint job and some plants.

TripAdvisor.com, the world's most-used travel website, began to take notice. Elated guests of Island Bay Resort were leaving an overwhelming amount of positive feedback on this travel information and opinion site. And while these guests certainly raved about many of the items I mentioned above, one of the main reasons they felt obligated to post a review on TripAdvisor was their love of, and loyalty to, the owners. Mike and Carol's names are almost always mentioned in customer reviews about their resort stay. Their service culture approach paid off…big time.

In 2011, Island Bay Resort earned the number 15 spot on TripAdvisor's coveted list of Top 25 hotels in the United States. Compared to the other well-known brands and large properties that made up the rest of the list, this was a huge honor for these small business owners. Almost immediately, requests for information about the hotel came pouring in. People wanted to know about this hidden gem in the Upper Keys. Consequently, NBC's *The Today Show* produced a special on the Top 25 hotels which specifically highlighted Island Bay Resort. This virtuous cycle increased the occupancy of the little hotel, which led to more positive reviews and eventually culminated in the resort landing at number seven on TripAdvisor's "Best Small Hotel" list the following year.

Mike and Carol Shipley are the poster children for how a brand's culture can be revolutionized, re-created and maintained. With a lot of hard work and a focused service philosophy that is unequaled, they have created a culture that rocks. I'm so proud of their success.

NOW Church

Ensconced in the race horse-producing township of Ocala, Florida is the non-denominational Christian mega-church known as NOW Church. The church volunteers, internally branded as The Core, support an extremely diverse congregation and the community in a variety of very cool ways that go beyond traditional church programs. These include a charity basketball tournament, an active children's church program complete with a branded, full-suit mascot and a broadcast-quality music program that would rival any on television. Yet none of this is what makes this church feel so alive for those who attend. Once again, all of the bells and whistles in the world will not make a business grow. The church, like any other business, is in the business to grow.

The down-to-earth preacher at the helm of this particular church family is Dr. Richard Perinchief. He also is a culture catalyst who has done some amazing things to really develop the culture of the church. His boldest move has been running it *like* a business. He has a Board of Directors, manages a budget and focuses on moving at the pace of society's culture so he can speak the language of the Millennials.

But Richard knows he needs to do more. He too is now taking a cue from the hospitality industry, and asked me to spend some time sharing the basics of guest service with his "Core" volunteers. Because that is how he sees the role of the church: to serve the customer. The church's ultimate customers are the ones that are not even a part of their internal club. Goal number one in *their* world is to get more people to join this extremely inclusive club in which everyone is welcome. What we discovered together during the process is that the basic pillars of unbelievable guest service resonate with any organization looking to grow the business and have a sustainable future. And that includes those organizations that may serve a higher power. This church has a culture that rocks.

Even in a religious, spiritual context, culture catalysts know how critical great service is to the overall brand.

SURPRISE AND DELIGHT

The real reason many of these unique examples I've shared are so memorable is that when they occurred, it was completely and utterly unexpected by the customer.

As a consumer, when is the last time you returned to your hotel room to find stuffed animals in your bed watching television? Or your toiletries, victims of airline malfeasance, cleaned and organized in your hotel bathroom? Or a business owner who made your day with a physical embrace and an authentic conversation? These examples are so rare and so far from the norm, that customers are simply shocked when they occur.

Sure, customers have a certain pre-conceived level of expectation they're going to get, but *not* knowing what's going to happen to them is also something that should be considered. This is what makes artists like Madonna and Bowie so great. It's not just the music, or the sets, or the costumes; it's also the unpredictable moments they spring on us that put us over the edge.

People love to be positively surprised. It makes consumers feel like they're special. The culture warrior examples I shared all included elements of unpredictability—and those are the moments worth sharing. So when you consider your service practices, focus a great deal of attention on your ability to surprise and delight a guest.

To be a competitive business, you must constantly separate yourself from the rest of your industry by being an innovator. The choice is yours. But at the end of the day, if your customer leaves your business with a welcomed sense of astonishment and revelation, he or she will also leave with a desire to return, if for no other reason, then to see what other magic tricks you have up your sleeve.

GREATEST HITS THAT ROCK	THIS IS HOW YOU ROLL
Consumers are Repetitious: People only repeat what they like. If you can create an unconventionally positive experience for customers, they will want to return.	• Name some businesses you frequent where you do *not* have good experiences. • What are some reasons that keep you returning to those specific brands? • List the guaranteed reasons your guests continue to buy from you or frequent your brand versus a competitor.
Culture Has to Be Developed: It doesn't happen by accident; Great brands painstakingly develop and continuously foster their organizational culture because they understand how critical their reputation is.	• Regardless of your brand's size, what is your specific strategy for maintaining your culture as your company grows? • In lieu of leadership always being around, discuss your level of confidence that there are enough competent decision-makers on the front lines to act in the best interest of the brand. • Discuss whether your company's employees are empowered to create "magical memories" with their customers, even if they're not part of the standard delivery process.

Make People Feel Special: Treat every single customer with whom you come into contact as if he or she is a VIP or your best friend, and that customer's experience will be practically guaranteed.	• Do your company's employees seek out ways to personalize or customize the experience for your consumers?
	  o If not, what is preventing your organization from fostering this?
	  o If yes, name some unforgettable moments in your brand that resulted from an employee's self-driven initiative to create an experience.
	• Name the areas of influence this group may have.
	• Debate how this mindset can be further developed into your company's service philosophy.

GREATEST HITS THAT ROCK

THIS IS HOW YOU ROLL

Share Stories of Service Lore:
By capturing and celebrating out-of-the-box initiatives used by employees to create unforgettable memories, you will create an environment in which other team members will seize a moment to surprise the guest.

- What are the specific formats your company uses to share unique service stories to all employees?
- How are these captured?
  o Written manual, video, online blog, verbal storytelling?
- If this is not currently done, what could be implemented to start capturing and sharing these service moments?

Employees Create Experiences:
Most positive experiences are based on human behaviors, not company initiatives; Hire and unleash competent employees who will decide to create unforgettable moments on their own.

- Name some stealth individuals working for your brand who are on the hunt to create memorable moments for customers, even though they will not be present to witness the magic.
- What systems does your organization have for identifying and hiring people who have a natural, insatiable desire to surprise and delight customers?
- What influence do you have in ensuring these memory-making individuals are being brought on board to create unique experiences?
- Discuss ways you can increase your impact and influence in this area.

8

FUNERALS, HEALTHCARE & HOSPITALITY

To dive deeper into the service industry and demonstrate how strong service practices can positively affect business success, I've compiled a case study on the cultural change possibilities in other industries, some of which could not be further from my own.

I have been fortunate enough to be invited to speak on the topics of organizational culture, guest service, employee branding, training, philanthropy, and various leadership topics at a variety of industry and non-industry conferences. Unbelievably, some of my biggest clients are funeral directors.

A good percentage of my sessions over the years have been in the "death care" industry. Unless you currently work in that field, your initial reaction is probably what I hear all the time:

"Seriously?
What possibly could the spiky-haired, former Hard Rock guy
talk about with funeral directors?"

My answer: The same things every other industry professional talks about —culture, service, engagement, branding, training and leadership. These crucial subjects matter just as much in death care as they do to restaurants and hotels.

On the surface, it seems like an unlikely pairing; the two universes appear as polar opposite as Taylor Swift and Kanye West. But the hopes and desires of these two business worlds are more alike than you would think.

DEATH CARE: A CASE STUDY

As in any other service-oriented industry, funeral homes are highly competitive. Business owners in this field are constantly searching for ways to differentiate themselves from the competition. Although this is an unfair generalization about the industry, I found that the majority of the funeral directors who hired me or responded well to my message were looking for an outside-the-industry perspective on how to enhance their service culture. It may have been that I was just a catalyst through which their networking groups could address other challenges, but customer service differentiation is my "most requested hit."

My impression, now based on conversations with literally hundreds of funeral professionals, is that the industry focused for so long on the product—caskets, urns, burial vaults, plots—that the service proposition had become rigid, formalized and predictable. Perhaps that is exactly what families want in a funeral service, as there are no perfect guidelines on how to deal with the loss of a loved one. And yet, when I think about today's generation, I wonder how *they* would like to honor, revere or celebrate a loss?

In my quest to bring something different to the death care industry, I encouraged funeral directors to take a cue from hospitality. Assuming the role of thought-starter, I lobbied on just about everything from physical infrastructure to alternative entertainment, with the hope some businesses would break out of their long-standing tradition of doing things the same way.

Consider a few of the best practices I present to funeral home directors when I facilitated sessions with them:

Blow Out the Building Design

When it comes to the actual design of a funeral home, I propose oversized furniture in the lobby and sitting rooms to offer families—their clients—more comfort. I've suggested "raising the roof," versus sticking with the typical low-ceilings I experienced, to help alleviate some of the sadness that may come from a pressure-filled enclosed space. And as visual backdrops become more and more common for indoor services, laptops, built-in LCD projectors and screens are must-haves for families wanting to show a PowerPoint slide show of pictures, quotes, music lyrics or scripture verses.

Enhance the Music Offering

Because music is a critical part of the modern generation's lifestyle, this is an area in which corners simply cannot be cut. Great sound systems—not just the crackly speakers originally built into the ceiling—should be a part of the viewing or service rooms. The system should include state-of-the-art speakers, quality microphones and an iPod docking station or sound chord jack to plug into the client's smartphone, allowing families to customize the experience with their own playlists. Funeral homes should also provide contact information for local musicians as an option for those who want this but do not have a personal resource.

Create Hospitality Events

We live in an era in which many families remember their loved ones by celebrating their lives. Thus, consider setting up the event to reflect the individual. Many services now resemble hospitality events: guitars might be used as decorations on the buffet line; music CDs might become food item labels; the loved one's Harley-Davidson motorcycle might even be parked inside the funeral home as part of the experience. Whether the funeral is "themed" around music, motorcycles, or even sports, funeral directors should recognize that families often want—and appreciate—the option to create a personalized event to commemorate the passing of a loved one. Funeral directors should alter their service practices to better reflect this shift in consumer expectations.

Consider Today's Generational Mind

As we'll continue to discuss in the coming chapters, today's younger generation is more socially conscious than ever. They seek out and support ways to leave a smaller footprint in the world. Utilizing recycled materials wherever possible will get noticed and be appreciated, but cremation and possibly even safe, biodegradable caskets could be options, as well. A funeral home should always be a reflection of its consumers, offering various avenues and mediums to affect whatever result a "customer" desires.

EVEN IN MOMENTS OF DESPAIR

Some funeral directors may be resistant to using these specific approaches in their companies, fearing that it will cut into their profit margins, alienate them from families that desire more traditional experiences, or be overwhelmingly difficult to execute. But having the ability to offer clients diverse options and a customized experience will certainly help put their funeral homes into a family's mental shelf space for when a need arises in the future. People remember the unique, even in moments of despair. The more you can personalize or customize the experience for the family, the more unforgettable the company. This is a tenet for any service-oriented brand.

No matter the industry, business owners should always self-evaluate and be on a constant search to evolve their companies. Understanding there is a world of different consumers out there, each with a multiplicity of needs in terms of what they want and how they want it delivered, is crucial to your organization's ability to succeed in a service environment. The funeral industry example is simply a case study for the creative ideas that even companies in *that* industry could implement to revolutionize their businesses. Regardless of the trade, each and every company can study and reshape its practices to mirror societal needs.

I do not personally know of any funeral organizations that have adopted *all* the ideas I've mentioned, but a few have implemented some. A few funeral directors contacted me later with success stories resulting from the time we spent together. One funeral home now *always* offers a local bagpipe player as a nice touch to the service. Another funeral director always provides personalized Starbucks coffee drinks to the immediate family at the viewing, knowing a warm cup of coffee is comforting during the process. Another owner even created a supervised children's area in the funeral home, complete with quiet games, to allow the adults to focus on the viewing in the next room without the distraction of active children.

During a networking session, one professional confessed he had been pretty determined not to implement change in his services over the years—until he sat through my discussion on customer service. Shortly afterward, a client requested that he allow family members to dip their hands in paint and place their palm prints directly onto the loved one's casket before lowering it into the ground. After some contemplation, he decided to honor the request. This funeral director later confided that he would not have endorsed this idea in the past, but that since my presentation he had become more willing to personalize the experience he offered. He now offers this option to everyone that uses his business.

A few funeral directors have shared with me they now do services and events with ice sculptures as part of the experience. One funeral home in California actually uses a Hummer as a Hearst to transport bodies to their final resting place. *That* one blew my mind. To be fair, that specific idea certainly did not come directly from my session, but it does demonstrate the desire from some to push the envelope. These business operators are reaching higher; they're undertaking a constant journey to improve, reinvent and enhance their service practices. These are culture catalysts who have created a point of differentiation…even in the way we honor death.

But the one who takes home the gold record for "Most Creative Innovation" in his service practices is the funeral director who installed an Icee machine in his funeral home. Just like the children's area at another business, this frozen, slushy treat was the business owner's approach to "entertaining" the kids while the adults made funeral arrangements close by. He freely admits the machine is both time consuming and the messiest piece of equipment he has ever dealt. Yet the unspoken comfort the families feel when the children are occupied while the adults have to make tough emotional decisions is well worth the daily maintenance. He even told me families now occasionally stop by the funeral home to get free Icees—which he is perfectly content to accommodate because he knows when there is a loss in the family, his is the phone they will ring.

Death Care is just one industry, made up of endless businesses, on a mission to differentiate itself from the rest in order to thrive and even survive. You may not initially think of your industry as hospitality-oriented, but we can all take a cue from brands that use serving people as their platform for success.

HEALTHCARE MEETS HOSPITALITY

Like funeral directors taking a page from hospitality's songbook, healthcare business operators are starting to sing that song as well. Hospitals are hiring executives from the hospitality sector. In fact, during a recruiting presentation at a local conference I attended, the speaker shared some data from the University of Florida showing that major hospitals were leaning more and more toward applicants that had hospitality experience on their resume. It didn't guarantee them the job, but when they were matched up against another similarly-qualified candidate, the one who had worked in a restaurant or hotel was the one with the upper hand in landing the gig.

Let me share a few examples of how experience in a guest-obsessed service culture can help out in any industry—especially healthcare.

Henry Ford Health System - Detroit

In May of 2011, Jessica Watson published an article on Henry Ford's online newsletter about Sven Gierlinger's appointment to Vice President of Customer Hospitality & Service Culture for the Detroit-based company. This was a newly-created position.

I was amazed to discover that Gierlinger's background included more than 20 years of experience in hospitality, including a stint as Vice President of Museum Operations at the Detroit Institute of Arts, one of the nation's top art museums. His accomplishments included coordinating a $158 million renovation of the museum and implementing a comprehensive customer service initiative that changed the workforce culture.

While working in the hospitality industry, Gierlinger opened six hotels in four countries in nine years, including Ritz-Carlton properties in the United States, Germany, Japan and Indonesia. He also holds a Bachelor's degree in Hotel Business Administration from the Bavaria Hotel Management School in Germany. Serious hospitality cred. Is there any doubt about the reason he was chosen by the Henry Ford organization?

This specific healthcare provider, was on the hunt for a service culture makeover.

Columbia Asia Hospitals - India

In February of 2011, *The Economic Times*, a non-industry specific, International media outlet for the world's economic news, featured an article detailing the transition of Tufan Ghosh's appointment as CEO at Columbia Asia Hospitals in Bangalore, India. Story co-authors Devina Sengupta and Shreya Biswas specifically noted that Ghosh was making this transition after 15 years with The Oberoi Group, a global chain of premium, five-star luxury hotels and resorts that has been voted many times over as "The World's Leading Luxury Hotel Brand." So, you can imagine the change of scenery was radical for Ghosh. But that was precisely why he was hired. Ghosh was an expert in the field of hospitality...and healthcare needs a radical infusion of hospitality.

Hospitals no longer want to be seen as tiresome rows of patient-care wards. As medical tourism becomes popular and competition among private hospitals heats up, these businesses are hiring executives from the hospitality sector. As was reported in *The Economic Times*, most people surveyed in India claimed not to use public health facilities, mostly due to their apprehensions about the quality of care, lack of accessibility, long waiting times and generally poor experiences. To ensure customer loyalty, innovative companies like Columbia Asia recognized the need to go the extra mile and provide personalized attention and care. To address this very issue, many of the executives in this hospital group were hired from the hotel industry.

HEALTHCARE'S CULTURAL MAKEOVER

In October of 2010, Shannon Kraus wrote an online article for *Health Care Design Magazine* focusing on the industry's initiatives to reimagine the patient/guest experience, from building design to guest-focused care.

Kraus reported that intertwining hospitality design with healthcare architecture is not, in itself, new. For more than a decade, healthcare architects have been using hospitality-like finishes to create destination-type settings that connect with their communities while appealing to patients. Super comfortable beds, fluffy bedspreads, warm wood flooring, balconies attached to rooms, soothing colors & pictures on patient room walls, music wafting through the corridors, meditation areas and gardens located throughout health pavilions are all part of this image makeover.

Lancaster General Hospital - Michigan

In that same article, Kraus also shared a great case study about a hospital in Lancaster, Pennsylvania, that had a clear mission when it planned its facility on a 70-acre site: "To create an extraordinary experience every time."

What? An "extraordinary experience" in a hospital?

Yep, that was the goal.

So the hospitality design approach was incorporated into every aspect of the project, creating more of a "life campus" than a hospital. The owner and design team visualized a "guest" room with health amenities, rather than a simple "patient" room. They envisioned waiting rooms as living rooms; the cafeteria as a restaurant-style dining area; a kitchen that could provide tasty, diet-friendly menus; a farmers market to introduce fresh produce to the campus. One of the central themes of the whole life campus is that it should be a place where people would actually come when they were healthy.

PATIENTS AS ROCK ROYALTY

The goal is to go beyond decorations and into the actual shaping of the architecture, the operations and the philosophy of the care being delivered. It is only *then* that integration can occur and the patient experience can be redefined from patient-focused care to guest-focused care, raising the bar for both design and healthcare delivery.

Surveys, such as those conducted by Hospital Consumer Assessment of Healthcare Providers and Systems, have shown that hospitals incorporating extra features and amenities score higher in patient satisfaction. But guest-focused care isn't about supporting an experience around the design. It's about creating a hospitality mindset—not just a mandate on brick and mortar finish qualities or amenities.

Today, a new wave of facilities is coming online that takes this a step further and considers the patient experience beyond just the rooms. This design approach views the patient as a "guest" first—creating a new, implied personal contract. While patients are something to be processed, guests are to be treated like rock royalty. So the idea of guest-focused care is about getting into the DNA of design and introducing attitudes that focus on the guest experience. The result is the renewed approach of "hospitality meets healthcare design" that goes further than it ever has in the past. A deeper cultural shift is required to truly integrate the two industries.

When we discuss the integration of hospitality and healthcare, it's hard to ignore medical tourism as a key segment of the market, evolving from lifestyle marketing in the hospitality industry. One of the first lessons in hospitality design is that 90 percent of what establishes the difference between a two-star hotel and a five-star hotel is service—not the building or the amenities. However, the design sets the stage for the performer to rock people's worlds.

This integration is more than a feel-good thing to do; there is also a sound business case for it. As many healthcare facility operators know, the driver today is patient satisfaction. Satisfied patients lead to improved market share, since most consumers choose their providers. They are also more likely to recommend a facility to friends or family.

FORCES OF MAGNETISM

Just as hotels are rated, healthcare facilities are being rated, as well. Hospital businesses are now creating scorecards that rank items from patient satisfaction to hospital outcomes and performance. Many of these are now being made public and are tracked in public forums. While this is controversial in the healthcare industry, it is indicative of healthcare's increased accountability to the consumer.

In 1990, the American Nurses Credentialing Center (ANCC) created "The Magnet Recognition Program" to recognize healthcare organizations for quality patient care, nursing excellence and innovations in professional nursing practice. Achieving Magnet status is a big deal. The designation is only awarded to hospitals that embody the highest service cultures. Amazingly, this once self-designated award created by healthcare employees to raise the bar in patient care, has now become an industry standard. Consumers now rely on this Magnet designation as the ultimate credential for high-quality nursing.

In these elite healthcare systems:

- There is no need to advertise for open positions; there are plenty of high-quality, candidates-in-waiting.
- Contract nurses are not needed; fulltime nursing teams are staffed 100 percent of the time.
- Doctors value all nurses on the team; everyone is perceived and treated with equal respect.
- Teams have development improvement plans, used regularly to seek continuous improvement.
- Nurses write and publish research papers—many on critical topics leading to financial impact.
- Magnet pins—envied and sought after by all in the industry—are awarded to all of the staff.

To apply for Magnet status, hospitals must prove their culture of communication, teamwork, patient service and supporting values in a very detailed way. To even be considered, a healthcare system must provide all-inclusive data from the previous 3 years. Once attained, however, Magnet status has a very positive impact on turnover and team engagement.

Lancaster General Hospital, mentioned earlier, has been one of these Magnet systems for several years, which makes sense given their quest "to create an extraordinary experience every time." Clearly, creating a positive culture can be accomplished—even in the most unlikely of businesses.

In every industry, the overall culture matters—now more than ever.

SERVICE TRUMPS PRODUCT – ALWAYS HAS, ALWAYS WILL

In the past two chapters, you have seen some of the most unique and interesting examples of outside-the-box service. These companies diligently and meticulously work to ensure that they are the chocolate in a world full of vanilla. They spend valuable resources like time and money to evaluate and understand their potential customers so they can tap into their true wants and desires.

In fact, these "monsters of rock" examples are the places—with the types of people—in which I like to spend my money. I imagine that the same is true for you. We helplessly hunger to be surprised by spectacular service, mostly because the great majority of companies simply do not feed our appetites.

All of the companies I've mentioned have created a culture to be envied by others. Even if the memory is tied to a process, like Independence Air's Happy Bag program or an Icee machine in a funeral home, the culture still had to be developed and supported. Additionally, the positive experiences that define and strengthen an organization's service culture are usually based on human behavior—the interaction between an employee and the customer, even if it occurred from a distance, like the shampoo bottle explosion and stuffed Disney character examples.

People who make a living in the hospitality industry will agree that out of everything they do, providing memorable guest service makes the only real difference between success and failure. This continues to be validated by countless studies and industry associations dedicated to measuring and assessing this service-to-sustainable success correlation. But even the average customer knows that great service—especially personalized service—trumps product, convenience, theme and even price, every time.

It always has; it always will.

The Container Store

One spectacular company that is consistently top-of-mind when I think about robust service cultures is retail specialist The Container Store. When the first location opened in Dallas, Texas in 1978, it offered such a mix of products devoted to helping people simplify their lives that it created an entirely new category of retailing: storage and organization. That first store was packed with items consumers simply couldn't find in any other retail environment—and while that delighted many customers, it seemed to confuse just as many others. The product collection—comprised of items like commercial parts bins, wire drawers, mailboxes, popcorn tins, burger baskets and milk crates—seemed odd to the casual consumer. Some could not understand why a store would sell empty boxes and crates. But when these solutions were employed in a home or office, they proved to save both space and time for Container Store customers. These products, literally and figuratively, became building blocks for organizing a person's life.

Today, The Container Store brand spans the country and offers more than 10,000 innovative products that help customers save space and time. As you can imagine, even the store layout is purposeful in its design. Each store is divided into lifestyle sections marked with brightly colored banners denoting "Closet," "Kitchen," "Office" and "Laundry." In their feedback to the company, customers don't just rave about finding the perfect product solutions for their specific needs; they also equate the physical store *itself* to a peaceful, organized oasis…especially helpful after a really stressful day.

You would think the wonderful products and the smart environment would be reason enough for the brand's reported average of 20 percent annual growth every year since its inception, yet once again, the company's leaders and most loyal fans do not cite either of these as the main reason for The Container Store's continued success. Remarkably, it's the unparalleled service delivered by caring, patient and cheerful employees that rock customers' worlds.

In addition to offering time- and space-saving products, The Container Store co-founders' original vision included the creation of an "employee-first culture" in which the associates would always be…in everything leadership did. Their belief was that if the company took better care of its employees than anyone else—by paying them better, training them more and treating them like business partners—those employees, in turn, would take better care of their customers than anyone else. This philosophy is actually written into the company's Foundation Principles and shared with every employee, along with the public, as part of the brand's commitment to transparency and accountability. The company's website offers some insight into this approach:

> *"It all starts with our commitment to hiring GREAT people! One of our Foundation Principles is that '1 great employee is equal to 3 good employees' in terms of business productivity. So why not hire only GREAT people? Most business people and many retailers have long ago given up on that concept. They just don't really believe it's possible to get great people to work on a retail sales floor. We are extraordinarily dedicated to finding and connecting with great talent."*

And they do. As part of the 1-2 punch, after the company hires these unbelievably GREAT employees, its intense focus turns toward training and development. The Container Store offers more than 263 hours of formal training for full-time employees in their first year—compared to the industry average of eight hours.

Wow! Be still my Training & Development heart. That level of attention focused on a retail employee's competence, self-confidence, growth and long-term success puts The Container Store into the "rock legend" category for me. This holistic "employee-first" philosophy is at the heart of The Container Store's culture and is the reason the company has enjoyed only 10 percent annual employee turnover, compared to the retail industry's average of nearly 100 percent. It's also why the brand has made Fortune Magazine's list of "100 Best Places to Work in America" every year since 1999.

Although the products sold at The Container Store are completely consumer-focused and the store itself is refreshingly hassle-free and organized, customers most relish experiencing an environment completely populated with GREAT employees who are competent, well trained and personable.

The Container Store is a culture that rocks!

MY EXPERIENCE IS IN THE SHOP

As much as I may like a product, the service experience is always going to be the winner. As much as I may *need* a product, the service experience is always going to make it better.

Let me give you another example.

Think about the automotive repair industry and your personal experiences having cars fixed. Anyone who owns a vehicle must go through this ritual multiple times, perhaps even several times a year, depending on the quality of the car, your ongoing proactive maintenance of the vehicle and your propensity for getting into accidents. You might put a car in the shop for something as small and relatively inexpensive as an oil change or tire alignment, or something as big and wallet-busting as a transmission repair or air conditioning unit replacement. It's a business that will forever be around and desperately needed as long as we continue to use complicated driving machines that require expertise to keep them going.

A repair shop that employs skilled mechanics and is fair in price is one of the greatest "finds" in life for a vehicle owner. Yet the rare, differentiating ingredient of "great service" tends to be an absent element in many automotive brands, necessitating our continued quest for the perfect mechanic. So the hunt continues.

As with the funeral industry case study, my experience and understanding of the auto repair business suggests that it also sees itself as a product-oriented business. It is not.

Most vehicle maintenance companies have not fully realized that their business is a service, of which the act of "fixing a vehicle" is just the by-product. The means to this end actually matter. It may not be as important for some of the older, more loyal customers enjoyed by some auto shops, but that clientele is quickly transitioning to the experience-starved consumers of the 21st century—and they require a bit more.

I would bet that the general driving public has had similar experiences and therefore shares my mindset: Nobody wants to go to the shop and everybody is going to be frustrated with the extent of the problem and the cost of the repair.

Isn't it possible to change that perception, if the experience is positive and the value proposition is high?

No doubt the repair work has to be done regardless and customers may not ever actually look *forward* to this inevitable disruption of life, but the overall experience can still be dramatically altered to make auto repair more palatable. I believe the service delivery alone could be so mind blowing that it might even become shockingly enjoyable.

I can easily imagine the numerous physical plant changes one could make to the repair shop itself, especially the waiting room, just to offset the hassle and disruption brought on by car trouble. In my mind's eye, when I think about a revolutionized vehicle maintenance waiting area, I envision a hotel lobby:

- Free premium and fair-trade coffee available—Pangeo, Green Mountain, Starbucks, Kuerig, etc.
- Self-serve containers of fruit-infused ice water—lemon, pineapple, melon, etc.
- Free WiFi Internet access
- Comfortable furniture with a mix of ergonomic and over stuffed seating
- An abundance of power outlets with easy access for laptops and phone charging
- Flat, plasma screen television monitors, versus an older, bulky unit sitting on a cart
- Warm paint colors on the wall
- Potted plants in the corners
- Recessed and directional lighting to, along with the paint and plants, help soften the room
- A black chalk wall for kids to draw on
- Up-to-date newspaper and magazines available, including inexpensive subscriptions like *USA Today, Entertainment*

Weekly, People, Rolling Stone, etc.
- Immaculately clean restrooms

Certainly there are some upfront capital costs here, but I would look at this as an investment likely to get an immediate financial return in the form of loyal customers—new clients and regulars alike. Instead of dropping the car off and then running to a more pleasing "staging" area away from the shop, this type of space would encourage me to want to stay. And although an enhanced atmosphere like this would still not be enough to guarantee my return, a premium, customer-focused environment would definitely lay the groundwork for a more value-oriented service experience.

To truly make a lasting impression and secure financial sustainability, an emotional experience needs to occur for the consumer. The authors of *The Experience Economy*—still considered one of the Top 100 business books across all industries—discuss this very point in the book as a key tenet in an organization's continued success. Great sustainable brands create memorable experiences.

There is a reason we continue to talk about cultural brands like Apple, Coke, LEGO and Zappos: they create memories. And memorable experiences help justify price.

How can an automotive repair business create a WOW! moment for customers?

The same way everyone else can: Surprise and delight them with some value-added moments of differentiation.

Consider what would happen if an automotive repair shop did the following for free…for *every* customer:

- Came from behind the service counter to offer a personable greeting—perhaps even handshake—versus the traditional "How can I help you?"
- Cleaned the dashboard
- Washed the windows inside and out
- Vacuumed the floor mats
- Topped off the windshield wiper fluid
- Placed a handwritten "thank you" card on the passenger seat
- Gave out an inexpensive gift, like a mini-flashlight, calendar, pen—even a lollipop for the kids
- Sent a birthday card to the customer on his or her special day

I'm sure there are many people who think the suggestions above go way too far…that these types of perks are reserved for high-paying, VIP members, not some random customer who came in for the discounted oil change that was advertised on the side of the road. But I think it's just the opposite. Vehicle maintenance shops should look for opportunities to stand out from the crowd and rock the world of every customer, regardless of the work provided. A shop owner wouldn't have to implement *all* of the ideas on the list— just enough of them to create a differentiation. Without these kinds of service extras, the business will always be looked at as a commodity, and the consumer will base his or her decision to come back on price of the product alone.

It's not enough. People want more.

Jiffy Lube

One company in this industry that gets it is Jiffy Lube. Started in 1971, the vehicle maintenance company was one of the first to "surprise and delight" its customers by throwing in many of the extras on my list…with *every* oil change. The value proposition was so high that the customer return rate skyrocketed, whether it was for another oil change or, even better, additional services. Like any decades-old company, the brand has seen its challenges. But with its recent physical store enhancements, a focused approach to training employees about products, a customer-obsessed service approach and aggressive development of store-level leadership, Jiffy Lube has propelled itself to the top of the class…not just in its own industry, but among *all* industries.

In January 2014, *Training Magazine* elevated Jiffy Lube to the number one spot on its coveted Training Top 125, above well-known businesses in highly lucrative industries like banking, insurance, manufacturing and healthcare. The quantitative and qualitative data that influences the Training Top 125 rankings includes training tied to business results, employee turnover, training technology use, leadership development, certification, training budget as a percentage of payroll and much more. Imagine, this auto repair company beat out companies Blue Cross Blue Shield, McDonald's, Capital One, Wells Fargo and Four Seasons for the top learning and development award.

The basis of its recent success is the company's collective mindset and crystal-clear focus. Check out the brand's core promise, as it was highlighted in the *Training* article:

> *"Jiffy Lube believes every driver deserves to be free from the anxiety of keeping his or her vehicle in top shape. To help customers 'Leave Worry Behind,' Jiffy Lube is committed to providing a high-quality, worry-free service experience that gives customers peace of mind, and reassures them that Jiffy Lube gets the job done right."*

Pretty amazing. Especially for an industry in which many businesses lack a written core promise or mission statement of any kind. Without clear direction, a company can expect dysfunctional results.

The article also listed these impressive facts about the robust training program that ensures Jiffy Lube's organizational alignment around customer service and leadership:

- Number of courses offered as instructor-led classroom sessions: 9
- Number of courses offered as instructor-led virtual classroom sessions: 4
- Number of courses offered as online self-paced modules: 120
- Total hours of system-wide training taken in 2013: 2.2 million

Even more impressive were the correlating measurable results—both internal and external—of this continuous, laser-like focus:

- Average length of employee service: 12 years
- Percentage decrease in turnover rate for technicians system-wide (last 4 years): 45%
- Percentage of job openings filled by internal candidates: 90%
- Percentage of new hires referred by employees: 80%
- Number of consecutive years of increased average revenue per customer: 9
- Number of consecutive years of improved customer service scores: 9
- Percentage approval rating by franchisees: 93%

There is no doubt here. Jiffy Lube did not get to rock icon status because of its product alone, as good as it may be. It's success is based on the experiences its employees deliver.

Product is no longer enough. Customers need more.

PRODUCT IS NO LONGER ENOUGH

Canadian-based Tim Horton's is the quintessential coffee culture in that country. Known as much for its sense of place in the community as its coffee, this company may still miss the overall experiential mark. Perhaps nothing will change the long-standing tradition of the gang meeting up at "Tim's" for a cup-o-Joe and some good ole conversation, but what if…?

Imagine what would happen if the brand pulled the same experiential levers that Starbucks does to create moments for its customers. The company would be unstoppable. But they don't. Tim Horton's doesn't do the extras—and that might be fine with its loyal, local and current customers, but it certainly diminishes the chances for growth outside of the country—unless the company dramatically changes its core offering, buys another growth-oriented concept or is bought out itself.

The brand is still the largest fast food concept in Canada and has more than 800 locations in the US—and even a few dozen in the Middle East—so there is no denying its success. But competition is getting fierce...even in its own backyard. There are just too many new, enticing brands that are providing experiences that supersede their products, and this especially resonates with the younger generation.

Only recently has the company stepped out of its comfort zone with Tim Horton's Café and Bake Shop, which does indeed layer in some premium products and a more experiential environment, but this concept only exists *outside* the borders of Canada. The country's slight aversion to US chains means this variation on the Starbucks theme is not always accepted by the locals.

Canadians love their Canadian brands. For sure, they love their "Timmy's."

I'm broadly stereotyping here, as there is definitely something to be said about a community-based, local joint, where the locals swear never-ending allegiance and loyalty, but future growth and sustainability have to be on every brand executive's mind. Tim Horton's is perhaps the greatest Canadian culture fixture in the country, but it cannot rest solely and forever on just its coffee, as good as it may be for many.

Product is no longer enough. People want more.

EXPERIENTIAL SELF EVALUATION

The quests of funeral directors, healthcare providers, auto mechanics and hospitality professionals are really no different than yours. On a daily basis, we all strive to find the exact equation for success while avoiding, at all costs, the pitfalls of failure. Different businesses may take different paths to find these answers, but there is one consistent principle that applies to all of us: Self-evaluation and creative thought will always aid in the effort to revolutionize your service practices and enhance your company culture. Personalized, attentive service is a game changer.

Take a moment to truly think about your business and compare it to the rest of your industry.

What is everyone else doing?

Now, do at *least* that, do more of it and do it better than everyone else.

Whatever industry you are a part of, these straightforward but powerful practices I have shared—and ones you will discover on your own—will facilitate future growth and immeasurable success in your respective brand. When building the pillars that will define your organization in terms of direct service to guests, it is imperative that your foundation is anchored to choices and mechanisms that will not only attract consumers, but create an experience that will propel those consumers back to your business time and time again.

Just remember: Service trumps product, price, theme and convenience… every time.

You have both the power and the opportunity to be the measuring stick for all other companies in your industry. It just takes a little extra attention to service to take your brand's culture to the next level.

Go for it.

GREATEST HITS THAT ROCK

THIS IS HOW YOU ROLL

Unpredictability Promotes Success:
The best service memories are the ones that are unpredictable—people love to be positively surprised.

- Share a positive experience you've had with a brand that involved some type of unpredictability and completely blew you away.
- How can *your* company deliver unpredictable WOW! moments for customers?
- Name the reward mechanisms you have in place for recognizing employees who provide unplanned positive experiences to consumers—and for fostering an environment in which more of these experiences can occur.

Service Trumps Everything:
The one true differentiator today is service—it trumps product, convenience, theme and price every time. Always has, always will.

- Discuss whether you think your company relies on product quality, price and/or convenience, versus the service provided, to set itself apart.
  o Debate whether that is enough for long-term sustainability.
- Discuss how prominent your brand's service culture is and whether it actually serves to differentiate you from your competitors.
- Identify the basic service offerings your competitors provide, especially their "differentiators."
  o Now, determine how you will match or supersede those initiatives.

Self-Evaluate:
Business owners should always be on a constant path to evolving and revolutionizing their companies. Only when you've truly looked at your brand can you determine the changes that need to be implemented. Do not get stuck in mediocrity because you are unwilling to consider other options, even those that may differ from the norm.

- What type of self-evaluation systems does your organization have in place?
- What short- and long-term initiative can be implemented to create an environment of self-reflection that will aid in your brand's quest to revolutionize service practices and enhance company's culture?
- Name all of your processes focused on addressing the multiplicity of consumer needs, both in terms of what they want and how they want it delivered.

9

ROCK STARS VS. LIP-SYNCHERS

"There's a difference between being a poseur and being someone who's so emotionally challenged they're just doing their best to show you what they've got."
- Billy Corgan, Smashing Pumpkins

Whether you're seeking a culture based on great service, a strong team spirit or high-level performance, you're going to have some challenges when you start to implement changes—mainly because culture, as I stated earlier, is a collection of *individual* human behaviors. Regardless of the results hope to achieve, the people you hire and cultivate will determine your ultimate business outcomes. So your obstacles to change can be overcome—just surround yourself with loyal brand ambassadors who have the skills to produce the desired results. If we want great guest service, then we have to find great service-oriented people to deliver it. If we want a high performance culture, then we have to hire high performers who can make it happen.

In Chapters 5-7, I focused quite a bit on the importance of the service deliverer—because I believe that is the secret ingredient to a service-oriented brand's success. When you onboard team members who organically become part of the tribe, who are willing to regularly go above and beyond to strengthen the brand, they take on "rock star" status. They bring the "spectacular" on a daily basis and perform as if they are playing for a packed house. Not because they *have* to, because they *want* to. Hiring and cultivating rock star talent should be the quest of all organizations in search of differentiation.

Unfortunately, the talent pool for almost any position, regardless of the industry, isn't quite what it used to be. Not only are the great ones harder to find, but the labor force is made up of an entirely different kind of animal. Compared to past generations, today's potential employees have different needs, different beliefs and different perceptions about work. Even the coveted top talent that everyone desires—individuals with both high competence and strong character—is often clouded with excess and unwanted traits.

Yes, top talent is out there, but like rock stars, they come with baggage. It could be the way they act, the way they look or the way they were brought up. However, today's potential workforce *is* ripe with talent just waiting to be discovered—perceived "flaws" and all.

KIDS TODAY

Each new generation seems to spark some literature attempting to educate the rest of the business world about how to deal with these "kids of today." I have a lot of respect for my business friends who are experts in generational training; they certainly have their fingers on the pulse of today's generation. They are well-positioned to explain the upcoming crop of employees-to-be and help us understand what hot buttons we need to hit or avoid in order to gain their loyalty. Between these resources and my own observations, there's no denying that today's generation is a different breed. But you need them—especially if you hope to create or enhance your company's culture.

With these initial challenges—namely hiring from a new and unique generational pool, then motivating and inspiring these new hires to become an extension of your culture beliefs and service practices—how does an employer or leader hire the right talent to represent his or her brand?

In this chapter, you'll find straightforward guidance on how to filter through that endless stack of applications and grasp a new generation of employees' attention by appealing to their individuality and desire to do meaningful work. If you can master this, you're ready to build a team dedicated to representing the positive culture and service practices that will ensure your company's success, even in cutthroat and competitive markets. This is a lynchpin initiative for creating a culture that rocks.

Let's go discover some rock stars.

BRING THE AUTHENTICITY

Lip-synchers suck. Seriously.

I understand that some musicians feel like they have to "mouth" the words to a song track when they perform in front of large crowds in order to ensure that the tune comes across as the artist intended. But once the charade is discovered, it demeans the performance and destroys the credibility of the artist. In other words, when it backfires, lip-synching does the exact opposite of what the musician wanted.

When it comes down to it, the difference between being a rock star and a lip-syncher is the authenticity of the person. Rock stars are authentic and envied for their star power, while a lip-syncher comes across as a celebrity "wannabe"—a fake. All the back-up tracks and AutoTune programs in the world can't help the lip-synchers. They will eventually be unmasked. Just ask exposed pop performers Milli Vanilli or Ashlee Simpson. Once revealed, they become toxic. Their fate is inevitable.

So as you sift through the pile of resumes on your desk and navigate the interview and hiring process, consider the vital role authenticity plays in your business. When people feel as if they receive an honest and true experience, they will almost certainly return. If the service seems fake or forced, however, repeat business becomes less likely.

As much as I give props to great service-oriented brands, even the great ones stumble every once in a while, inevitably because of a flawed interaction between an employee and a guest. It happens even to the biggest and the best, and it's rarely because of a product or a process that an experience is less than expected. Human beings, after all, are endowed with "free will"—that's why companies need to hire as many rock stars as possible, to minimize the possibility of mistakes. And it all starts with screening for authenticity.

Employees that are engaged in the moment and understand what it takes to send the audience into a frenzy—thereby creating mind-searing performances—are rock stars. They know they're on stage every day and that they're playing for an arena full of fans. They know that to make a difference in the consumer's mind to solidify an unforgettable memory, they have to bring something spectacular every day, every shift and every hour. The special moments they create don't have to be as spontaneous or surprising as the ones I mentioned earlier—there are different paths to the destination of customer fulfillment. The process of punching in everyday and considering how to make a difference in the eyes of the fan is really the tricky part. You can teach it to some degree, but the great majority of these authentic experiences occur because you hired an employee who is simply wired in a way that drives him or her to work hard at creating memorable experiences for your guests.

Actual rock stars do not just sell music, they sell an overall experience. Great organizational cultures do not just sell a product or a service; they realize it's about the experience. It's those mind-blowing performances that create differentiation among the organizations in your industry.

KISS MY GRITS

The most experienced talent is not always the right fit for your service philosophy. This may seem to fly in the face of the original approach to Hard Rock Cafe staffing, since company founders Isaac Tigrett and Peter Morton initially only hired mature, 30-year old women, but their approach was deliberate; their reasoning had little to do with potential employees' previous experience or tenure in the industry. They were looking for a very specific service mindset which would, they believed, create memorable experiences for guests.

And that required hiring unique employees.

To really envision the prototypical employee that perhaps Morton and Tigrett sought, you'd have to be a fan of American television shows in the1970s. Characters like Lucille Ball and Carol Burnett later infiltrated the airwaves and may have continued to influence the Hard Rock's idea of the perfect service conduit, but in my mind, no one fits the image of the quintessential

Tennessee truck stop diner waitress better than the irreverent character of Flo, of Mel's Diner, on the hit television show *Alice*. I'm sure those of you who are old enough can hear the immortal words "kiss my grits!" ringing in your ears right now. Flo was known for chewing gum, complaining about the workload and even slinging a few insults at the guests who pushed her buttons, but she also had her "regulars" who kept coming back for more—because she created experiences. She was one-of-a-kind. She was real. She was memorable. She was unapologetically authentic.

The original Hard Rock Cafe servers were *just* like that. They were a bit irreverent and almost always unpredictable, but guests loved every moment of the experience because it was different. It was the spirit of Rock 'n' Roll come to life. That edginess may not be as readily acceptable in today's society or in every market, but consumers still crave "different." In a 21st century Hard Rock environment, rock star employees know how to tow the line between being edgy and being disrespectful.

- What is your prototypical employee profile?
- Is there even an ideal employee for your brand?

When making your own hiring decisions, you have to first consider the type of mold you are trying to fill. It could be someone like Flo, or it could be very different: perhaps someone who is young, trendy and extremely attentive and polite. Every business has particular needs that should be evaluated before the hiring process even begins.

If you don't know the shapes of the holes you are using, how can you find the pegs that will fit?

FROM WAITRESS TO M.B.E.

To fill Hard Rock's employee ranks, it seemed as though "day one" waitresses, with mid-century diner names, like Eve, Betty and Delia, were pulled from right out of a classic black and white movie script—they looked and acted exactly as you imagine they would. Unlike the made-up television character Flo, these 30-year-old spitfires were the real deal. They were one-of-a-kind and memorable to anyone who shared a moment with them.

More than anyone else, original server Rita Gilligan became the company's quintessential rock star. It was an unintended role she fell into, but one she gladly accepted.

Ironically, Rita confided to me on a number of occasions she didn't feel as though she was the best technical waitress around, but that her infectious personality and natural gift to talk saved her every day—and made her a lot of money at the time. Rita eventually owned several homes—one for each of her kids.

I would say she made a pretty comfortable living out of her attitude.

Turning thirty just six days before the opening of the original Hard Rock Cafe, Rita barely met the company's hiring requirements when she was interviewed by Peter Morton. However, she ultimately became the face of the brand. And then the amazing happened. In 1998, due to her well-known service approach and years of dedication to tourism in the United Kingdom, Rita Gilligan was awarded the M.B.E. (Member of the British Empire), the highest civilian award you can receive from the Royal Court.

Can you believe it? Rita started her career as a server more than twenty-five years prior to receiving this award, yet her uniqueness became legendary. So much so that an entire country recognized her amazing performance in the service industry.

When she retired, Rita continued to act as the organization's "cultural attaché," spending the majority of her time spreading the heritage of Hard Rock. She told the early company stories as only she could, tracing Hard Rock's progress from the craziness of a fledgling cafe to the global entertainment brand it is today.

In fact, for many years the London Hard Rock Cafe displayed table tents informing guests that Rita would visit the restaurant on the first Thursday of every month, completely decked out in her perfect white diner dress, paper hat and collectible guitar pins. And she did—every week. She methodically made her way to every guest in the cafe to share stories, take pictures and sign autographs. Unless there was a major holiday in the UK, *Rita Day* was one of the cafe's busiest days every month; customers flocked to the restaurant to get some one-on-one time with her.

In terms of meeting our goals in this book, it's important to understand why consumers were drawn to Hard Rock on *Rita Day*. You see, people were attracted to this event because Rita offered them something they couldn't get anywhere else: an unbelievable cultural and service experience.

Consumers are categorically enthusiastic about differentiated events. When a company can combine one part music history, one part good food, and, most importantly, one part fantastic and personalized service, the stars align and customers will be blown away. For an organization that sells a product or delivers a service as its business model, differentiation must be part of the brand culture—this is critical to its long-term future.

UNIQUE PEOPLE = UNIQUE EXPERIENCES

As a business owner, it is your responsibility to create the "Rita experience" if you have any hope of ongoing, sustainable growth. Do not be confused. This is not about throwing an event. This is about hiring and unleashing rock star employees who can create their own experiential events with their guests, who in turn form unforgettable memories about your brand.

Once again, the deliverer matters.

Rita Gilligan is living proof that one person in an organization can make a difference. She almost makes me advocate "cloning." I wish there were a way to easily replicate what she did on a daily basis, because her talent wasn't taught in a training class. As Lady Gaga would put it, she was "born that way." Thankfully, some hippie American restaurant owners took a chance and let this redheaded Irish girl loose among the paying guests. And it paid off. Rita became not just the face of the brand, but the epitome of the service Hard Rock strived to offer day in and day out.

Rita and the rest of the forty-six original employees created the type of cultural model we all aspired to achieve at Hard Rock. Unfortunately, the type of talent pool pillaged by Isaac Tigrett and Peter Morton in 1971 doesn't seem to exist anymore, in almost any industry. Still, that specific part of the founders' plan—to seek employees who are demonstrably unique or off-center—is still the brand's quest. And by the way, this is no big secret from the rest of the hospitality industry. They all know it. All of Hard Rock's competitors know that having a unique staff is the key, but many are scared to take in that same crop of crazy.

When I talk about "crazy," I am not alluding to people who may be mentally unstable or dangerous, but rather employees who are more outspoken, confident, witty and quick-thinking than the average person. Most of these traits would be celebrated and sought after in any service-oriented company. So, I don't look at "crazy" as being a negative characteristic.

Although many companies pride themselves on being inclusive of all types, the majority of employees now entering the workforce seem to be made of a "different cloth"—one that is often difficult for an employer to accept. And that's the point where some brands create differentiation. They *want* these unique individuals.

Progressive-minded organizations realize that unique experiences are created by unique people. Unless companies seek to discover and hire a person like Rita Gilligan, who naturally shows up with her own unique characteristics, they will have to spend a lot of time trying to train their employees to do things differently. Because *that* is what consumers crave now: different. Brands that continue to provide the same generic service they have delivered for years—as tepid and forgettable as everyone else—will surely become obsolete.

Unfortunately, being different than what society deems traditional and safe is a deal-breaker for too many companies. Brands like Starbucks and Apple, and entrepreneurs like Fish Morgan, relish the off-center mind, because they know that "crazy" leads to "unique."

WHERE FREAK FLAGS FLY

Perhaps in the more rebellious brands, like Harley-Davidson or Hard Rock, the employees just seem to be a bit higher on the crazy scale because their personalities are just *bigger* than society's norm. They're louder, more daring, even a bit more aggressive—and they proudly fly their visual freak flags. No doubt the way many members of today's potential workforce look—colored hair, unshaven faces, visible tattoos, multiple piercings—reinforces the reluctance of other organizations to venture down this hiring path.

Hesitation to embrace society's misfits continues in most industries. Part of this hesitation is indeed purely about aesthetics—the way the potential employee looks. But some of the nervousness revolves around hiring people that are just too far off-center.

Translation: Unpredictable behavior is scary for most people.

Another factor is the perceived attitudinal baggage and sense of entitlement that comes with today's generation—and this *does* present some challenges. But all of these traits collectively lead to interesting, memorable experiences-waiting-to-happen.

It's exactly these nuances that made the rock group KISS so mind blowing. Most music historians agree that while the individual band members didn't have the best voices…or the instrumental playing chops…or the most well written tunes, no one can disagree with the group's performance art. These guys were the masters of creating an experience. Their painted face make up, themed costumes, character personas and stage theatrics, complete with pyrotechnics and fog machines—as over the top as all of that may have seemed—coalesced into an unforgettable experience, forever seared into young minds everywhere. The band understood showmanship and the need to veer from the status quo—and they delivered the goods at every performance.

Loyal fans who identified with these rock gods became card-carrying members of the KISS Army, swearing allegiance and promising to "rock 'n' roll all night and party every day." It was all part of the KISS experience, and millions were drawn into it. Many of the band's musical peers freely admit that KISS influenced them to develop their own unique performance style. Younger up-and-coming artists proudly point to the band as the reason they started performing in the first place. They were unique—and people responded.

It's ironic that as "dolled up" and "packaged" as KISS was, it was the band's unapologetic authenticity in bringing something different to the world that made its members rock star models for so many others. And for that reason, I still have my membership card.

All of this is just fodder for the mind if you're in an industry or a company that sees this example as too extreme. But I do hope synapses are firing off by the thousands inside your brain, searching for what "unique" could mean to your brand. Because I still believe that unique people create unique experiences.

This kind of unstructured employee profile will not work for every company, but if the quest is really to differentiate yourself from the rest, then hiring at least a few out-of-the-box thinkers can't hurt the brand's chances of standing out in the consumer's mind.

WORK EXPERIENCE IS NOT ENOUGH

Industry statistics are clear: If you can convince restaurant servers to smile with their teeth showing, make genuine eye contact with customers, kneel down or sit down with guests at their tables and even touch guests on the shoulder at some point during the meal (traditionally taboo in the industry), those servers are practically guaranteed a sizeable increase in gratuities versus what they would ordinarily get from their customers. Memory-making techniques like these, used by the original Hard Rock Cafe staff, are the stuff of training legends.

Decades ago, these experiences sprang organically from people who were hired with a particular disposition. Now, however, it takes training programs to get employees to create memorable experiences. This mentality does not always come with work experience.

Work experience is not enough. In fact, *repetition* of mediocre service practices only leads to *engrained* mediocre service practices. We may think we need years of experience in every position, but we don't. We need "different." The ability to deliver unique guest experiences is far more valuable than an employee's tenure doing the same job year after year. People expect more.

There is value in being different, both financially and strategically. The best employers "hire for attitude and train for skill," a notion that rings true today more than ever. Of course we would also like experienced, competent, smart, hard working employees, but these are often not the ones who will create memories for guests. It's the unique and unpredictable ones who truly leave lasting impressions on consumers.

UNPREDICTABILITY CAN BE COOL

How do you think a guest would react if you or one of your employees were to surprise them with something unexpected? For example:

- What would happen if a call-center employee impulsively offered to pay for a customer's shipping cost of an item? Not because something was going wrong, but because the employee recognized the importance of delighting a regular and valued guest.
- What would happen if a bartender noticed a returning customer—one who was at the bar for the first time the night before—and decided to make him a drink "on the house" as a way of saying thank you for the patronage? What do you suppose the customer would say about the place after he left?
- How do you think a receiving clerk would respond to getting an order delivered from a box company in which the sales representative has thrown in an extra supply of free boxes and a kind note…just to solidify the relationship?
- What would a homeowner do if a lawn fertilizer company noticed that her yard needed some big time care compared to the neighbors and stopped by to offer her a free, no-strings-attached fertilizer spray, just to keep her in the good graces of the neighborhood?

These unexpected moments are the types of subtle techniques that smart companies use to stoke the relationship fire between brand and customer. Of course, not every idea has to cost money. There are also little-to-no-cost experiences just waiting to be created. For example:

- How would a customer feel about getting a personalized birthday card from his auto insurance agent (even if it was an electronic card via email)—not with the intent to sell more policies, but for purely creating an unexpected memory and keeping their relationship front and center?
- How do you think a person would feel if her hairdresser said he loved her new look so much that he wanted to take a picture of the stylish cut and post it on his Facebook page? Don't you think she would be on 'cloud nine' over this type of fashion attention?
- What would happen if an airline ticket agent noticed a passenger's team jersey and made a positive comment about his baseball team, even reaching out to give him a "high five"? How would that passenger feel about that unexpected moment over a shared love of a sports team?

- How would a customer feel if her local print company, in an impromptu tweet to all of the company's Twitter fans, singled her out to say how much they appreciated her?

I hope these examples of unpredictability help to get the juices flowing in your own mind as you think about how you can create differentiation between your brand and the competition. To echo my earlier point, *not* knowing exactly what's going to happen to a guest in your business could be part of the experience. Unpredictability is cool. It's refreshing. It's exciting. And it gets rewarded.

It isn't the only way to create memories, but surprising and delighting your customers is a great no-brainer to having your culture stand out from the rest.

IRREVERENCE: A GOOD THING?

Is it bad if an employee tries to impress a customer so much that he or she goes too far in the quest to be different?

Maybe in most companies, but not for me—and I suspect not for others, as well. Like many experience-starved consumers, I welcome an employee's endeavor to create differentiation.

Don't get me wrong; I'm not saying it's alright for employees to do whatever they feel like regardless of the consequences. But as a business owner, I would much rather have to pull an individual back from the brink and remind him or her where the boundaries are than try to get an entire organization of safe automatons to do something unique and memorable.

So it's no surprise that Hard Rock team members are constantly asking for "forgiveness rather than permission" when it comes to their interactions with guests. This approach makes sense in a music-inspired environment, but no doubt scares many other organizations. It shouldn't. The reason it works for Hard Rock and can work for you is that the current and future generations of customers crave memorable moments more and more each day. You just have to figure out what those moments could look like in your world and then unleash the organizational ropes that bind your staff.

EXPERIENTIAL OWNERSHIP

Even if this exact approach doesn't work for every company, you can still cultivate a spirit of "experiential ownership." That is, if the end-goal is to turn your customers into raving fans, then empowering your employees to make memory-searing moments—as if *they* were the business owners—should be relished and celebrated. When your staff takes ownership in creating authentic, unforgettable experiences for clients, they will be inspired to do more. The guests will love the memories they forge and employees will be jazzed to create them. If we really do hire for attitude, as many of us claim to, then let's get out of the way and let our employees use that attitude to WOW our customers.

This idea may still shock many executives and Human Resource professionals who fear that it will result in an employee counseling session, a customer complaint or, even worse, a guest lawsuit. But deep down inside, those same company professionals know "right fit" employees are the ones that make a real difference in company culture and drive an organization's sustainable future.

Still, can an empowered employee in your organization avoid being rude and disrespectful while skirting the edge of irreverence...and be internally celebrated for it?

For example:

- Would there be any harm if a sunglasses sales associate at a mall kiosk noticed an approaching shopper with a cowboy hat on and said, "What's up, Tex?" Are you too unsure of how someone might take that greeting?
- What would happen if a cable company employee answered the phone, "How can I rock your world?" Would you be too scared of how the customer might actually respond to that?
- How would guests at a theme park respond if, when they ask a tour guide to take a picture of them, that park employee turns the camera around and takes a "selfie," adding himself to their vacation pictures? Of course in today's era of digital photography, many people will just delete the picture, no harm done—but some will keep the shot as a captured, unforgettable moment of the overall experience. Would you discipline the employee or quietly celebrate his moxy?

TRIP TO NEVERLAND

One of the great business cultures that enjoys an almost cult-like following is Chick-fil-A, an American quick service chicken restaurant. The company's product is fantastic, often touted as the best chicken sandwich in the fast food industry. But as great as the product is, it's not the reason I assign the company rock icon status. This cultural fave of mine tops the charts because of *its* "irreverence" and "unpredictability." These might seem like odd word choices for describing Chick-fil-A, but I believe this brand marches to the beat of a different drum than its competitors.

It is widely known by the general public this privately-held company has a faith-based heritage, one which sparked some controversy when the brand's founder made some personal religious comments in a published interview. These comments turned off quite a few members of the public, even leading to a boycott of the restaurants. But they also caused even more fans to rally around the brand, solidifying its unique culture in their eyes. And it has paid off, big time. In 2010, well before the controversy, Chick-fil-A surpassed McDonald's to claim the number one spot in single store sales, generating an average of $2.7 million in annual revenue per location, versus the hamburger chain's $2.4 million. And Chick-fil-A is doing it with fewer operating days…because of the company's faith and family philosophy, its restaurants are closed on Sundays. This amazing story continues to be written.

Chick-fil-A realizes that product—as good as it is—is not enough. It is only part of the equation that contributes to the company's years of growth, financial success and rightful place as a culture warrior. The key ingredient in this recipe for success is the employee.

As many fans of the restaurant chain will attest, Chick-fil-A is "religious" about the people it brings on board to represent the company. I mean that literally. Whether you're a fan of the brand or not, you can't dispute that it hires "right fit" employees. In fact, company management goes to great lengths to ensure it. In addition to having a customer-obsessed philosophy, each associate's value system matches up with that of the organization. There is no conflict between personal interest and the brand's ultimate mission. So the attention to detail, sense of urgency and genuine care demonstrated by employees doesn't just come *across* as authentic…it *is* authentic. When an employee responds to every request with "It's my pleasure," I actually believe that it's their pleasure to be pleasant and helpful.

When I go to Chick-fil-A, I usually go through the drive-thru because it's quick. The associates' sense of urgency is valuable to me. But just as comforting is their attention to detail. To this day, I have never experienced a mistake in my drive thru order at Chick-fil-A. Never. I cannot say the same about any other fast food business.

Just recently, I stopped by Chick-fil-A for lunch and actually went inside to order. As I stood at the order counter, I had my hands on my hips in curiosity while I contemplated the menu board. Jose, the quick-witted employee at the register, instinctively said, "Well, hey there, Peter Pan!" alluding to the wide-stance way I was standing…exactly as the character stands in the book, movie and on stage. We both immediately busted out laughing.

That was *it*. That was the moment that this employee turned me into a lifelong, raving fan.

Here was an attentive personality who understood the value of being on the hunt for a moment of opportunity—and then pouncing on it. He was not trying to be offensive or condescending, rather he was taking a risk to provide some unpredictability. Instead of letting that moment pass, like most businesses would probably prefer, Jose took advantage of that window to create something memorable for me. And it worked.

I had never remembered the name of an employee at a fast food restaurant before, but I won't forget Jose's. In that singular moment, he rocked my world and solidified my loyalty.

Well done, Chick-fil-A. Well done.

Are any of these examples too irreverent for you or your brand? Because these are the moments I suspect many other consumers are thirsting to experience. In an era of "same-ole, same-ole," a little irreverence and unpredictability is a good thing.

Take the time to figure out what you will allow…and then roll the dice.

I bet the results for your culture will be phenomenal.

GREATEST HITS THAT ROCK	**THIS IS HOW YOU ROLL**
Win the Talent War: The war for talent is on— suit up for battle if you want "rock stars."	• What is the prototypical employee profile for your company? • How do you define "rock stars" in your organization? • Discuss your brand's realistic ratio of authentic "rock stars" (top talent) to lip-synchers (those who are going through the motions and faking it). • Debate whether or not your brand has a competitive edge in hiring the best talent available.
Understand the Options: "Rock stars" can always get another gig, regardless of the economic state of affairs.	• Talk about the specifics of your company's turn over, especially if you are losing great employees to other companies or other industries. • What type of pay and benefit initiatives are in place to attract and retain top talent? • Discuss whether changes to pay and benefits are necessary for attracting these "rock stars." • Debate whether the organizational culture is strong enough to influence top talent to leave another brand and join yours.
Hire "Different": Unique, unpredictable and irreverent talent creates memories.	• Debate whether your brand stands out from the competition because of your employees. • Do you work with "off-center" people who naturally create differentiation that leads to memorable moments? o Name these employees. • Discuss whether your business has enough employees who are capable of bringing a unique service delivery to the business. • Debate whether your customers are regularly surprised and delighted with unexpected moments.

GREATEST HITS THAT ROCK

THIS IS HOW YOU ROLL

Celebrate Unique Behavior:
Enforce standards, but give out "permission slips."

- Debate whether your organization is rules and policy-oriented or if it allows irreverence and unpredictability to be fostered.
- Discuss whether employees are empowered to do whatever it takes to create an experience for consumers.
- Discuss whether employees are regularly chastised for being irreverent in their approach to creating desired experiences.
- What would have to happen for this to be embraced by the organization?

10

IN SEARCH OF...3C EMPLOYEES

"It comes down to building your own world out here on the road. It's who you surround yourself with."
- Brad Paisley

Every day, companies are becoming more cognizant of the fact that sustaining an organization's culture is primarily dependent on hiring people who can live and exude it. This drive to hire culturally-sound employees wasn't always a popular approach. In the past, most organizations focused more on a person's ability to do the job, the amount of work experience he or she has accumulated and, as much as it's possible to tell from an interview, the person's general trustworthiness. Culture most likely wasn't a huge factor in the hiring process.

Times have changed. While that criteria is still, as it should be, front and center during the hiring process, there is now a broader acceptance of the importance of "right fit" employees. As I mentioned earlier, there are still many company leaders who do not see or understand the value of culture and will shrug it off as a nice-to-have by-product of the brand, versus a sought-after characteristic, but many others are starting to come around. And if those naysayer leaders were to do a little self-study about the successful companies that are constantly in the news for their brand health—The Container Store, Five Guys Burgers, Whole Foods, etc.—they would notice that their strength isn't solely rooted in their employees' base skill-sets or job experience, but rather in the way those associates have magnificently represented the organizations' values and overall culture.

In a July, 2012 *CNN Money* article, Fortune Management reported on this heightened awareness in corporate boardrooms across the U.S. The article specifically pointed to the rise in Chief Culture Officer appointments. This executive level position is tasked with keeping an eye on the overall culture, especially for those brands that believe culture drives everything the business does. An organization's hiring approach would obviously fall into this position's sphere of influence.

An applicant's ability to perpetuate the company culture is now as critical as any other hiring factor—perhaps even more so in some brands. Apple Computer's co-founder put it this way:

"Find people who are competent and really bright, but more importantly, people who care exactly about the same things you care about."

- Steve Jobs

Jobs was not discounting the benefits of diversity in an organization's workforce, rather he was singling out the importance of an overall values-match between a company and its employees. He also clearly believed that intelligence and work experience were not enough in his world. This supports the thoughts I shared in Chapter 1 about surrounding yourself with different yet like-minded people in order to positively affect company culture.

Brands today are only as good as the care and attention they put into ensuring that every employee has all three "C"s:

- Competence
- Character
- Culture

It used to be that the first two "C"s were enough, but now you need all three: solid Competence, strong Character and a Cultural fit. All of these are unseen qualities that will not necessarily show up on an application or a resume. Instead, these have to be discovered during the interview and onboarding processes.

Competence
This is the ability to actually do the job required. It is still vitally important, as you can't just rely on your employees to smile their way to success or simply look good. You have to have faith that they can perform their assigned functions with excellence and take personal responsibility for helping the company be successful. This is where previous experience—explored with some well-chosen interview questions regarding specific job tasks performed—can come into play. If the potential hire has no previous job experience in the position, he or she should at least have the capacity and willingness to learn the job. This too is part of competence.

Character
This is best described as trustworthiness—a person with "character" is worthy of another person's trust. One would hope that a potential hire's value orientation matches up with the brand's, but there are some timeless principles that transcend any specific company or industry. Basic traits like honesty, professionalism and integrity are a few of the key elements any employer would want in an employee's character. It may be hard to pre-determine whether or not someone is willing to steal from you, likely to lie to you or will inevitably do something completely contrary to the company's policies, but these are definitely detrimental to the trust factor. These are a few of the traits any employer would seek to weed out.

Culture

Obviously, the entirety of this book is centered on this concept. In this context, however, culture refers to an employee's ability to accurately and willingly represent the brand. Based on the potential hire's personality, enthusiasm, appearance and answers to questions, both during the interview process and the initial training, a smart leader can tell if someone possesses the cultural DNA of the organization. It may be crystal clear to some managers that an interviewee would be a perfect fit, but for others, it may just be a "gut" feeling. They might not be able to say why, but they know the company juice is running through the potential employee's veins. It's this unique element that is now in big demand. Culture is not the only cherished characteristic, but it is a critical and equal part of the equation.

Rock star employees will have all three "C"s, but the reality is many employees do not—and the one that tends to get "thrown under the bus" and disregarded is culture. Why? Because some employers retreat to the only position in which they feel comfortable, relying primarily on competence and whoever can do the basics of the job. Unless the individual is an entrepreneur with no employees, a leader cannot do the work him- or herself and therefore must rely on others. The easy route is to fill a position based on the person's experience and the ability to do basic job tasks. The harder decision involves hiring a "right fit" employee who oozes culture, and then supporting that person in the development of competence.

It would be great if we could find employees who possess all of the technical and attitudinal skills we desire, but if we have to err in favor of one of the qualities, we should go for the cultural fit. Brand-oriented leaders understand that culture is everything and therefore must play a crucial part in the employee profile. This may still feel unrealistic for some, but twenty years of studying culture and service have left me confident that when company leaders shift to this approach, they inevitably feel better about the experiences created for consumers—and the long term results that follow.

THE "IT" FACTOR

When I was at Hard Rock, I regularly travelled to company properties and discussed various issues that concerned the management team—from providing unparalleled service to driving top line sales to finding organizational efficiencies. As part of those onsite visits, I would conduct management one-on-one meetings to get a clear picture of each manager's growth, challenges, hopes and fears. One of the exercises I would employ in those discussions was to discuss their department personnel, specifically the highest-and lowest-performing staff members. Inevitably, their top employees were not just the ones who produced the best results or were the most likable, but also the ones that best fit the culture and positively represented the brand. They had the "it" factor—that *something special* that was hard to teach or even find in a policy manual—which made the difference between a paid employee and a brand ambassador.

When I had those same conversations with the General Manager about the managers on the team, the GM also opted for the leaders that understood and represented the culture. Perhaps this was an unfair position to put them in, but I would literally ask each General Manager the following question: "If I forced you to choose only one of your six managers to go to war or start a new business with, who would you take?" They *always* chose the "culture guy" or "culture girl." It never failed. I can assure you that most of their selections were not the business-oriented, marketing-savvy, number-crunching managers that you need to drive sustainable growth; they always leaned toward the *one* leader that team members would follow and feel inspired by—the one they felt *truly* represented the brand. They had the "it" factor. Again, this does not mean that the other characteristics are not important—because they are—it's just that for this brand, culture trumped them all. No doubt this heightened focus has contributed to Hard Rock's decades of success.

To be clear, I'm not advocating a complete shift to one characteristic over another, but as a capitalist interested in making money and having a sustainable enterprise, I'm convinced that we need to focus on more than just work experience and ability to do the job. As a business owner, it is imperative that you hire for the "it" factor. Your specific "it" factor may not be attitude. It could be determination, or innovation, or maybe even attention to detail. Whatever "it" is, it's clear that experience is not enough, nor should it be the deal breaker in a hiring decision. Employers must figure out exactly which skills fit their business the best and hone in on those characteristics during the interview process. As I mentioned before, focusing too much attention and energy on a resume can influence your overall impression of a potential employee and prevent you from hiring a true cultural hero. Understand your needs and look at the silver lining of each and every potential employee to make sure you find exactly what you are looking for.

If you happen to work in an industry in which there really *is* a labor shortage, even when the economy is struggling and unemployment is high, then you will eventually have to hire some team members who don't have enough experience—so you may as well take a chance on the candidates who demonstrate a unique attitude and personality and then train them in the specific and technical job skills. But if your organization's internal stakeholders agree that you do indeed need a different type of brand ambassador, then they'll have to be prepared for the qualities that come with those employees. Because these new hires look and act differently than those that have come before. They have different needs and expectations. They tend to shake things up. And those issues may be big concerns for your company.

The good news: These new and unique people also come with novel attributes, characteristics and, eventually, experiences for your consumers.

Is your company willing to take a chance on the trade-off?

GOT TALENT?

If service is what you intend to improve, then you will most likely acknowledge that, above all, this is a people issue. It's time to suit up for battle and deploy your key initiatives aimed at solving the front-end issues of your Employee Life Cycle: recruiting and hiring the right people. Those that do not address this fundamental issue immediately will fall behind the rest of the competition. Since unique employees create memorable experiences, those brands that snatch them up early and solidify their loyalty will blaze past competitors that have failed to realize the value in hiring "different." Customers of these proactive brands will be feasting on mind-blowing performances. Their competitors will be serving up a healthy dose of elevator Muzak.

To create differentiation, we need to find rock stars.

In North America, we're in the midst of a labor shortage that we knew was coming for nearly a decade, and by now everyone realizes they are in a war for talent. It's here. It actually began years ago, even before the global economic pains of 2008—rising commodity costs, increasing gas prices and the collapse of the housing and credit markets—set in. And oh yeah, don't forget about the skyrocketing cost of healthcare. Collectively, these issues put almost every industry into a downward spiral. But before all of that occurred, the talent war had already begun. And it will continue into the future. This will always be a challenge to an organization's culture and survivability.

My knowledge and experience of this challenge are limited to the U.S., but I know every country has its own set of issues and obstacles around hiring. If it's not the economy or the unemployment numbers, it's something else. As an employer, it is essential your business model includes a game plan for the changing times so you can maximize your search for talent.

People Report is an organization dedicated to tracking, measuring and analyzing people-oriented data in order to derive assumptions and identify best practices that will make hospitality the industry of choice. In a report of its annual findings published just a few years ago, this association came to some startling conclusions about the industry's future.

The United States population only grows about 1 percent per year

—around 3 million people. I won't bore you with all of the statistics, but the impending problem was clear: There were not enough physical bodies being born in the U.S. to supply hospitality's labor needs.

To pile it on a bit more, the industry learned a second kick-in-the-teeth statistic: The hospitality industry, second only to government in size, would soon be overtaken by healthcare, groceries and education, both in growth rate and number of overall employees. Additionally, those industries were starting to go after the same employee demographic as hospitality—yet they were grabbing them earlier in life, providing them with superior pay and benefits and offering them a better quality of life.

Ouch. The pond is getting drained far too quickly.

Many companies have already felt the cold hard fact that there are simply not enough great potential employees out there to "mind the store." And the great ones that are out there are not exactly banging down the door for a job. They already have one. In fact, any time a recession hits the United States and unemployment rates increase, most of the good employees just stay where they are, happy to have a job, but all the while knowing they could go elsewhere and easily get another. Regardless of the economic environment, top performers realize that they are in a much better position to test the waters, avoid commitment to a single company and eventually decide what their next career choice will be. Why?

Because they can.

Rock stars can always find another gig.

TOP TALENT HANGOUTS

Armed with this knowledge, you would think more organizations would start morphing—changing with the times—to better reflect what's going on out there. Sadly, not enough are. But while many are missing the mark, the savvy employers are already moving. They realize great service is the true differentiator, so they focus on the service *deliverer*. And the answer can't be found in their training practices; it's going to be in their recruiting approach.

Perhaps you are lucky enough to work for a company that fosters internal promotions and truly takes the time, care and attention to groom talent and develop leaders from within the organization. Sadly, there are too many that either don't do this or don't do it well. As a result, there is a constant churn of new employees coming and going through the revolving door.

In this environment, an organization never gets to the next level—the sweet spot—because it never reaches the "developing leaders" stage. Instead, too much time, energy and money is spent on the wrong hires, who either self-select out of the brand or get let go early on. So when the organization needs to re-ignite the culture or is on the hunt for future leaders, it has to go outside to find them.

Even in an unbelievably competitive industry like hospitality, great talent is still available—but these talented individuals no longer show up, fill out an application and then wait for the phone to ring. Remember, the good ones have a job somewhere else. It may not be their ultimate career choice, but they have a job. Therefore, like a savvy music producer, business owners must aggressively search for great talent. And once they see it, they will, as Rihanna sings, "shine bright like a diamond" among the rest.

Rock stars clearly stand out in a crowd.

So where are they? Where does the top talent work? Well, if you believe what I do, that unique people create unique experiences, then we must first find the places where unique people hang out and work.

You could certainly try to pillage from the brands that I have highlighted in this book, but good luck with that approach—these companies have already figured out that culture is the way to long-term success and their workforces are populated with an army of committed brand agents, many of whom have sworn loyalty for their entire careers. It would take a lot for one of them to bail on a chart-topping, iconic brand like Google, Zappos.com or Pike Place Fish Market. So perhaps the better approach is to seek out the *undiscovered* misfits.

Regardless of your specific industry, I would start looking in the types of places where I have personally experienced customized and individualized service, such as:

- Hospitality (of course), including Coffee Shops, Restaurants and Hotels
- Cosmetic Sections of Big Department Stores
- Museums and Theme Parks—specifically for tour guides
- Improv Acting Studios
- Tattoo Shops
- Social Media Blogs

Although these specific businesses may not work for your employee profile, you should still seek out the types of hubs where unique people are drawn.

SEEKING EYEBALLS

Another way to attract great talent is to step up your influencing superpowers and get them to come to you. This may require a change in the way your organization recruits, but consider implementing some unique ways to get rock star eyeballs on your brand.

If you can create brand-specific recruiting collateral that both accurately represents the brand and stands out from the rest of the "help wanted" ads, you'll have a much better success rate in attracting the exact talent you want and need.

Here are a few spectacular recruiting ads that do just that:

Venti, in Starbucks' language, means "Large." That's all this ad needed: two words, in brand speake—for potential hires to Dream Big about working there.

FEEL FREE TO ACTUALLY ENJOY WHAT YOU DO

Work on an awesome Team with amazing benefits, endless opportunities, and have FUN doing it!

SOUTHWEST®

TIRED OF LONG HOURS AND TOO MUCH TRAVEL???

WE'D LUV FOR YOU TO JOIN OUR INTERNAL AUDIT TEAM!

Based out of Southwest's Corporate Headquarters near Dallas Love Field, Southwest Airlines' Internal Audit department has various openings for FUN-LUVING Financial, Operational, and Information Technology Auditors with 3-7+ years experience.

► Candidates must take Internal Audit seriously- but not themselves.

► Certification (CIA, CPA, CISA, CFE) is required for some positions.

► Travel is less than 20%!!

Southwest is considered one of the "Best Companies to Work For" as recognized several times by *FORTUNE*! We have FUN, work hard, and fly for free!

BENEFITS AT A GLANCE:

► Unlimited space-available flight benefits to any Southwest destination for you and your immediate family.

► Outstanding medical coverage with plans currently starting at a $10 monthly Employee contribution.

► Our 401k plan matches dollar for dollar up to 7.3%

► Our Profitsharing plan rewards our Employees for their contribution to our overall financial performance (paid out 7.9% in 2006).

► Casual dress environment- which means you have the freedom to be comfortable and wear shorts, jeans, and tennis shoes to work!

For more information please contact:
Greg Muccio
People and Leadership
Greg.Muccio@wnco.com
or visit
www.southwest.com/careers/

An extension of Southwest Airlines' popular television commercials, in which you are "free to move about the country," this variation is aimed internally for potential hires.

Pretty confident approach, some would say, for this talent management software company. But this is exactly the type of branded recruiting tool that completely matches Cornerstone's culture.

And a few of my all-time favorites from Hard Rock:

Tapping in to its inner AC/DC, the brand uses song lyrics to resonate with people who would want to work in a music-engulfed environment.

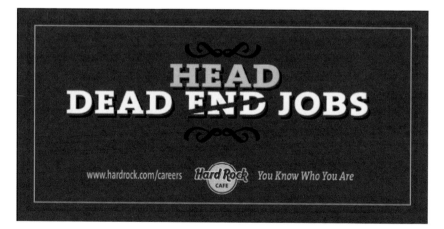

Although we mentioned this in Chapter 3, you would have to be a little bit older, a music aficionado or a part of The Grateful Dead's cult following to know that fans of the band are Dead Heads. The person who would know that is exactly who the brand is trying to attract and recruit.

My favorite over the years and the one that won Hard Rock a few recruiting awards. Humorous, authentic, a little irreverent…perfect!

Not working here **Hard Rock** CAFE must really SUCK

Every time someone joins us here at Hard Rock Cafe, they tell us how there's just no comparison. We've built a business out of having fun...and that makes us a great place to be.

- Restaurant Managers
- Kitchen Managers/ Assistant Kitchen Managers

To work here, you have to have at least three years of high-volume, full-service restaurant management experience.

The World's Original Theme Restaurant · Top Salaries · 100% Paid Family Medical & Dental · Three Weeks Paid Vacation (after one year) · 401K Plan · Huge Advancement Potential · Opportunities From Coast-To-Coast · Relocation Package · Philosophical Approach To Success

If your current job sucks, send your resume...quick! Hard Rock Cafe, General Manager, 215 Peachtree St. NE, Atlanta, GA 30303; fax (404) 681-1025. No phone calls, please.

Interested in other worldwide opportunities? Forward your resume to: Tracie Berg, Recruiting Coordinator, Hard Rock Cafe, 5401 Kirkman Road, #200, Orlando, FL 32819. Fax (407) 370-5125. EOE

One of my more recent "finds" during an online image search is an employee recruiting ad from Apple with the headline that reads "Close Your Windows, Open a Few Doors"—a not-so-subtle dig on Microsoft Windows—making the analogy that career doors will open for those who join Apple Computers versus its competitor. Like the other ads, this one made me take notice…exactly what Apple would want from a potential rock star hire.

All of these examples could be used in traditional print advertising, Internet web banners or social media campaigns. The goal is not just to elicit interest from like-minded candidates, but also to start these same potential employees on their cultural education.

With a simple piece of brand-relevant collateral like this, don't you think these companies are more likely to get the top talent they seek than the organizations that are not as culturally dialed in?

EMPLOYEES-IN-WAITING

So owners, executives and managers of today actually have to go out there and mine for great talent if they have any hope of strengthening their culture. First, they have to discover *where* great employees are currently working—then they have to convince those talented individuals to come and work for *them*. Tough thing to do and still find time to run a business. And this problem is not exclusive to the hospitality industry—or even North America. Many organizations in other industries, are facing the same challenges.

Unfortunately, it's not going to get better unless someone in the organization is willing to make some tough hiring choices—which includes insisting on all three "C"s.

Hire the most unique, service-oriented talent available and everything else falls into line. When you hire off-center but guest-obsessed employees on the front end, the training process also gets easier because you're starting with passionate, committed brand champions who seem to pick up tasks quicker and are willing to go the extra step and deliver unparalleled experiences for the customer…all while giving your veteran staff an infusion of positive morale. These individuals certainly make a manager's job much easier.

Onboarding these authentic new hires, however, is not an easy fix for organizations in need of a cultural overhaul. The "right fit" employees-in-waiting I've described here are a part of a different breed—a generation with different needs. But if you're armed with the right knowledge, you have the opportunity to not only identify those needs, but meet them as well—ensuring that your company will be chock full of unique employees, all diligently working to propel your business to the top of the charts.

GREATEST HITS THAT ROCK	THIS IS HOW YOU ROLL

Discover the "Right Fit": Work experience is not enough—err in favor of hiring "right fit" employees.	• Do the majority of your employees have all three "C"s—Competence, Character and Culture?
	• Discuss whether your hiring practices rely more on work experience or attitude.
	  o Is it the right mix?
	  o If not, what should it be and what are some things that can be done to move your company toward this goal?
	• Discuss whether your company is willing to take a chance on the trade-off of hiring more culturally relevant employees versus more competent ones.
	• If you wanted to shift to a more attitude-oriented profile, what would have to change?

Find the Top Talent: You have to mine for great talent—the good ones already have a job somewhere else.	• What is the company's strategy for seeking out potential employees that currently work elsewhere? • Name all of the companies, industries and locations that would be the best places to find top talent. • Discuss how you will communicate with and attract potential hires you encounter, that are currently working in other jobs.
Create Brand-Specific Recruiting Collateral: Unique ads that stand out from the competition will attract the desired talent.	• Debate whether or not your company employs unique recruiting initiatives to attract unique employees. • Name the methods currently used for recruiting. • What are some things that could be done—short- and long-term—to better attract desired talent?

11

THE ISLAND OF MISFIT TOYS

*"I used to think anyone doing anything weird was weird;
now I know that it is the people that call others weird that are weird."*
– Paul McCartney

One of the best places to enhance a company's culture is at the hourly-paid, non-management level, specifically with employees at the front end of their careers. At the very least, the goal should be to "stop the bleeding" of an anemic culture and, by positively influencing the "new blood" coming on board, prevent it from getting further watered down.

You may recall the 1964 cartoon classic "Rudolf the Red-Nosed Reindeer," which comes on television every Christmas season in the U.S. My favorite part in this stop-motion holiday special is when Rudolf and Hermey the Elf stumble upon the Island of Misfit Toys. In this abandoned land, you would find a train with square wheels, a boat that wouldn't float, a spotted toy elephant and, instead of a normal wind-up Jack-in-the-Box, a Charlie-in-the-Box. This is the place where all the broken toys live because nobody wants them.

Ironically, this is the analogy I proudly use to describe the Hard Rock staff.

The company has indeed become the Island of Misfit Toys for many employees. It's a safe haven for physically and attitudinally diverse individuals that no one else wanted. But the brand does not look at these folks as charity cases. Rather, these are unbelievably great, service-oriented people who happen to look and behave differently, but who nonetheless can do an amazing job. They were just square pegs in round holes to previous and potential employers. Yet they eventually found a home—a place where they could be accepted for who and how they are—the Hard Rock brand.

As one of my mentors, MK, often said in his presentation to new company managers:

"We'll take people how they are; we care what they contribute."

Therein lies the symbiotic relationship between people who are different and culturally-focused brands.

FEEL FREE TO RAP

As you may have noticed from my gushing comments earlier in the book, another one of my favorite company cultures is that of Southwest Airlines.

There are a variety of reasons I have such love for this Dallas, TX-based air carrier, including the company's:

- **Boarding Process**—so effective that it baffles my mind why other carriers have not tried to replicate the format
- **On Time Departure & Arrival Record**—the best in the industry; partly due to the boarding process, but certainly because of the brand's commitment to efficiency
- **Baggage Fee Process**—the company charges none, while every other airline proudly does just the opposite
- **Flight Change Policy**—again at no cost, realizing that passengers' plans change all the time…providing a hassle-free sense of comfort when booking
- **Safety Record**—although some minor incidents have occurred, to date, they are one of the only major carriers without a major crash or passenger loss of life

These are just some of the reasons why Southwest Airlines have generated 40+ consecutive years of profitability, even during financially tough years when many of the other major carriers struggled to survive. However, despite these well-known and relished policies and programs among Southwest's frequent fliers, the signature characteristic of the brand, which most passengers admire, is the company's employees. The brand hires some pretty unique characters and then encourages them to have fun and create a loose, comfortable flying experience for their passengers. I have been on many Southwest flights where the flight attendants crack jokes or sing throughout the traditionally stale safety announcements. Everyone knows how important the instructions are, and the crew never takes away from the message. But by having some fun along the way, people actually pay closer attention to the details.

However, no *one* individual can top David Holmes, the Las Vegas-based flight attendant who delivers the flight safety announcements in a customized rap song. Yes, he actually raps the entire safety announcement…and he's great. He started doing it in 2009 on just a few select flights, but then a video of him doing the routine quickly went viral on the Internet, making him an instant celebrity. He's been rapping the announcements ever since, and the company has actually encouraged it. David is a rock star and his catchy hip-hop performance creates an experience people will remember—and associate with Southwest Airlines—for the rest of their lives.

This unique employee took the company's recruiting ad—to "Feel Free to Actually Enjoy What You Do"—literally. And he does. He's a misfit who has found a home.

Of course Southwest is one of several major air carriers that have sought to "up" the entertainment factor in their formal safety announcement videos, but none of them can compete with Virgin America Airlines' bold approach. This brand has truly capitalized on our desire to be surprised and delighted by creating an unbelievably great, five-minute safety video…in the form of a music video. It's fantastic!

This highly informative demonstration, with its irresistibly catchy song, will capture the attention of everyone on the airplane, regardless of how frequently they fly. The video went viral on the Internet within days of being launched—it's *that* good. This is no doubt the start of the Airline Safety Announcement Video Wars. Expect competitors to produce more irreverence in the near future, hoping to catch up.

This chapter is about tapping into unique talent pools and bringing the best on board. But since I singled out a unique Southwest flight attendant who refreshingly delivered an otherwise mundane message, I couldn't help but call out Virgin America as another organization that has brilliantly tapped into our lust for memorable experiences. This airline simply took David Holmes' approach and formalized it into a consistent format that could be spread throughout the company (and the Internet). For sure some unique people at Virgin were involved in this daring idea, from the Marketing personnel who initially threw the idea on the table to the company's CEO, Richard Branson, who signed off on it.

Misfits were involved. And we're better off because of them.

THINK DIFFERENT

Like Starbucks, Zappos or Harley-Davidson, I realize that unique people create unique experiences…the type of experiences I believe the average consumer craves today. Those companies that can open up their diversity policies to include the "crazy ones,"—a tactic celebrated in Apple's viral, one-minute video, "Think Different"—will surely deliver more memorable moments for their customers.

But that type of employee may be too extreme for most.

Not all companies can strive to attract misfits, nor would we want them to. We don't want every brand to be the same. But we *all* want more companies to be great. And every company *wants* to be great. Still, we can each appreciate the imperative of attracting—and loving on—top talent. Finding and hiring the best available talent is every company's quest. It's Business 101.

RACK 'EM UP

Speaking of "thinking differently," there's one company that certainly knows how to *work* differently—it's part of the mantra at Rackspace, a global leader in business Information Technology infrastructure. While the name may not be widely-known to the general public, Rackspace is considered a rock star brand by companies that run databases, applications and websites. The Texas-based company operates several data centers around the world and delivers the best-fit product for meeting each organization's IT needs, be that dedicated computer servers, the public "cloud," a private "cloud" or some combination of these platforms.

Since its inception, Rackspace has chosen a different path than its competitors. As cloud-based technology became a reality, the founders worked with NASA to develop OpenStack, an open-source, scalable operating system that makes data easy to move from one data center or service provider to another. This branded technology has now become the fastest-growing cloud platform on the planet. And here's the kicker: Rackspace makes it readily-available to everyone. While other cloud vendors focused on developing proprietary technologies that would handcuff organizations when they needed to change or share their data, Rackspace shook up the industry by providing its cloud code to the world, allowing any business to use it. Utilizing this technology, companies are able to customize better and scale faster, all while knowing they have the flexibility to control company data any way they want to.

To create an added layer of client confidence, Rackspace guarantees the availability of the network, power and infrastructure systems 100 percent of the time, offering customers a five percent credit on their monthly fees for every 30 minutes of downtime. The company also guarantees functioning hardware components at all times and provides replacement parts for failed components at no cost to the customer. So between the stellar product, the infrastructure flexibility and an appealing financial guarantee, Rackspace garners immediate brand loyalty from its clients.

The organization now hosts hundreds of thousands of customers worldwide—including more than 40 percent of today's *Fortune 100* companies. Yet, as good as their product and systems are, they're not the only reasons Rackspace has enjoyed years of success. The company's firm commitment to the central cause of serving their customers is what elevates them to cultural rock icon status. The organization's internally-branded, award-winning *Fanatical Support* helps customers successfully architect, manage, troubleshoot and deploy these critical business applications with an overwhelming amount of positive support and care. And that's only possible through committed employees.

This cloud-hosting company has made a deliberate decision to hire its own breed of misfits—known as "Rackers"—who enjoy creating experiences for clients. Rackers are self-proclaimed technology geeks that are flat-out customer-obsessed. To recognize and celebrate this obsession, each year the brand presents its coveted *Fanatical Jacket* Award—a literal straight jacket—to a deserving Racker who has provided outstanding customer service. Individuals who truly deliver *Fanatical Support* to clients are nominated for the jacket, which is the highest award a Rackspace employee can earn. It is representative of the organization's commitment to rocking peoples' worlds.

Remember, this is a technology and data hosting company, yet creating Fanatical outcomes is the desired mission of every employee in the brand. And it shows. Consistent, gushing employee feedback on the workplace environment has elevated Rackspace to Fortune's list of the "100 Best Companies to Work For" nearly every year since 2008.

Fantastic.

As proof of Rackspace's spectacular internal culture, the company's website has an area dedicated to employees—working in spaces reminiscent of Zappos—sharing their personal stories through videos and blogs. Rackers talk about everything from how they create moments for customers to trends in the industry—and some simply profess their undying love for the brand. But the ultimate act of loyalty was committed by the company's former Head of Culture Branding, who had the brand's logo tattooed onto his shoulder. That's crazy…and I love it.

Brand loyalty runs rampant in this company.

Rackspace is a great example of a company that seeks out and hires unique individuals to deliver memorable experiences, even in an industry not traditionally known for its world-class culture. This brand is proof that any business can create a culture that rocks.

WHAT'S NEXT?

Now that I have defined the difference between rock stars and lip-synchers, mulled over where they may currently work and how you can recruit them to your organization, let's go a little deeper into what your ultimate workforce will inevitably look like. Since team members make the difference in the guest experience, we need to better understand them if we have any hope of hiring, training, developing and retaining them.

The next few chapters will focus specifically on the current generation that makes up today's workforce, but I'll throw in some nuances that will differentiate the *future* talent pool, as well. I'll share the key drivers that fuel their engines to set the stage for you to better secure their loyalty and, ultimately, your company's position as an employer of choice.

THE TIMES THEY ARE A-CHANGIN'

In 1965, the wildly successful singer-songwriter Bob Dylan made a significant change to his musical style. To "amp up" his sound, the troubadour shifted from acoustic guitar to electric guitar. This was a drastic transformation by any measure: Bob Dylan adapted his style and altered his approach to reflect the changing times. Hence the name of his album, *The Times They Are A-Changin'*. For some, that was the moment the "every man" artist sold out to the popular sound of the day and became a part of the mainstream money-making machine.

This is the type of inflection point I envision when considering today's workforce. I compare that turning-point moment in Dylan's career—and the way it felt to his most loyal fans—to the way the employee base has evolved over the last 50 years. They both represent significant cultural shifts.

Although it certainly hasn't been as dramatic or instantaneous as Bob Dylan's conversion, the talent pool has slowly transformed over the past half-century, evolving from a laid back, subtle acoustic vibe to a louder, more in-your-face, aggressive electric sound. That is, employees have discovered the amplifier. And they have plugged in.

Because wow, have times changed!

All you have to do is sit by the front door of any business and observe as the youth of today strolls in to apply for a position to know things have dramatically changed over the last five decades. This is not a negative comment about any specific generation—I both celebrate and long for this type of uniqueness and diversity—but the reality is talent is quite different today. Potential employees have priorities, needs and learning styles that are vastly different than those of generations past. They look different, behave differently and have different expectations of an employer. These are crucial traits for businesses to understand.

Let's take a look what makes these individuals tick.

WHO ARE YOU?

It's been called the Nintendo Generation, Echo Boomers, Generation Next and Generation Y, but let's refer to the group of people born between the years 1981 and 2000 by its most widely-used moniker: the Millennial Generation. Like every generation, Millennials have a variety of priorities. For our purposes, understanding these needs is critical if you want to use them to benefit your business.

As a record number of Baby Boomers exit the workforce and Gen-Xers move up to fill their executive ranks, the Millennials have become the predominant entry-level workforce. Every organization taps into the Millennial ranks sooner or later. Many companies are already there and clearly have their culture steeped in Millennial entrepreneurship—and now they have to turn their attention toward the next generation.

The employees of tomorrow (born after 2001) will require a much more experiential and tech-savvy approach than even the Millennials. While some have labeled this up-and-coming group Generation Z or the iGeneration, I prefer the more appropriate and unique name "Digital Natives," because it captures the way this group lives symbiotically with technology—it's the only life they know. In fact, Digital Natives can be compared to an infamous race of villains on the popular TV show *Star Trek*. Sci-fi fans will instantly know exactly what I mean when I compare our future workforce to…The Borg.

The Borg is a race of beings composed of both organic and cybernetic material co-existing in a single symbiotic life form. They are half human, half robot entities that cannot survive without both parts. Digital Natives affectionately remind me of this fictitious alien race as they are practically born with a technology chip in their heads, allowing them to easily access and wield technology as if it were a natural part of their existence.

The reason I'm singling out these specific generations (Millennials and Digital Natives) is that organizational culture, as I've defined it, is simply a collection of individual behaviors. If you belong to a company that sells a product or provides a service and your goal is to create memorable moments for your consumers, you're going to have to rely completely on human beings. And if you believe as I do that smart and pleasant employees can certainly deliver good service, but only unique ones can create memories, then attracting and understanding the "misfits" you'll eventually want to hire is too important to dismiss.

KEY CULTURAL DRIVERS

Understanding the key drivers and hot buttons of your labor force is essential to planning for their needs and adjusting the organization to accommodate them. We need to revolve our internal business systems around them, rather than trying to fit *them* into our internal business systems.

The innovative and flexible organizations that understand this will boldly rush toward this group of talent, like first-in-line concertgoers racing to the front of the stage when the venue doors are opened. They recognize specific traits in the potential employees of today and have moved to reshape their internal organizational cultures to address their high-value needs. Your company can do the same when it understands these critical traits.

Here are the key drivers vital to understanding Millennials and Digital Natives. They are:

- **Experience-Obsessed**—they crave memorable moments in their personal and professional lives
- **Identity-Oriented**—they covet individuality as a priority and see it as a non-negotiable in life
- **Visual Learners with Short Attention Spans**—they prefer and respond to photos, graphics and video over text
- **Technology-Dependent**—they are savvy about technology and heavily rely on it for functionality in life
- **Purpose-Driven and Socially Conscious**—they want to do meaningful work, usually something bigger then themselves, and they care about the planet and social causes

In order to leverage this unique crop of talent to represent and perpetuate our organizational culture, we need to be able to relate to them, value them and appreciate their unique attributes and behavior. Therefore, as we move through the next few chapters together, we will focus on understanding how each of the key drivers directly affects and motivates these groups.

GREATEST HITS THAT ROCK	THIS IS HOW YOU ROLL
Celebrate Individuality: Truly celebrate the differences in others—this mindset fosters unique experiences.	• Do you personally value the difference in others; do you look at wide diversity in thought, action and physical make-up as a benefit to the company? • Determine whether diverse teammates bring different perspectives to the business. • Discuss whether you think your work environment values the differences in others. • Debate whether your brand would have any issues with integrating some "misfits" into your organizational workforce. • What would be the pros and cons of infusing the brand with this type of uniqueness?
Revolve the Business Around Employees: Innovative organizations reshape their internal cultures to address employee key drivers.	• Discuss current organizational systems that have evolved and now revolve around your employees. • Identify other business processes that still need to be adjusted to address employees' high-value needs. • How prepared are you personally to recruit, train, develop, communicate with and retain Millennials and Digital Natives? o How prepared is your company?

12

EXPERIENCE & INDIVIDUALITY AS WEAPONS

"I'd rather be hated for who I am, than loved for who I am not."

- Kurt Cobain, Nirvana

It is not my intention to get into generational training here, as there are far more experienced experts—some of them friends of mine—that already play in this space. Additionally, the hot buttons that I will lay out in the next few chapters are but a sampling of a much longer list of lifestyle nuances that matter to today's talent. However, after years of observing behaviors and producing educational content for the "next generations," I've compiled this whittled-down, combined list of characteristics I believe will profoundly affect an organization's culture.

EXPERIENCE-OBSESSED

The initial key driver for today's talent is the desire for memorable moments in their lives, both professionally and personally.

We know from the previous chapters that customers want memorable experiences—and we have covered this specific expectation in detail. The great news is that this is now a generational key driver for potential employees, as well. These individuals also long for mind-searing experiences in their lives, including at work. So all of the points I made earlier about guest expectations can now be applied to both the consumer *and* the employee.

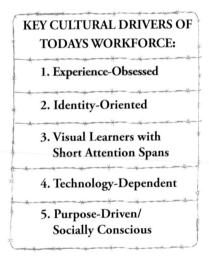

KEY CULTURAL DRIVERS OF TODAYS WORKFORCE:

1. **Experience-Obsessed**

2. **Identity-Oriented**

3. **Visual Learners with Short Attention Spans**

4. **Technology-Dependent**

5. **Purpose-Driven/ Socially Conscious**

In other words, it is not enough for us to create great experiences for our customers; we now have to do the same for our workforce in order to create a sustainable culture.

Take a look at one of my favorite brands, one that deliberately seeks employees who are experience-obsessed.

Wawa

Based in Wawa, Pennsylvania, this family- and associate-owned chain of convenience stores of the same name has served as a staple for Northeastern U.S. locals for decades—and is now taking the entire East Coast by storm. With its simple core purpose, "Fulfilling Lives, Every Day," Wawa has created a way to make "convenience" a positive experience.

At first blush, the environment is unlike that of any convenience store I have ever experienced: immaculately clean locations, spacious product aisles, extra large restrooms, flat-screen video monitors and digital signage, outdoor seating and popular music playing throughout the store. Then there's the product itself. Sure, the shelves are stocked with the traditional small convenience store fare, but the company also offers high quality, Wawa-branded products that rival any deli or coffee shop offerings. They are known for their built-to-order hoagie sandwiches, freshly made smoothies and premium coffee drinks.

Wawa also sells gasoline, but that's almost a nice-to-have amenity. I'm sure the company makes a lot of money selling gas, but even its print collateral and television advertising do not focus on this part of the business, except to guarantee quality fuel for every purchase—another rarity. In fact, everything at Wawa comes with a money-back satisfaction guarantee to the consumer.

I could go on and on about the self-serve computer touch screen menus that improve accuracy and delivery speed for food orders, or the no-surcharge ATMs that offer free cash withdraws for Wawa customers, but I believe these are just process-driven, brick-and-mortar springboards from which the brand ambassadors create positive experiences. With a rallying cry like "Famous for our hoagies, loved for our people," you would expect Wawa's cultural amplifier to be its employees…and it is.

"Wawa" is the Native American word for the Canadian goose found in the part of Pennsylvania in which the company was founded. An image of a goose in flight serves as the Wawa corporate logo—not just to honor this heritage, but also because the company employs the principles of teamwork, group consensus and encouragement…all inherent elements of a flock of geese flying in formation. To ensure this internal culture exists at every location, the brand goes to great lengths to recruit, hire, train, develop, inspire, motivate, recognize and reward the right-fit associates who deliver service memorable enough to match the cool environment Wawa has created.

Because employee turnover is one of the biggest threats to a business' success, Wawa has purposefully created an employee-centric universe that both attracts and retains service-oriented talent. Take a look at just a few of the company's stand-out benefits and programs:

- Full medical & dental insurance benefits, including prescription drugs, offered to employees
- Associate credit union
- Education assistance plan
- Wellness reimbursement program
- Philanthropic community involvement programs
- An average rate of 25 percent internal promotion into management
- Associate stock ownership plan, which more than half of the brand's employees engage in, collectively securing 40 percent ownership stake in the company

Just a quick reminder: This is a convenience store!

These generous benefits clearly reflect Wawa's commitment to its employees and have no doubt contributed to the extremely low turnover the company enjoys, but for an employee to reap these rewards, he or she has to demonstrate a guest obsession every day. To that end, team members *themselves* need compelling reasons to keep coming back. Wawa knows this is paramount to its ongoing market domination.

By using the same techniques you employ for courting customers, you can attract and recruit the "rock stars" you need to create memorable experiences.

Getting them to stick around, however, requires the creation of some real internal experiences for employees.

INTERNAL EXPERIENCES

Financial benefits aside, consider the following suggestions for creating unique experiences for your staff members:

- **Surprise and Delight:** Seek out opportunities to throw an event or party for your employees; offer random discounts on specific brand items; solicit answers to trivia questions or company procedures in echange for prizes like company logo items, gift cards or concert tickets.
- **Give Recognition:** Publicly acknowledge and reward employees for specific instanes in which they've gone above and beyond the service basics; rewards might include certificates, pins, badges, etc.
- **Peer to Peer Rewards:** Create an authentic staff-on-staff recognition program that does not involve leadership; when done properly, this is a great morale booster, and it's a type of program that will take on a life of its own.

- **Random Acts of Kindness:** Every once in awhile, buy several $1 lotto tickets and hand one out to each member before or during the shift; based on this suggestion, create your own "random act" that makes sense for your business.

- **Surprise Delivery:** Order up a surprise delivery of a type of food that makes sense for your brand (e.g., pizza, chicken wings, mini-burgers, hot pretzels, frozen drinks, cinnamon buns) or even have a food truck stop by once a week.

- **Play Games:** Create employee games and contests (for prizes) that are designed to enhance business results; employees will drive sales, push particular products, and create organic marketing…all while having fun.

- **Change Attire:** Implement "Dress-Down Fridays" or "Blue Jeans Days," where employees can wear something more casual than the business' norm; "Theme Weeks"—employees dressing as their favorite musicians during Grammy Award week, for instance—are both great fun and great for morale.

- **Invite Family:** Foster an environment in which spouses and kids can be included; this could be at a company BBQ or dinner, an annual conference or a "Bring Your Kid to Work Day."

- **Show Holiday Spirit:** Encourage work groups and teams to get into the various seasons by decorating the office during Christmas, dressing up and having Halloween costume contests, wearing green on St. Patrick's Day or celebrating the company's birthday.

- **White Elephant Gifts:** Consider implementing the popular and hilarious secret gift exchange during the end-of-year holidays.

- **Pot Luck Lunch:** Encourage Quarterly or monthly all-staff "pot luck" lunches in which everyone brings a covered dish to eat in a more communal setting, versus the daily grind of individuals doing their own thing.

- **Suggestion Box:** If you don't already have open dialogue sessions to solicit employee feedback (e.g. Quality Circle Meetings), create a non-threatening, anonymous Suggestion Box to gather feedback—and then act on those ideas to make the company better.

- **Cross-Training for Staff:** Schedule individuals—or allow all team members—to work in other positions through an intern or passport program; this will both increase company knowledge and enhance collaboration.

- **Boss Swap for Leaders:** Implement a program in which executives and managers work in entry-level staff positions for a day (perhaps once per year or Quarterly); walking in the employees' shoes will help them develop humility; this is always fun for the employees, as well.

- **Go Teambuilding:** Consider holding non-work team building events, such as Go-Carts, Bowling or Miniature Golf.

- **Movie Night:** Host a team movie night complete with popcorn, Twizzlers and beer; my team at Hard Rock used to watch only "rockumentaries" to build our music knowledge and perfect our craft, but the best part was hanging out together and watching a movie.

- **Internal Talent Show:** This is another opportunity to get employees together once a year, in this case to perform in front of each other (e.g. sing, dance, act, read poetry) while eating and drinking.

- **Group Break:** Pick a specific time of day (e.g. 3:00pm) to take a 15-20 minute break as a team; have a collective cup of coffee, watch videos or play pool, table tennis, etc.

- **Beer Thirty:** This is a little more riskier, but some progressive companies select a time at the end of the work week to stop business early and share cocktails as a group.

- **Book Club:** Start a monthly book club and have the team collectively read a business book over the course of a month or two, then discuss and share insights together.

- **Handwritten Notes:** Take the time to hand-write a personal note to each team member, letting them know how you feel about them and how important they are; have the note waiting for employees as they arrive for or finish a shift.

- **Philanthropy:** Identify a specific charitable cause that will rally the team together for something bigger than the job; take the group to do a philanthropic activity (e.g. working in a food bank, cleaning a park, feeding the homeless, starting a food can drive, etc.).

- **Ongoing Development:** Offer opportunities for employees to continue learning; create a self-development pathway, providing free e-Learning courses or even bring in guest speakers to teach various subjects.

These are just some thought-starters to help you brainstorm and create the type of internal experiences that today's employees expect from companies they want to work for. And creating a work environment that fosters these types of experiences is a great start to revolutionizing a brand's culture.

IDENTITY-ORIENTED

The youth of today need freedom to express themselves in the way they look, dress, talk, behave and interact with others. Having a personal identity that doesn't conform to any particular set of rules or guidelines is a high-value need of today's entry-level workers.

Part of Hard Rock's competitive advantage—among other hospitality companies and even other industries— is in the way it celebrates individuality and provides a respite for those that just don't seem to fit in elsewhere. That is

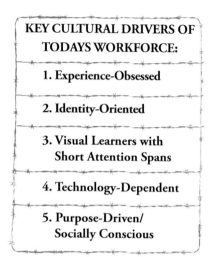

KEY CULTURAL DRIVERS OF TODAYS WORKFORCE:

1. **Experience-Obsessed**

2. **Identity-Oriented**

3. **Visual Learners with Short Attention Spans**

4. **Technology-Dependent**

5. **Purpose-Driven/ Socially Conscious**

not to say these employees couldn't do the work that's available out there, but rather, in many instances, they were not even given a chance because of the personal identities they displayed.

Just like Rock 'n' Roll, the prototypical employee at a Hard Rock property is going to be a bit irreverent, at times unpredictable and probably a little off-center. In my early years with the brand, the team members I served with skewed a bit higher on the crazy scale than your average restaurant employee. They were either missing something in their lives or they were "faulty" in some way and in a constant search to fill or fix the missing part. They were truly broken toys. And it was the inclusive, welcoming arms of a brand that embraced these individuals for the misfits that they were.

We may not be able to make the same generalizations about today's new crop of employees, but Hard Rock still seeks out people that are differ- ent. And so should you. Brands who "get it" recognize the importance of a strong organizational culture, and culture is made up of individuals. The employees of today and tomorrow come engrained with the high-value need of individuality.

Here are a few elements that define an employee's individuality needs:

- **Visual Identity**—they want to look the way they want
- **Permission Slips**—they want the freedom to act outside the box without fear of retribution
- **Vocal Forum**—they want to be able to speak their minds and be heard
- **Devil's Advocate**—they want to challenge the status quo

As U2 front man Bono once said,

> **"To be united is a great thing. But to respect the right to be different is maybe even greater."**

The four physical and attitudinal identifiers listed above should help "in-tune" employers re-shape their brands' hiring standards to better reflect the individuality that is a priority for today's workforce. Let's look at each one.

Visual Identity

Today's potential employees choose to be different—and that includes the way they look. It's easy to discuss the wants and needs of today's talent, but it's hard to take a chance on an individual that so differs from your norm... especially when it comes to the way someone looks.

When a person's individuality manifests itself physically, it might be displayed a number of ways: customized clothing, amount and type of jewelry, a unique hairstyle, extravagant makeup application or even something a bit more permanent, like tattoos, body piercings and colored hair. These artistic embellishments on the Millennial body seem to be the signature markings of today's youth.

The reality is that more people are getting inked up and pierced today than ever before...and at an alarming rate. This physical self-expression helps to tell an individual's personal story. For many, it is a visual representation of his or her personal culture. Part of the attraction, specifically with tattoos, is the permanence. As Hard Rock communicates in its brand collateral, a tattoo is the mark of a risk-taker. It clearly screams to everyone:

"I am not scared of commitment. I am in it for the long haul."

Contrary to what you might think, many of Hard Rock's employees don't join the company completely covered in tats or sporting multiple piercings... they evolve into it. In fact, most of the staff came to the brand from some other hospitality company in which they were not afforded the luxury of expressing themselves aesthetically. It's only *after* they've joined this inclusive tribe that they discover they have the freedom to paint from the entire color palate. And they begin to morph into literal rainbows of expressionism.

Sixteenth-century painter and sculptor Michelangelo made a similar comparison more than 500 hundred years ago when he described his process for sculpting a piece of art. He famously stated that he never actually *created* a single statue; all he did was chip away at all the excess rock to reveal what was already there. Allowing people to have this much freedom of self-expression does the same thing—it creates unique, living pieces of art.

Earlier, I generalized the amazingly unique people I've met and worked with during my career as the crazy ones. I suggested that they were perhaps "broken" in some way. I do not see this as negative; I just think we are all a little broken on this inside and are just looking for a place that accepts us for the way we are, including the way we look.

I've found that many Millennials have battled with some type of acceptance issues in their lives, and that a percentage of them have the scars to prove it. Some just hide their scars, while others have no problem wearing them on the outside—both emotionally, via their behaviors and attitudes, and visually, through mohawks, multi-colored hair, body piercings and tattoos. To many, it's actually a rite of passage, an outward badge of honor to bare their inner stories. This helps define who they are, in a society that historically tries to compartmentalize people with labels and stereotypes.

As this body art becomes more and more acceptable, the shock value is receding. These days, it really isn't a big deal to see someone's exquisite tattoo peeking out of a sleeve or in full view on someone's forearm. Tattoos and body-piercings might not ever become *so* popular that they become the norm, but society is definitely loosening up its rigid standards a bit.

A clean, professional look is desired by every company, but some brands are now re-defining how "professional" can play out in a business world replete with unique characters. If you are part of a company or industry in which this would be too extreme, think about what changes you *can* make to edge toward the workforce's need for visual identity.

Are any of the following scenarios possible?

- **Men can grow facial hair**—but only on vacation or if he at least appears to "have a plan" when growing a mustache, beard or goatee
- **Unique hairstyles and color allowed**—as long as it is clean, safe and sanitary

- **Makeup can be worn however desired**—including color of eye shadow, eyeliner thickness and design
- **Fingernails can be colored**—with any solid color of fingernail polish
- **Tattoos are allowed**—but must be in good taste; no bad words or naked people showing
- **Multiple earrings allowed**
- **Facial piercings are allowed**—but limited, safe, sanitary and in "good taste," such as the eyebrow, nose or chin

Even though these human decorations will not prevent someone from actually doing his or her job, the idea of shifting an organization's culture to allow this high-valued element of individuality is just too much for many organizations to swallow. Still, can your brand do more? Because visual identity is critical to today's employees.

Permission Slips

The need for potential employees to be different is not just an aesthetic one; they also need a wider playing field than most. Think of a ball player who has to perform within a certain set of boundaries on a court or ball field—except today's talent requires more area to roam and the freedom to play "outside the box." Diversity in thought and action is as critical to the Millennial, as oxygen is to you and me. Try to place them in a box and have them unconditionally conform to a set of rules or policies with which they may not identify or agree, and the result will be monumental failure for all.

As my colleague Brandon Hill wrote into one of Hard Rock's e-Learning courses:

> *"It would go over about as well as a Slipknot concert at a retirement home."*

Which is to say…not very well. Even if you aren't familiar with this hard core rock group known for its scary rubber masks and matching, serial-numbered industrial work clothes, you get the idea.

As I mentioned in Chapter 9, if you want today's employees to take ownership of the business as if it were their own, you have to give them the executive-at-the-moment empowerment to create experiential memories for customers—A.K.A. "permission slips." This approach is relished and celebrated by guests, but it is also a key element in your employees' individuality.

Remember, current and future generations crave memorable moments more and more each day—both as consumers and employees. Your brand just needs to figure out what those moments can look like in your world and then let the staff loose to forge some memories.

Will there be mistakes? Sure. Is it possible that some employees will go too far in their quest to rock someone's world? Of course. But an employer shouldn't be afraid to dole out a virtual permission slip from time to time if it ensures the possibility that unscripted and memorable experiences are being created. Empowered employees are the ones that make a real difference, in both the company's culture and its sustainable future.

Vocal Forum

In terms of attitude, today's workers are on a quest to have their voices heard. They have strong opinions about how things should be done and they have no problem telling someone—everyone—how to do them. They need people to listen to them and, more importantly, appreciate them for their ideas. They need the ability to speak their minds when particular value systems are not aligned with theirs—or whenever the moment strikes them. They need the permission to articulate their opinions with expressive bravado, especially at work, without having to endure the traditional organizational hierarchy or the fear of retribution for disagreeing.

Society has taught us that the "squeaky wheel gets the grease," meaning that those individuals who speak out the most or the loudest tend to get the attention. In an environment of self-indulgence and the quest to be famous, having a voice in the world is perhaps the biggest driver of today's youth. Whether they speak confidently in front of others or use the more subtle power of the pen; whether they choose a loud microphone for hundreds to hear or opt for a reserved one-on-one discussion—people need to be heard. And now social media provides the biggest stage of all for those willing to listen. As evidenced by the millions of personal YouTube videos uploaded every day by fame-seekers of all ages. It seems that everyone wants his or her moment in the limelight.

That moment can be trivial, like being thanked in the company newsletter for suggesting a new process that saves the organization money. It can be grandiose, like having the opportunity to speak up in a team meeting about a company policy that no longer works…and then having that policy changed. It can be self-indulgent, like having a blog or posted video go "viral" on the Internet. It can even be self*less*, like orchestrating a change to an entire community policy in response to a wrongdoing or societal need.

Regardless, the need to be heard is intoxicating to today's youth.

Millennials and Digital Natives also take cues from their public heroes—

actors, athletes and musicians alike. They may not emulate these heroes in every way (at least we hope they won't), but they do see the influence their rock icons wield with their fame and status. They hear rocker Neil Young talk about the importance of biodiesel-fueled vehicles versus those that rely on oil-based gasoline…or the punk rock members of Green Day speak out against an injustice done to lesser-known, imprisoned musicians in a different country. They watch in awe as country music icon Willie Nelson continues, as he has for decades with his Farm Aid music festival, to marshal the entire country to rally around farmers. And they see Bono's quest to eradicate AIDS from the planet, commanding the ears of U.S. presidents and other world leaders. So of course our current and future workers see the rewards that come with stardom. People listen.

Speaking out—and truly being heard—is powerful to your future workforce.

Devil's Advocate

Challenging the status quo has become a generational art form. Again, I am unfairly generalizing an entire age group, but many of these young individuals often *do* feel entitled. Because of that mindset, they want and expect to make things better in their own world. They therefore have no problem questioning why things are done a certain way, or pushing back when they think something is wrong.

No doubt some businesses see this challenge to authority as a negative, but smart leaders realize that there is a massive advantage to having a few "devil's advocates" on the team. Doing things the way they have always been done will continue to garner the same results. Even if the current processes yield great results, there is real value in always seeking to produce more or make processes better. Status quo challengers play this vital role on the team. Every professional in team dynamics or team organization I have ever encountered would validate this balanced approach.

Two of the instructor-led courses I have frequently taught over the years are "Building Rock Star Teams" and "New Team Transitions." Common to both of these sessions is the focus on having a diverse team, inclusive of all personality types and strengths. Business owners who see the value in this type of dynamic team know that team management will be more time-consuming, but they also know that the rewards are worth the effort. This is why behavioral assessments like the Myers-Briggs Type Indicator (MBTI), True Colors, DiSC and StrengthsFinder are so popular…particularly when everyone on the team starts to realize how different they are from one another and how they will all have to capitalize on each others' strengths in order to drive positive results.

One of the better behavioral assessments I have seen lately, The Collaborative Harmony Index (CHI), was developed by my friends at *Banding People Together*. This performance improvement company is comprised of a select group of rock stars, hit songwriters and collaboration experts that came together to help organizations get the most out of their talent. Their purpose and mantra is "Improving Performance Through Effective Collaboration," but this tagline does not fully capture the unique experiences they create. During a bandleader-led session with *Banding People Together*, participants identify their own collaborative and communication styles, discover the songwriting process, then actually write and perform original songs. It is a complete blast for the participants and a truly memorable shared experience. Just going through *that* process is worth the price of admission, but the experience is elevated to new heights when it's combined with the CHI assessment.

Founder Alan Schaefer and his rock star band of merry men created this crystal clear, highly intuitive and fun assessment to help teams understand how each member learns, communicates and collaborates—all using famous recording artists as metaphors for different behavioral styles. Taking the Collaborative Harmony Index assessment helps you discover if you are more like a pop artist, a jam band, a singer-songwriter or a crooner...all very different performance styles, each successful in its own genre. You might be confident that you know which artist or style you most identify with, but you would be surprised to see what your CHI report reveals. There is real science and expertise built into this assessment, but because it is immersed in the spirit of Rock 'n' Roll, both the process and learning of the results hit a high note with just about everyone. Smart, helpful and fun...this assessment is "edutainment" at its best.

One of the many discoveries a participant may uncover in taking an assessment like the CHI is that it's absolutely okay to be a devil's advocate and challenge the status quo. But while behavioral assessment tools are helpful in identifying and validating personal behavior types, it is then up to the leader to assemble a robust and diverse team in which all organizational holes are filled—and that means including team members who feel comfortable challenging your day-to-day norms. We need them. It's healthy to have individuals call out the leader, the team, or the organization when decisions go against the brand's values, against an individual's values or against the law. These individuals are vital to a team's continued success. And if challenging the norm is done in the true sprit of collaboration and with the goal of perpetuating the team's success, it can be a great thing.

I have always played this role when I've been part of a team. I did it at Hard

Rock and I still seem to assume this position when I work with networking and industry associations. I once had an executive accuse me of challenging the status quo all the time just for the sake of doing it. I think that executive was right. I wasn't trying to be negative to the suggestions being discussed or the initiatives that were in place; I was just always on the hunt for a better way of doing things. I wanted to ensure we were not just "saluting smartly and charging up the hill," as if we were in a military environment. I thought there needed to be an inquisitive and opposing view. That's why books like Marcus Buckingham's *First, Break All the Rules* are so appealing to me.

The associated counter-culture cliché "if it ain't broke, *break* it" resonates with me. I always look for ways to break old systems and enhance their effectiveness. And I'm a Gen-Xer! With our current and future generations, this personality trait seems even *more* innate. We should not stifle that trait; we should embrace it. We need some yins to our yangs.

Devil's advocates who challenge the status quo are a good thing.

CELEBRATING INDIVIDUALITY

With these particular generational nuances, today's workforce can easily be compared to the broken toys no one else wants: Potentially great talent, just looking for a home where they will be accepted for who they are. And once they find that home, they're committed. For what does a company get from those "broken toys" in return for embracing a diverse employee culture like this?

Loyalty.

Team members who enjoy the freedoms at work like the characteristics I have shared here tend to stick around a bit longer than those that don't. And why wouldn't they? Given the chance to be themselves and make a living hanging out with other diverse people—versus conforming to a rules-oriented, stifling environment—don't you think most people would choose to move to the Island of Misfit Toys? I think the choice would be clear.

As Barry Manilow once said,

"Misfits aren't misfits among other misfits."

Unfortunately, these characteristics are going to be real problems for the companies that refuse to adapt. Perhaps the elements of individuality create too big a hurdle for some organizations to jump. Or a unique aesthetic look for the employees just doesn't fit the brand and would scream of unprofessionalism to customers or the industry at large. Maybe empowering staff members to create authentic experiences—experiences that might require them to seek forgiveness for going too far versus permission for trying something daring—is too scary to allow. And encouraging a person or group to constantly challenge organizational norms and decisions is just asking for a full-time thorn in the side of the brand, since entertaining a counterpoint requires more time, energy, patience and open-mindedness.

When companies stack up the characteristics of Millennials and Digital Natives and only look at their potential downsides, they are apt to avoid hiring for or cultivating individuality. Which means there is an entire untapped portion of the workforce, made up of potentially great employees, who, because of how they look and act, will never get a chance at some careers—and *that* leaves a larger talent pool for progressive-minded brands, which actually foster individuality, to fish from. Companies like Harley-Davidson motorcycles, whose brand purpose is to "fulfill dreams of personal freedom." That motto isn't just for the consumer; it resonates with employees, as well.

As Lady Gaga has professed many times, both in interviews and in concert,

"Don't ever let a soul in the world tell you that you can't be exactly who you are."

The reality is, many companies do just that. And it makes total sense for those brands. But many organizations—even complete industries—could be more inclusive if they really wanted unique experiences to be created for their customers.

For today's talent, the high-value need of individuality is probably a bit safer in the world of hospitality...for now. Foodservice employees already enjoy long-standing freedoms that come with working in a service-oriented profession. However, many other industries are beginning to skinny-up their policy manuals, loosen their age-old restrictions and give their employees the autonomy to showcase their personal cultures. And those same companies are the ones with proven growth on their side.

How's the talent war going for your brand?

Celebrating individuality is one of the keys to winning the battle.

GREATEST HITS THAT ROCK

THIS IS HOW YOU ROLL

Today's Workers are Experience-Based:
People crave memorable moments in their lives—professionally and personally.

- List some of your company's internal practices that employees would consider memorable for them.
- Discuss whether your employee benefits truly reflect your current employees' needs.
- Do some changes need to be made to your company's offerings in order to better attract and retain future employees?
  o What are they?
- Debate the type of out-of-the-box, non-financial experiences that could be implemented to create a cultural-rich environment.

Today's Workers are Identity-Oriented:
Employees need the freedom to express themselves—in the way they look, dress, talk, behave and interact with others.

- Think about your company's appearance standards and discuss whether they are current and relevant to today's workforce.
- Could the policy be adjusted to include facial hair, visible/tasteful tattoos, multiple ear piercings or a nose ring on an employee?
- Debate whether your organization could foster a "permission slip" environment, allowing team members to make in-the-moment, unscripted decisions to create memories for customers.
  o Would this be widely supported and encouraged or frowned upon?
- Are employees able to freely speak their minds if the company's value systems are not aligned?
- Discuss whether team members are confident that they can articulate a difference of opinion with leaders without fear of retribution.
  o If not, what can be changed to allow it?
- Can you name your team's devil's advocates who challenge the status quo?
  o If so, discuss whether the organization sees them as healthy brand agents interested in perpetuating the brand's success.

13

COMIC BOOK COMMUNICATION

"I wish myself to be a prop, if anything, for my songs. I want to be the vehicle for my songs. I would like to color the material with as much visual expression as is necessary for that song."

- David Bowie

VISUAL LEARNERS WITH SHORT ATTENTION SPANS

Another characteristic of today's workforce is that, above all other learning styles, they are visual learners—and this is further complicated by their short attention spans.

The individualistic lifestyles of today's workforce demands that we communicate and provide training content in an entertaining way that addresses issues in both focus and concentration. The way kids learn and play today has seen an enormous shift. There is already a massive chasm between the way we learned and retained information growing up

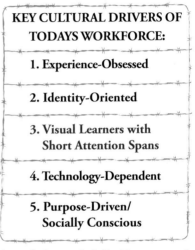

KEY CULTURAL DRIVERS OF TODAYS WORKFORCE:

1. **Experience-Obsessed**

2. **Identity-Oriented**

3. **Visual Learners with Short Attention Spans**

4. **Technology-Dependent**

5. **Purpose-Driven/ Socially Conscious**

and the way the youth of today develops knowledge and skills. Young people learn more visually than ever before.

In the course of my History and Children's Education studies in college, I learned what I had already suspected: People learn differently, but visual learners are the most common. I know there are auditory learners who learn best by sound, but in today's iPad-based, video game-filled society, where the written word is becoming a lost art, the visual now prevails as the sensory style-of-choice for gaining and retaining information.

People today need graphical assistance when they learn. Photos, drawings, simple graphs and models all help the learner to grasp information more quickly—and have more fun doing it. Sometimes just a simple piece of artwork added to a printed page of text is sufficient to keep the learner engaged enough to continue reading. And that's just where the power of visual learning tools begins.

As a training professional for Hard Rock, my approach was not to simply sprinkle pictures sporadically throughout the training materials, but rather to replace complete pages of text with photographs and drawings. Visuals should be the focus of training, not just a helpful aid.

Additionally, today's young people have extremely short attention spans in just about everything they do. They expect a healthy dose of interaction and entertainment to be embedded in their learning, as they constantly crave sensory stimulation. They have little patience for sitting through lecture-filled classes or reading massive amounts of content on text-heavy pages. Therefore, when you train or communicate with these new employees, it is crucial to implement the most efficient methods for enhancing their retention. As a result, you both maximize learning potential and minimize your number of poorly trained employees.

Your internal company collateral actually both reflects *and* affects your brand's culture. Let me share a few ideas you might consider for enhancing this part of the business culture.

PRINT COLLATERAL

Knowing that most people learn visually and have short attention spans should give us some clear direction for positioning our communication conduits. For example, if your company still produces physical print materials, there are some fundamental things you can do immediately to start tapping into the Millennial mind.

Here are a few tried and true design elements that can be implemented in any employee-level collateral:

- More Graphics
- Less Text
- Bullet Points, rather than sentences and paragraphs
- Lots of White Space
- Consistent Typography

All of the elements above contribute to the internal branding of an organization. Each one plays a part in the overarching culture of the company—at least internally. Let's dig deeper into each of these elements—and others—and look at some of the best examples.

ICEBERG, RIGHT AHEAD

I equate this visual collateral design approach to that of an iceberg. As you may know, the portion of an iceberg that you see above the surface of the water is only 10 to 15 percent of its total mass. The majority of the ice actually lies below the surface.

When it comes to my collateral design approach, this is how I think of an organization's brand. The visual part of the iceberg is analogous to what the public sees. That small portion is the external brand experienced by the consumer …and it's the only thing that matters to your customers. However, when it comes to organizational culture, it's the 85 percent below the surface that truly matters. This is the portion of the iceberg on which we should focus our energy. This is the Service-Profit Chain in action: Focus on the internal employee environment and your team will deliver the external culture the public expects.

All of the cultural drivers of today's workforce help make up the internal branding and culture of an organization. This includes internally-created processes, systems and tools—especially print collateral for the employees. If done right, the internal, below-the-surface environment is so "on point" that it naturally bubbles up to the surface for the world to see. It's an inside-out approach.

In many ways, internal branding for employees is just as important as external branding for guests. And it's the one I have always focused on as the vehicle for achieving true, sustainable internal results in any business.

THE DISHWASHER MUSE

Regardless of the tool or process I was creating, the 19-year old dishwasher who spoke very limited English became my muse.

This imaginary employee was always my audience, the person to whom I was delivering information. I constantly thought about that person and wondered "How would he or she want the material presented?" By catering to this profile, I could assume the content and design was sure to fit everyone. If someone who spoke little, if any, English could fully comprehend the Employee Handbook, anyone could. This approach helped quite a bit in the structure and design of any collateral I ever created, particularly materials for staff-level, front line employees.

Not only did the materials feature great instructional design, but they also echoed the language of the generation. Some employees even told me that the training materials spoke directly to them, helping them better understand the brand, rather than just learn a specific job function. A cafe busser once confided that he was so proud of the Employee Handbook, he used it as a coffee table book at home. Crazy, huh? Remember, these were training manuals… with policies and procedures in them. Yet this is the reverence with which a few Hard Rockers held these materials.

It appeared that, by indirectly speaking the Millennial language through print training manuals, I was on to something. As simple as it seemed, those initial staff manuals are what put me on the map—at least in my own little

Training world. Those start-up materials and concepts influenced everything I produced from then on, and they have become a staple of my print repertoire…a model I could easily replicate for other organizations and industries. The print materials were basic and simple, but they offered a strong message and direct guidance.

Anyone can craft materials like this, especially with today's technology. If you still produce print materials for your employees, I would challenge you to take a hard look at how they are designed and whether or not they match your company culture or today's workforce.

So, how did I come up with an approach that seemingly spoke to an entire brand's workforce?

I tapped into my childhood.

THE SUPERPOWERS OF A COMIC BOOK

Like many people my age, I grew up on comic books. Through their visual representation, I experienced fantastic storytelling and mentally traveled to exotic places filled with adventure and wonder. I learned not only how to tap into my creative side, but also how to better communicate in the world. All of this through a visual landscape of stapled pages.

Even in my early work life, I always felt that company materials should be more like comic books than training manuals. So, when I ultimately had an opportunity to take ownership of the training material design at Hard Rock, I re-created the manuals to be *just* that. I guess I just assumed that since it worked for me, others would respond favorably, as well. And they did.

Not only did this approach attack the visual needs of the employees, it took their short attention spans into account, as well. When they flipped through the pages of a manual that had little-to-no text, but instead panel after panel of pictures, graphics and drawings, they were like the teenagers of the 1950s seeing Elvis Presley perform for the first time. It changed everything.

What I learned in the process of creating these visually stimulating materials was they also had great instructional design principles behind them. The fundamentals of graphics versus heavy text, bullet-points versus paragraphs and even generous white space between content areas all contributed to the success of the manuals and added to the brisk pace with which employees blazed through them. With this simple tweak, the Employee Handbook and department manuals became the voice of the Millennials…at least in print form.

Take a look at the examples on the next few pages, all of which resemble the basic format we used to create Hard Rock's training materials. Once you review these visual aids, it should be clear how you too can implement these valuable tactics into your employee manuals.

NOTES

Subject Title

As you can see above, the "Subject Title" is much larger, bolder and even in a different typeface than the rest of the page. The remainder of the content in the body of the page is in a much thinner lettering style, so that the reader can easily read the text.

On the page are two different types of images that enhance the content and provide interest for the reader:

• Drawing (usually from employee)
• Actual photograph

Of course, less text is the way to go. Bullet points are also used in the above and are much easier on the eyes to quickly capture information.

I also made a conscious choice to use the staff manuals as a workbook. Therefore, I gave up ¼ the page to dedicate for the team member to capture their NOTES.

• This section is also designed in a light grey, to again provide some depth to the page.

Section Title

As you can see, another use of a larger font for a small section title on the page is used above.

Some things to consider when using graphics:

Text caption

1. Put a shadow on the pics to provide depth.
2. "Float" drawings with no border.
3. Give credit to the employee who drew the image underneath the artwork – this will provide "buy in".
4. Place the various graphics in different locations on the page, versus being in a standard horizontal row...this breaks up the eye.
5. Don't be afraid the break the "firewall" or "tattoo" plane (as shown here) – this also provides some depth to the page.

9.

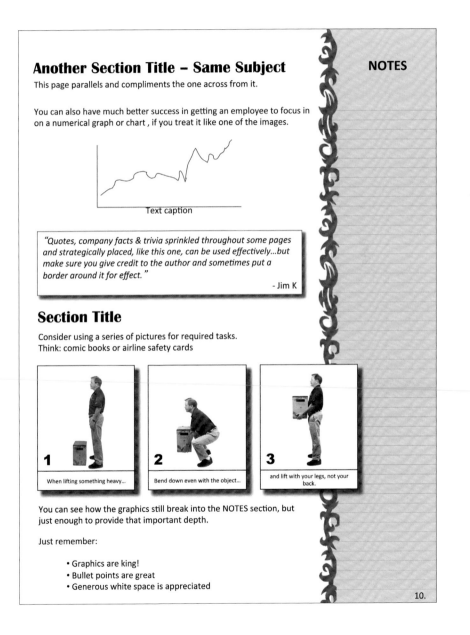

Another Section Title – Same Subject

This page parallels and compliments the one across from it.

You can also have much better success in getting an employee to focus in on a numerical graph or chart , if you treat it like one of the images.

Text caption

> "Quotes, company facts & trivia sprinkled throughout some pages and strategically placed, like this one, can be used effectively...but make sure you give credit to the author and sometimes put a border around it for effect."
>
> - Jim K

Section Title

Consider using a series of pictures for required tasks.
Think: comic books or airline safety cards

1 When lifting something heavy...

2 Bend down even with the object...

3 and lift with your legs, not your back.

You can see how the graphics still break into the NOTES section, but just enough to provide that important depth.

Just remember:

- Graphics are king!
- Bullet points are great
- Generous white space is appreciated

NOTES

10.

A GUIDE TO GREATNESS

You may have noticed that I embedded a few of my instructional design principles directly into the samples on the previous pages, but here are the main elements I would incorporate into any training manual for entry-level employees in today's world:

Typography/Fonts

Typography refers to lettering styles, otherwise known as fonts. Companies that have clear, non-negotiable style guidelines know that fonts are important to an organizations' overall branding. Some organizations do a fabulous job of identifying brand standards and guidelines early in the company's inception—guidelines that include everything from logo usage to color palate to lettering style. Others never see the need to create structure like this in their material development—or they simply relinquish control of the content creation and production to an inexperienced employee. Eventually, someone tries to get creative by adding all different types and sizes of fonts to make the material "cool"—when in fact it's a hot mess.

Once your company develops approved lettering styles for all external marketing and consumer-directed messaging, I would use the same fonts in all internally-branded collateral, as well. I would recommend picking only one or two fonts…one bold style for page or section titles and another more conservative, thin and legible style for text. This creates a very clean and consistent look. This element of print design may not be as critical to a new hire in terms of learning, but it is an easy way to immediately clean up your materials as part of your overall culture makeover.

Titles & Copy

Page and subject titles are always larger than the rest of the text on the page. If your brand employs two different fonts, I would use one—usually the wider, fancier font—for titles, and the other for the copy text. The lettering style that is easiest to read is best used for all of your narrative.

Bullet Points

Knowing what we now know about the way today's talent likes to receive information, you should always consider the most effective and efficient way to provide content. To address short attention spans, always look for opportunities to put content into a bulleted format. Do not feel obligated to write everything in narrative form with complete sentences. It may seem small, but every little bit of time you can save for the person reading and understanding your content will be appreciated. Certainly I would always want to use proper grammar, but where I could eliminate words and provide content in bullet points, I would.

White Space

Another pitfall for writers and designers of company new-hire materials is the overwhelming desire to fill the entire page with text, thereby using fewer pages and saving some money. They see white space as a cost, rather than a benefit. But readers need to breathe a little "psychological air" as they go from concept to concept, which is what white space on a page provides. Learners need to feel as though they are getting through a page of content at a relatively brisk pace. Creating a training "novel" will only turn off new employees and prevent them from engaging in the content or retaining the information. White space is cool. I would always encourage someone to use it liberally in the company's learning and development collateral.

Photos & Drawings

Today's employees will respond more favorably to pictures and graphics than written words in any context. They will also retain information better. When it comes to imagery, you have several options. You can use actual photography, clip art pulled from the Internet or customized drawings. I am not a fan of "pre-packaged" or "produced" artwork that everyone can use, so I have always erred in favor of taking my own pictures or enlisting employees to help draw pictures. The latter, by the way, creates instant buy-in of your content, especially if you give the artist credit in a caption underneath each drawing. Graphics can be used to enhance content or provide more interest to the end-user, but I would also seek to use graphics for actually teaching or communicating specific information. Of course, sometimes graphics are purely "eye candy"—visual entertainment weaved into the educational content—but employees need that, too.

Graphic Design

When you do use photos and drawings in your materials, focus on making them look professional. It's not enough to just grab an image and throw it onto a page. Find a graphic designer who will make these images pop off the page and make a statement. Consider the following:

- Place shadows behind images to give them more depth.
- Eliminate any borders so the images "float" seamlessly on the page.
- Place graphics in different places on the page, versus in a standard horizontal or vertical row; this breaks up the page and creates interest.

Interactivity

If your collateral is in the form of a workbook in which the employee will be writing, consider carving out part of each page as a "Notes" section. I was willing to give up 25 percent of each page for this purpose, even knowing that this would increase the number of pages in a typical manual. It was worth it to create that flexibility and "interactivity." We even branded this area, using a "fire line" or tattoo design as the page divider and then additionally shading the Notes area grey to give the page some depth. To really break up the page for your end-user, don't be afraid to let a picture cross the "dividing" line into the Notes section.

Statistics & Graphs

Unless you are part of a company that lives solely off of metrics, I would use this type of content sparingly. I have found that using a percentage statistic or a graph to make a point from time to time is extremely effective, but completely disastrous when used too much. Pick and choose when to "bring the thunder" and enhance your point. The same principle applies to using quotes. Sharing an inspiring comment from an appropriate person is great for employee manuals, as long as it's done sparingly. If you decide to sprinkle quotes throughout your document, consider throwing a border around them to change things up and help the quote stand out from the rest of the page.

When you combine all of these elements, your branded materials will become more visually reflective of the employees you'll be hiring. I even decided to brand the name of our employee training materials, seeking something more inspirational than "department manual." Thus Hard Rock's *Guides to Greatness* were born. The idea was to make these simple pieces of collateral part of the overall internal employee culture, offering new hires a developmental pathway to something bigger than themselves.

Was I too grandiose in my reach? Perhaps. But I would rather shoot for the stars and hope to achieve greatness than play it safe and end up as a forgettable garage band.

SAFETY CARDS & FURNITURE INSTRUCTIONS

While I was there, this visual approach carried over into every piece of internal training material Hard Rock produced for its employees. Pocket-sized job aides, safety posters and test materials all were re-imagined to include these approachable design elements. It wasn't too long after our Marketing team transformed the brand's consumer-facing collateral that I adopted those same style standards for our internal customers—the employees. We ultimately created the most culturally-branded employee collateral in the industry, a fact my team could be proud of—and one that was validated by several industry awards.

As a result of our efforts, the onboarding materials were actually fun for employees, instead of being a necessary evil. New hires had a real feeling of accomplishment when they studied. And they retained the information better. Much like passengers responding to an airline safety card or consumers responding to IKEA's famed furniture-building instructions—both of which include few-to-no words——our employees knew exactly what to do with very little instruction. It was precisely what we needed at the time.

Surprisingly, this approach also addressed some other issues, as well...

Global Understanding

Collateral that is predominantly visual in nature helps include employees with language barriers, such as English as a second language. Although Hard Rock is an American concept, the company operates around the globe. It would be safe to assume that many of the employees in other countries would require onboarding and training materials in their native language. However, the visual approach of our documents made this largely unnecessary. Employees could understand the content, regardless of their property's location in the world.

Cost Savings

Translating documents is expensive and most translation companies base their prices on word count. Imagine the savings Hard Rock enjoyed when the pages we translated—for a particular property or market—contained little text and lots of photos. In fact, many of those properties actually opted for the English version, since there were no major issues in understanding the intent of the information. This was a pleasant surprise.

Help for Struggling Learners

Another cool by-product was how inclusive these materials were to employees with learning disabilities or dyslexia. They may have mixed up the order of the words or letters in a sentence or struggled reading from left to right in school, but they overcame those obstacles at Hard Rock, simply due to the visual nature of our manuals. Not that the company went out of its way to hire people who struggled academically, but it was great to know the organization could look beyond human limitations and provide internally-branded collateral that would supersede a person's impediment. That rocks.

"Edutainment"

The training materials at Hard Rock allowed all types of learners from around the planet to both easily grasp the content and, later, have their new knowledge validated. In other words, the materials were both entertaining and instructionally sound. This is "edutainment"—education that is entertaining for the end-user. By offering employees different ways to learn new and unfamiliar information, you open doors and opportunities that may otherwise be closed. More times than not, employees desire the entertainment but welcome the education if it is presented in an interesting way.

WHAT'S IN A HANDBOOK?

It used to be that the Employee Handbook was a small pamphlet of guidelines that highlighted the few things an employee had to avoid to keep from being fired. That's where the name comes from: It was supposed to be a book the size of your hand. But as the company grew, the Handbook got thicker; more rules were implemented to keep everyone in line. The content had to be straightforward—albeit stale—to alleviate any potential misunderstanding of new-hire job responsibilities. Over time, as employment litigation increased across industries, so did the Handbook's number of policies and amount of legalese—brands favored protecting themselves over content creativity. And then one day you notice your company's little book of guideposts has become this monster book of laws, stifling what remains of the brand's written culture…at least in this document.

I now think that the Employee Handbook for most brands is a direct reflection of the company's culture.

It certainly doesn't tell the whole story, but this important piece of mandatory collateral is perhaps the first physical impression of the brand's culture to which a new hire is exposed. So we should think carefully how this content is presented.

As I did in the materials I produced at Hard Rock, some companies have figured out a different way. They see the Employee Handbook as a necessary tool, but believe the means to that end can take a different path.

Here are a couple of my favorite examples:

Zappos

Zappos.com, the now infamous shoe company known for its online and offline guest-obsessed service, has become one of the go-to brands for making a point about internal company culture. Those lucky enough to tour this company's Las Vegas headquarters have experienced this phenomenon up close. The office environment at Zappos makes most visitors drool with corporate envy—and causes many HR professionals to freak out as their conservative minds try to envision this culture in their own companies.

When you take the experiential tour of the company's offices, your "culture magician" tour guide will start off with a brief history lesson. You'll learn about the shoes that first inspired the brand as well as the company's obsession with customer satisfaction. Perhaps a little more interesting than your average corporate office tour, but still typical. Then the craziness starts. As you roll from department to department—including the "Stairway to Culture" and the "Goals Club," in which employees write on the walls—each one seems to throw a bigger party than the last. Every employee seems excited to see the group come through their area, as evidenced by genuine smiles, warm greetings and noise makers of every kind—maracas, cow bells, kazoos…you name it, they play it.

As part of the experience, you'll get to meet and talk with Zappos' Founder & CEO Tony Hsieh, who works out of a cubicle and calls himself the "Head Monkey." You'll also get a polaroid picture of yourself wearing a crown and sitting on the "I'm Royalty at Zappos" Throne. Great fun, all around.

The tour showcases one of the greatest collections of unique people you will ever find. These brand ambassadors are not afraid to show off their individuality. In fact, they are encouraged to do so. They are an amazing reflection of the company's overall culture.

In an environment like this, would you expect the brand's written materials to be any less creative?

When a new employee joins the Zappos tribe, he or she receives—in addition to a "Core Values" packet—an inspirational, book-bound compilation of photos and testimonials from every employee in the company. Every single team member contributes to this *Zappos Culture* book. As you can imagine, the book grows exponentially as each new hire gets a chance to leave his or her mark—visually and verbally—for all to experience.

Although it's not really considered an Employee Handbook, but rather a more organic, non-traditional vehicle for onboarding, this compilation piece is as critical a part of the Zappos orientation as anything else. It certainly adds to the sustainability of the culture. Visitors who tour the headquarters also receive a copy of this culture book as a gift. It's a pretty sweet gift, a fabulous read and it's hard to put down.

Valve Software
In April of 2012, *Fast Company* Magazine featured an article about the highly-visual and fun Employee Handbook of Valve Software, maker of the popular video games *Half-Life* and *Portal*. The brand prides itself on the cool company culture that permeates everything it does…and that includes

its written materials. Like Zappos, this organization has realized that the language used in onboarding needs to match its unique culture.

It started off as a light-hearted survival guide—created by Valve veterans and passed down to "newbies"—to help new-hires know what to expect when they come on board. But what began in the spirit of fun turned out to be one of the most enviable Employee Handbooks in business today—not just because of its look and feel, but also because of its effectiveness.

Check out this sample page from Valve Software's Employee Handbook, portions of which anyone can find on the Internet:

Fig. 2-4 Methods to find out what's going on

step 1. Talk to someone in a meeting
step 2. Talk to someone in the elevator
step 3. Talk to someone in the kitchen
step 4. Talk to someone in the bathroom

Awesome, isn't it?

Of course there are pages woven through with policies and procedures, but who wouldn't be entertained by the content shown…and as a result pay more attention to the serious and necessary stuff?

Greg Coomer, one of Valve's product designers and founding team members, was quoted in the same *Fast Company* article as saying:

**"Company culture is a result of a tremendous amount of energy.
There's a broad understanding that if we don't put that energy into maintaining it,
it's very easy for it to erode."**

Even in print, there is a better way to capture a company's culture and ensure that it rocks for the foreseeable future.

INTERNAL BRANDING

Imagine taking your current materials, regardless of the state they are in, and morphing them into something as visual and effective as the examples I have shown you here. You may already be there in the development of your external brand, but your internal employee manuals may still need a little love. If they look more like comprehensive rock festival riders, complete with the boring, text-laden legalese of artists' non-negotiables, than the beautiful, highly visual, concert tour picture books they *could* be, then it's time for a collateral revolution.

In other words, we need comic books, not "heady" novels.

I am not suggesting that your company's collateral should look exactly like what I have described or shown in this chapter, but I wanted to share some proven best practices via these materials that have great instructional design and have won some awards for re-engineering training along the way. These design principles would work in any company, industry or environment, but the cultural look and feel still need to match up to your specific employee profile and brand. Think hard about your organization and what the physical materials should look like for your employees; then see if there are clear opportunities to enhance their effectiveness.

Internal branding for your employees is a big part of creating, protecting or revolutionizing a company's culture. In the iceberg analogy, it's the unseen bulk of the brand that lies below the surface.

Like Zappos' Culture book and Valve's Employee Handbook, the *Guides to Greatness* are what employees found particularly interesting and successful at the time. But great brands cannot become complacent. What worked 20 years ago for Gen-Xers may not apply to or resonate with future generations.

The Hard Rock brand wisely continues to evolve its collateral, keeping the content and delivery style fresh and relevant. The company's Learning and Development team recognizes the need to keep moving at the pace of today's workforce.

And that is about moving beyond print collateral and into distance-based learning technology.

Businesses today have to amp up their communication and training methods if they have any hope of attracting, identifying and retaining the tech-savvy talent pool of today.

GREATEST HITS THAT ROCK

THIS IS HOW YOU ROLL

Today's Workers are Visual Learners with Short Attention Spans:
Employees today need graphics-based material with simple, bite-sized messaging. Internal branded materials should be enhanced to resemble comic books, airline safety cards or IKEA furniture instructions.

- Does your company use print materials (manuals, workbooks, posters, wallet cards) for employee training and communication?
- Discuss whether your company's internal print collateral effectively represents the brand.
- Debate whether your materials include instructionally sound design elements like graphics/images, less text, bullet points and white space.
- What would it take to transform them into training tools with more graphics & less text?
- Would your employees feel proud to show their training materials to others outside the company?
- Discuss whether the materials in their current condition are effective for an employee to whom English is not native.
- Does your organization's internal collateral utilize the same branding elements (fonts, colors, logo, style) as your external Marketing collateral?
- Discuss the types of opportunities you have for improving the look and enhancing the effectiveness of your materials.

174

14

THE RISE OF THE MACHINES

"Technology is huge; I wanted to learn about it. People might say that's odd, but I think it's odd if artists aren't interested in the world around them. I'm always chasing that."

- Bono, U2

In order to stay relevant, companies should always strive to be at the fore-front of training and communicating with new employees. For your organization or industry, that may mean overhauling your physical print materials to make them more visual and effective—and that alone might seem revolutionary. But for most companies, staying relevant is about speaking the "speake" of the current workforce…and that is all about technology. To increase our chances of building short-term loyalty, we need to communicate with the newer generations on their turf, with their toys.

The reality is…print communication is a dying medium.

When I speak about organizational culture in front of younger audiences, I will often go back afterward and look at the Tweet Stream—the record of all the Twitter posts made during the event, about the event—just so I can see the conversation that was happening at the time I was ranting about physical printed collateral. Sometimes I will see sarcastic posts like "What is this thing called 'print' that he speaks of?" I know these comments are made in jest and, in fact, I actually do not spend a lot of time talking about print materials when I am in front of a live audience. Still, their points are valid. The concepts I've shared about that specific medium are solid and will definitely reflect a company's internal culture, but print communication is becoming obsolete.

Messaging through electronic media is now the way of the world.

TECHNOLOGY-DEPENDENT

Millennials and Digital Natives have certainly learned the art of delivering and receiving information at lightning speed, all while also multi-tasking on whatever else happens to be going on in their lives. When away from work, your employees can listen to their download-ed music, watch Internet-streaming

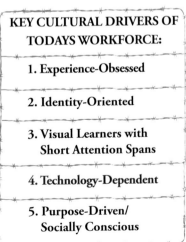

KEY CULTURAL DRIVERS OF TODAYS WORKFORCE:

1. Experience-Obsessed

2. Identity-Oriented

3. Visual Learners with Short Attention Spans

4. Technology-Dependent

5. Purpose-Driven/ Socially Conscious

television shows, Instant Message with their friends and upload pictures to their Facebook pages all at the same time…on a single device…while doing their homework. Do you think a monumentally thick, text-laden Employee Handbook is going to resonate for them at work? It won't. And it's up to you to cater to your employees and create training and communication that meets their needs.

Because we know people respond more favorably to visual stimulus than written text, having content delivered in an exciting, real-world format is certainly going to kick the entertainment and retention level up a notch. There are numerous electronic media options you can easily implement into your business that will maximize both communication and the educational experience.

Following are a few thoughts and resources.

Video

Stand-alone videos, perhaps in the form of physical DVDs, might be the first step to enhancing your organization's communication.

Videos are actually an inexpensive option these days. You can produce your own culturally-sound, branded videos internally or even outsource their creation for a great price. Again, having a visual representation of your culture—like a video—helps preserve and perpetuate its existence. And unlike an instructor-led presentation—which relies solely on the storytelling prowess of a facilitator—a video ensures consistent messaging for any desired content.

Although I am a fan of videos, I should point out that they are one of the least effective of all the electronic mediums, mostly because the format is stagnant. Once produced, a video immediately starts to depreciate, because as the company goes through changes—and it will—that video's content becomes less relevant. Specific processes, brand facts and even the on-camera personnel delivering the content all change over time. So unless the video content is timeless, the process of keeping it up-to-date is costly and time-consuming for an organization going through rapid change.

However, if all of your current training is built solely around instructor-led classes and print materials, adding some videos may be the easiest way to spice it up. For some organizations, this would be like bringing fire to a caveman for the first time. It's a start.

Internet

It's probably safe to say that most people in North America and Europe now have direct access to the Internet, whether it's through a computer or a mobile device of some sort. This is certainly true of the younger generations that comprise your future workforce. Utilizing the World Wide Web could be a great option for reaching your workforce.

From an external branding stand point, marketing experts will of course push Internet platforms like Facebook, Twitter and the company's own web page. But knowing that today's workforce is largely technology-dependent, there is also a critical *internal* use for online media.

Many websites exist solely to provide general knowledge or teach people how to do certain tasks. If you want employees to learn how to effectively change a vacuum bag, lift a heavy item, make a Classic cocktail, shift gears in a standard automobile, replace a watch battery or utilize a coffee hand-press, then websites and search engines like YouTube, Google or Wikipedia might be great options for a company to leverage as part of its messaging.

Some brands invest in creating their own password-protected websites for customized training and communication purposes. Obviously, this is a cleaner alternative than using the more generic sites, but both have value. In either case, the Internet can be a valuable part of a company's internal branding.

I've seen a lot of public speakers effectively use Internet weblinks in their presentations; it's an inexpensive and entertaining way to bring visual content to the audience. I have done the same over the years, but recently I've started using more interactive tools to get the audience involved in the experience. I have fallen in love with Internet-based audience response systems. This technology allows attendees to answer a question, via their own mobile devices, then captures and populates the responses, in real-time, directly into the presenter's slides for all to see. It's a real Wow! factor. When I use this tool, I am as much interested in showcasing the cool technology and its potential uses as I am in the actual answers to my question. I am trying to point out that today's workers both desire and expect this type of interaction when a company trains, develops or communicates with them.

My resource-of-choice is www.polleverywhere.com, which has various pricing levels (including a free option) based on the number of responses allowed. It's rare that I do not find a way to incorporate this technology into my sessions.

e-Learning

As companies get bigger and/or expand geographically, distanced learning has become the preferred solution to the dilemma of how to quickly and cheaply disseminate information. It isn't just the future, it's the here and now.

Shortened from "electronic" learning, e-Learning is a great option for brands willing to put some infrastructure in place. Whether you're purchasing educational content from a third-party vendor or creating customized content internally, having information that can be immediately accessed by or delivered to everyone—and can be easily changed at any time—is a benefit worth exploring. For many organizations, there is real value in allowing employees to engage in education electronically on their unique timetable, when they are ready to learn—whether that learning occurs in a controlled office space or on a mobile device at home, on the other side of the world, in the dark of night, in their underwear (just as an example, of course).

Most e-Learning is not cheap, especially the content that needs to be customized to fit culturally within the brand. But this up-front cost may be nothing, in the long run, compared to the cost delivering the same information by instructor-led, print or video means. Additionally, if the e-Learning content employs great instructional design principles and a good mix of education and entertainment layered with interactive elements like simulations, participatory exercises and thought-provoking validations, then your end-users will actually enjoy the learning experience.

At Hard Rock, we decided on a blended approach to e-Learning. The culturally-critical topics, for which it was important to have our logo, fonts, colors, messaging and unique people represented, were the ones whose content we committed to creating internally. Subjects like "Music Appreciation," "Memorabilia," "Hiring Rock Stars" and the type of differentiated service experience we needed our misfit toys to deliver could not possibly be covered in off-the-shelf products. These topics either did not exist or would have fallen short of the specific philosophy we needed to communicate. On the flip side, there were several managerial-focused, task-oriented, even compliance-driven e-Learning courses that were perfect for the brand to purchase and make available to our leaders, with no need for customization. Subjects like "Running an Effective Meeting," "Influencing Decision Makers," "Responsible Alcohol Service" and "Enhancing Your Listening Skills" did not need the same cultural dunking as other brand-critical topics.

Smart Phones

The lightening quick growth of mobile devices since the turn of the Century is unparalleled by any other form of electronic communication. And cellular technology was just the beginning. Our eventual transition to "smart phones"—handheld devices with the ability to access the Internet, take pictures, record video and, yes, make phone calls—changed everything.

Smart phones are super-encyclopedias with access to all the world's information literally in the palm of your hand. Think about how incredible that is. With more power in each smart phone than the computers we used to initially send astronauts to the moon, these devices have become so indispensable to today's young people that they wouldn't know what to do if you stripped them of the technology. And many companies do. Some organizations have a zero tolerance for employees accessing their smart phones during work time, while others actually embrace the tech.

With the advent of smart phones came the creation of Apps, or customized applications. The generational phrase "there's an App for that" implies that someone has created a unique application to allow a smart phone to access specific data or information. There are Apps for downloading music, for identifying which direction is North, for locating your favorite coffee shop from your current location, for identifying star constellations, even for managing company projects. If the App doesn't currently exist, chances are that someone is about to invent it, just to customize people's lives a little bit more.

Smart phones can be used to enhance a company's culture.

Some brands have created external company Apps to help consumers have customized experiences with their products and services, while others have created internal applications to keep their employees engaged and informed. For the willing, the cultural applications of this technology are limitless.

One of my favorite culture crushes is on a technology company called HotSchedules. This Austin, Texas-based brand prides itself on making life in hospitality better, for both employers and employees. HotSchedules has created software that allows team members to check their work schedules and switch shifts right from their smart phones, without ever making an actual phone call or talking to a manager or colleague in person. This software has turned one of the industry's most mundane and frustrating processes into something simple and pleasurable. This is a big deal in the foodservice world.

This same technology also allows managers to communicate with each other through a virtual managers' log. Written communication among restaurant and hotel management staff is standard practice for staying abreast of these operations. But HotSchedules figured out a way to eliminate the physical, written binder replete with time-consuming, illegible notes that every manager has to read at the start of his or her shift—even if that shift occurs several days later—and replace it with technology enabling an individual to view this information in real-time from anywhere, with just a smart phone or computer. Not only does every manager know what's going on in the establishment at all times, but now the General Manager can instantly contribute to the conversation or decision-making process, even when he or she isn't technically working the shift.

This was revolutionary stuff when HotSchedules first came onto the scene. This is an example of a great company helping other companies effectively manage their own cultures.

Tablets

Just as culturally influential as a smart phone, the handheld tablet has revolutionized the way people communicate and work. It may have been Apple's Steve Jobs who first introduced us to the iPad, but it didn't take long for virtually every competitor to put its version of the tablet on the market.

Tablets are basically a hybrid of a smart phone and a laptop computer, with just about all the functionality of the two...it just can't make calls like a phone or store data like a computer. Okay, it's probably not the best analogy. But in almost every other way, it's the perfect combination. In addition to accessing to the Internet, I've seen more and more young people regularly using their iPads for everything from taking notes at a conference to watching movies to reading e-books on the road. I've heard many Millennials claim to no longer use a computer at all; the tablet does everything they need.

Just before I left Hard Rock, the company's Cafe division was moving closer and closer to putting its entire management training program directly onto a tablet. All of the tools, processes, forms, videos, projects, and training agendas would be pre-loaded onto an iPad that each Manager-in-Training (MIT) would receive during his or her Day 1 Orientation. Since the cafe properties were already configured with wireless Internet, accessing the company's e-Learning program via this training tablet would be effortless. Although the existing training program, with its printed 3-ring binder, on-the-job training, practical projects and some digital learning, was considered to be highly effective and credible, this progression to a technology-rich, instant-access platform was the next logical step in the program's evolution.

Imagine a new manager showing up for training, only to receive the entire program on a fully-loaded, flexible handheld device with complete access to all things "Hard Rock." So cool. We even talked about allowing managers to keep their tablets after their initial onboarding, just as a nice hiring bonus. Now that would be awesome.

I'm sure there are other companies that treat managers to the same type of innovative onboarding. I am convinced that this is exactly the type of technology use that will be appreciated—and eventually expected—by our future workforce.

A BLENDED APPROACH

Maybe a simple hybrid of the two worlds, consisting of both print and electronic media, is your next logical step. Or perhaps the printed manuals could be used for some things, while online content is helpful for others. No doubt some people still respond favorably to inert stimulus like print, while video content is the only thing that will resonate with others. And since some people learn better visually while others respond better to sound, you are more likely to hit a bigger audience by offering more options. By blending electronic and print media, you can reach all of the various learning styles and increase the chance that your workforce will retain the desired information. This is precisely why more educational practitioners push for a blended approach.

QR Codes

Perhaps physical print materials will always be your content tool-of-choice, but you can still dramatically enhance these pages with the addition of QR Codes. Short for "Quick Response," a QR Code is a two-dimensional, optically machine-readable label that, when attached to an item or printed page, provides more information to anyone who scans it. The user has to download a smart phone App first, but then he or she can then scan any QR Code to discover whatever information is available.

Unfortunately, QR Codes are actually quite ugly and tend not to fit very well into established brand standards. Below is an example:

Not very sexy, from a design standpoint. But a QR Code doesn't have to be black and white or even that rigid in its use. Most companies that use them do not even know that these can be effectively used in different shapes and colors—virtually any design element. Macy's Department Store, for example, had a great holiday campaign in which a colored QR Code was incorporated directly into its iconic star. The functionality of the scan was retained, but the effect was far less unsightly. Here's Macy's brilliant design:

Today's generation of QR Codes are dramatically better in design, color and imagery, with the intent to increase interest and exploration. When I solicited opinions about using QR Codes in collateral, my friends and I collectively came up with some alternative approaches. Take a look at these creative uses and ponder if something like this could work for your culture—externally or internally:

The biggest challenge with QR Codes are their misuse. While some brands have had great success using them in their marketing efforts, most have seemed to use them simply because they were the newest tool to come along and have therefore seen very little traction in their use. Social Media gurus and Marketing experts have come to distain the way QR Codes have been used in the public domain. But as an internal communication and training tool...I think they have tremendous potential.

Imagine a new employee flipping through your Employee Handbook or a Department Manual, only to come across a QR Code embedded in the pages—especially if they were displayed in a unique design like the ones I created above. The employee could take a break from the static pages of traditional text and graphics and scan the barcode with a smart phone (which you know he or she will be carrying) to get additional information via audio podcasts, video clips or website links. If it's used correctly and the content is valid, you have another interactive way to engage the employee and enhance learning.

Even old-school trainers can't fight cool and effective toys like that.

Podcasts

Another format that could be considered a hybrid is a podcast. Individuals and companies have been using this type of digital media for years with great success, in part due to easy access. The format got its name from the advent of the iPod and was originally designed to present audio programming in a downloadable format for portable listening devices. Now these broadcasts come in just about every format imaginable, including video, and can be accessed from any of the devices and media we have discussed so far.

If it's done right, this format can be both the easiest to distribute and the most well-received of them all. If the company culture will support it, a person or team might produce a series of podcasts designed around critical message points that both staff members and/or managers can follow on their own timelines. Employees can listen to—or watch—these one-directional messages on any device they choose.

Hard Rock had great success putting out Quarterly management video podcasts to communicate leadership concepts, training content and other company hot topics that needed to be consistently rolled out to the global enterprise. The production involved a one-person camera crew videotaping an on-screen host who read a five-minute script from a teleprompter. Topics ranged from interviewing standards, to handling guest complaints, to properly filling out expense reports. Our video producer, Graham Cohen, spent a little time adding in some graphical elements, but the overall production took about a day before we were able to launch the episode.

The series was internally branded *Take 5*, since each podcast would only include five bullet points, focused on a single topic, delivered in less than five minutes. Because these messages were visual, culturally consistent and only as long as the time it would take to have a cup of coffee, these podcasts became the preferred management communication conduit for our team, creating both credibility for the department and desire for more education.

If an electronic environment doesn't currently exist, perhaps a podcast series would be a great way to introduce technology into your organization and create more consistent communication and branding.

FUTURE-PROOF THE BRAND

The way your internal materials are designed, the training methods you use and the way you communicate within the organization can all help beef up your company culture. However, just like any other best practices I share, an electronic platform may not currently be the right vehicle for your industry or brand. Still, it's important to note that your impending workforce will continue to be technology-savvy and dependent. *You* may not be ready, but *they* are.

Regardless of your method of choice, your goal should be to develop content with compelling and instructionally-sound processes that speak directly to today's budding talent. Adopting technology is just one of the ways you can help future-proof your brand. By getting in front of it and harnessing its power, you endear yourself more to the employee. It's imperative we think like they do and ultimately provide information the way they like to receive it. This helps ensure new employees will learn and retain your messaging and create the sense that you understand their needs…the way they like to learn and communicate.

This internal focus may be just as critical to your brand as the customer-facing culture we discussed earlier. One affects the other. And when it comes to culture, everything matters. These initiatives might just be the little things that collectively could rock your brand's world.

GREATEST HITS THAT ROCK

THIS IS HOW YOU ROLL

The Times They Are 'A Changin':

Unlike generations past, there is a shift in the way Millennials and Digital Natives prefer to learn and communicate. They will be tech-savvy and so should we.

- Do you have Millennials and/or Digital Natives as team members in your organization?
- Is your company's leadership aware that these generations require access to and communication through technology?
- List all of the employee programs/initiatives in your company that utilize technology.
- Discuss whether your company has a well-developed and inspiring orientation video to educate new hires about the brand's culture.

Focus on the Future:

Distanced-based learning is the future. To stay relevant and at the forefront of training and communicating with new employees, delivering information through electronic mediums should be considered and celebrated.

- Does your organization utilize online training?
- Do you already have training available for access on a mobile device?
- Are your company's employees encouraged to utilize their mobile phones for learning?
- Discuss the obstacles that might keep you from moving toward this e-Learning direction.
- Name some easy, low-cost things that can be done immediately.

Consider a Blended Approach:

Organizational processes will eventually have to change to match up with today's workforce.

- Debate how the organization would respond if any of the following were implemented:
  o Digital Hiring/Onboarding - web-based application process; pre-hiring electronic behavioral assessment; online orientation videos
  o e-Learning - electronic content (management courses, audio/video podcasts) accessed, via mobile device, from anywhere
  o Text Messaging - staff communication (shift scheduling, management-to-staff mass messaging) driven through cell phones/smart phones
  o Blended Training - electronic content taken as pre-requisites for instructor-led classes; QR codes added to internal print materials

15

PURPOSE IS INSTRUMENTAL

"You don't have to be singing about love all the time in order to give love to the people."
- Jimi Hendrix

Loyalty to any single company seems to be a rarity these days. People "job hop" like Cher changes outfits during a show. Internally, employees of today constantly ask, "How does this work in this job specifically benefit me?" If things don't gel with their idea of good quality-of-life—because of the pay, benefits, hours, environment or even the leadership—then they have no problem moving on to greener pastures—because they can.

In the previous four chapters, we focused on how employers can create a culture that rocks for their specific business by understanding what resonates with the new generation of employees. Now we'll take this guitar riff even further and discuss the pivotal role "purpose" plays in an employee's overall attitude toward an organization.

PURPOSE-DRIVEN & SOCIALLY CONSCIOUS

Purpose, in a business context, can manifest itself in a couple of ways. It might deal with an employee's "big picture" understanding of the company's overall mission, beyond his or her singular role. It might also be philanthropic in nature—maybe the brand goes above and beyond its day-to-day responsibilities to help those less fortunate. Both of these manifestations are important to and widely expected by today's youth.

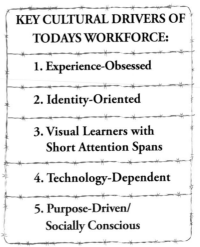

KEY CULTURAL DRIVERS OF TODAYS WORKFORCE:

1. Experience-Obsessed

2. Identity-Oriented

3. Visual Learners with Short Attention Spans

4. Technology-Dependent

5. Purpose-Driven/ Socially Conscious

People are purpose-driven. They naturally want to do meaningful work and grow both personally and professionally. It doesn't matter what type of work they do; people need to know that their work matters.

I believe that most people want to contribute to a meaningful cause. They need to clearly understand their roles—how their pieces of the puzzle fit into the grand scheme of the organization. Communicating this cause is a responsibility many employers struggle with. Perhaps the leadership doesn't have time to talk about it or they don't know how, but my experience in these environments has been that the employers simply see their employees as conduits for getting the work done. After all, the employees are getting paid. Isn't that enough?

It's not. People need more.

If your company's ultimate mission is not communicated up front and discussed on a regular basis, your employees will fill in the blanks and come to their own conclusions, which may or may not align with your own. And sometimes those conclusions can be perceived negatively. Without direction, even really competent and caring employees will do the best they can, yet still not deliver the exact experience you want or your consumers need. The employees aren't to blame. If team members are never taught or motived to aspire for more within the organization, they will surely continue to just "punch the time clock" for you...no more, no less.

Employees need purpose. It is a key cultural driver for today's workforce.

As leaders, this little bit of commitment on our part will help solidify an employee's commitment to the brand. As much as any of the other factors we've discussed so far, purpose is a major part of the driving force behind today's employees...and, eventually, your organization's culture.

TAKE TIME TO BE KIND

Another key factor in an employee's quest to find the perfect company is the role the organization plays in the community. Philanthropy is an instrumental part of the meaningful work they desire. With a socially conscious talent force waiting to be courted, what your brand stands for carries enormous significance. Fans of music want to follow artists they admire and respect, just like employees want to work for employers they can emulate and ones that offer a positive image they recognize.

When it comes down to it, it's all about what you stand for in the minds of your employees and consumers. Take an introspective moment to reflect on your company and ask the following questions:

- What does the company stand for?
- Do we have a mission?
- Is the mission purpose-driven?
- Do we support the community, beyond just selling a product?

Philanthropy is not just some feel good initiative with little merit—it can be great for business. In fact, brands like Whole Foods, TOMS, Panera Bread and Chili's each have proven business metrics on their side when they insist their company's sustained success is, in large part, due to their charitable initiatives. So, although it's not the sole reason to do it, philanthropy can be a profitable and signature part of the brand's culture.

CONNECTED CAPITALISM

Unless your company is a not-for-profit entity, your ultimate business goal is, of course, financial success. But it doesn't have to be the only goal—and there's more to success than just making a profit. There is a better way.

A group of my friends and colleagues, led by Cinnabon President, Kat Cole, started a discussion around the concept of "Connected Capitalism," a business philosophy introduced by former Coca-Cola Chairman and CEO Neville Isdell. The basic tenet is that companies should connect the bottom lines of their businesses with a social conscience. Like the other popular philanthropic models of Caring Capitalism, Creative Capitalism and Conscious Capitalism, the common denominator is "capitalism." The idea isn't to forgo capitalism for pure, non-profit altruism, but rather to turn a profit while using the weight of the brand to be an agent for positive change in the world.

Isdell espoused that while capitalism is a great model, people have grown weary of corporate greed; the Millennials desire something more than just making money. Brands interested in long-term sustainability need to change the way they *practice* capitalism if they want the *benefits* of capitalism to continue. Financial results alone are not going to be enough. Business and society need to be better-connected going forward.

Yes, even capitalism needs to go through a culture change.

The fundamental essence of Connected Capitalism requires business leaders to make four critical connections:

- Your business to the communities you serve
- Your business with civil society and governments to address relevant large-scale problems
- Your philanthropic initiatives to causes directly related to the core of your business
- Your business with the values of your employees

As our core group collectively dissected, debated and made sense of the connections above, we each committed to modeling this purpose-driven philosophy in our own brands going forward. What started as an open discussion among friends evolved into a collective voice for change and, ultimately, our cultural commitment to revolutionize the way we did business in our own communities. This commitment came with the additional explicit intent to influence others to join our efforts.

Thus the Changers of Commerce were born.

Over the years, this small group of like-minded souls has grown in number and influence; we now meet a few times a year to focus on grass-roots efforts to perpetuate the Connected Capitalism movement in a variety of pragmatic and organic ways. Some of the deliberate approaches we have used to communicate our message include videos, blogs, speeches, conference events and, most importantly, our own actions. Because of the influence the Changers of Commerce have had on me personally, I have integrated Connected Capitalism into my own business model.

Let me give you just one example based on this key pillar of doing business differently.

NO KID HUNGRY

Share Our Strength is an organization dedicated to eliminating childhood hunger in the United States. It employs many tactics and programs toward this end, but it's the *No Kid Hungry* campaign and associated activities that specifically resonates with me. *No Kid Hungry* works to connect kids to effective nutrition programs like school breakfasts and lunches and summer meals. The work is accomplished by a network of private citizens, government officials and business leaders who implement innovative hunger solutions in their communities and break down the barriers that keep kids from healthy food.

Sadly, in August of 2012, CNN reported that 40 percent of all food in the United States was going to waste. This baffled me, because I knew that, at the same time, one in five kids were reported as going to bed hungry. The contradiction is mind-boggling. If the situation weren't so serious, the paradox would be humorous. But this crisis is serious. And it could be easily solved with some focused attention.

Unlike many diseases for which we don't yet have a cure, we *absolutely* know the cure for hunger: Food.

The restaurant industry should own childhood hunger in the United States.

Can you imagine what would happen if restaurants—the second largest industry in the U.S.—got behind the movement of eliminating hunger in this country?

They would crush it.

That would be awesome to experience and see during my lifetime. And I want to be a part of it.

I have spent the majority of my 30 working years in hospitality, specifically in restaurants. Since foodservice has been my core business, it only makes sense that my "give back" cause-of-choice would be food or hunger-related. Out of all the great and deserving charities, *No Kid Hungry* is my conduit. In addition to participating in the various programs and activities this brand executes regularly, I look for opportunities to engage my own community in hunger-related issues. Additionally, a portion of the proceeds from this book—and all of my speaking engagements—goes directly to *No Kid Hungry*.

I don't share this example to pat myself on the back; I do it because this is the way things ought to be. Business as usual cannot continue in the future. To have any hope of long-term sustainability, companies need to figure out ways to be better connected to society.

People want to be a part of something bigger than themselves.

Give them a reason to join your band.

THE UNDENIABLE POWER OF PHILANTHROPY

Philanthropy is not a hard thing to do. In fact it usually doesn't even require money—just time and support.

Philanthropy can be anything from cleaning up a beach or river, to organizing a recycling drive, to working in a food bank—all of which can be facilitated on your company's own timeline. It can also rally around designated dates and causes. For example, your company's philanthropic initiatives could support putting on an Earth Day event each April or implementing Breast Cancer awareness initiatives in the Fall. It just depends on what makes sense for your organization.

There are literally thousands of deserving charities and causes that need assistance of some sort. They can be well-known, global opportunities or small, local causes…and each can potentially resonate with your employees.

But the brand *has* to do something. It's now expected.

Following are a few reasons—some with quantifiable business results—to engage the brand in philanthropy:

- **Great for the community & environment:** Who doesn't see the value in recycling, beach/river/park cleanups, hunger relief, sustainable products, feeding and clothing homeless, etc.?
- **Engages and galvanizes the entire organization around a powerful and worthwhile goal:** Teams solidify when the job is more than a paycheck.
- **Gives employees an emotional connection to the brand and their jobs:** People want to do meaningful work.

- **Employee morale is higher:** Team members who do purposeful, meaningful work are happier.
- **Employee turnover is lower:** When team members are happy, they stick around longer.
- **Provides a differentiator that reinforces your brand's positioning with guests:** More socially-minded guests make purchasing decisions based on issues they care about.
- **Offers positive media and public relations opportunities:** This may be less a reason than a good by-product, but once the outside world discovers the good work a company does, the brand will get credit in the form of free advertising.
- **Provides opportunities to get strategic partners more involved:** Vendors become part of the culture, versus just financially supporting the company's regular business.
- **Removes barriers between managers and team members:** Working side-by-side toward a common purpose is a great equalizer.

Collectively, these outcomes lead to increased profitability…some directly, others indirectly. There are real dollars attached to reducing employee turnover, securing free advertising and having a strategic partner fund an initiative. But even the most nebulous, indirect outcomes above can be correlated with a brand's success. Being an active community partner, developing a work environment in which employees are happy, rallying around a cause bigger than the brand's core business—these will all surely have long-term impact on a company's culture.

Just to be clear, identifying and acting on "purpose" isn't just about a company writing a sizeable check to a charity. That is definitely commendable, but it's not enough. Socially conscious employees are not passive observers. They want to participate, in some way, in the preservation of the planet and human kind. It would be awesome if that conduit just happened to be the employer.

IS EMPLOYER LOYALTY DEAD?

People say employer loyalty doesn't exist anymore. But start up an authentic cause-oriented group within your company—if one doesn't already exist—and you will see people flock to it. Even better, let your employees' values guide your philanthropic efforts. Support the causes that resonate with them and achieve an even more powerful shift in the organization.

One way Hard Rock International brings its purpose-driven values to life is through the creation and support of the Ambassador Program. This is an employee-led philanthropy group that exists at each property and strives to make the local community a little bit better. This voluntary program supersedes the company simply writing checks for well-known causes. Members of this group are completely engaged, getting involved in charitable causes because they *want* to, not because they *have* to. Ambassadors meet regularly and seek out no-cost opportunities to help their communities, many times rallying around a colleague who has fallen on hard times. Just by the existence of the Ambassador program, the job goes above and beyond slinging drinks and making burgers for many Hard Rockers.

- Is there a local cause your employees wish to wrap their arms around?
- Does one of your team members have a personal connection to a particular cause?

A quest for this information is time and energy well spent, because finding a way to make an impact beyond the scope of your day-to-day business could be the catalyst that will revolutionize your company's morale, productivity and long-term success.

NO-BRAINER RATIONALE

Setting up an employee-led, volunteer philanthropy group is a simple process:

- **Share your philanthropic thoughts and goals with all of your team members**—use all-staff meetings, department meetings, postings in an employee area or any combination thereof.
- **Solicit an initial core group**—one member from each business function or department to represent the entire company or property.
- **Allow the group to determine its own structure**—whether meetings are open to everyone in the company, just a select few from each department, or only formal elected officers.
- **Support the group's causes**—encourage the volunteer-employees to identify the local causes and activities they would like the brand to support.
- **Support the group's ongoing needs, where possible**—offer meeting space, food and beverage, t-shirts, etc.
- **Get out of the way**—allow it to take a life of its own; through

passionate, committed employees, the process will manage itself.

If you'd rather not instill this type of formality in the process, then just create an open forum in which team members can show up, voice their opinions and participate in something meaningful. Even *that* would be a great start.

Today's generations are looking to offer up their loyalty to those companies that are truly active in making their communities better.

Do you think this is too grandiose a concept to apply to your organization?

Ask any 19-year old what he or she now looks for in an organization and some language around "giving back" or "doing the right thing" is likely to pop up. This is how the Millennials grew up, and they expect this to be common-practice in businesses today.

AT THE END OF THE GAME

Just a quick reminder: If you are considering starting a cause-related group or integrating some community service work into your business, it *must* be voluntary. Philanthropy cannot be mandatory. It doesn't work like that. Philanthropy never works if someone is forced to participate. In fact, power and hierarchy cannot have any role in charity work. That's the beautiful thing about engaging in some collective company volunteer work: All levels and titles are obsolete when you are working together to re-build a storm-ravaged home or participating in a cancer walk for an unseen victim.

Philanthropy is one of the great equalizers in the world. Remember, one of the main reasons to engage the organization in something bigger than the core business is that it removes the barriers between leaders and team members.

Consider this little-known Italian proverb:

"At the end of the game, the King and Pawn go back into the same box."

In the board game of Chess, some pieces, like the Queen or a Rook, are more powerful than others—partly because these pieces can move more than just one space at a time and even in any direction the player wants. Pawns, on the other hand, are limited in their movement and are considered the least powerful pieces on the board—yet they have a critical role in the game. They protect the more powerful pieces, often having to be sacrificed for the greater good. Pawns can also can advance to a place on the board where a player can swap them out for more powerful pieces. The King, as you would imagine, is the ultimate prize. If one player can get the other player into Check Mate, meaning the King has nowhere to go without himself being captured…the game is over.

Why the quick overview of chess? Actually, to point out that it's *just* a game. As limited or powerful as a piece may be considered *during* the game, all of the pieces become equal partners *after* the game, as they're haphazardly tossed back into the box they came from. This is the essence of philanthropy. Doing good works for a cause bigger than yourself levels the playing field. Titles, power, status, influence…none of that matters, when the game of life is played.

I have attended many multi-day seminars with built-in "service" events, usually as low-commitment, pre-conference electives, where I have found myself stocking backpacks for kids at a food bank or pressure-washing a much-needed playground…all while working with and talking to some other like-minded conference attendees for the first time. But the shocker for me is what happens after the charity event.

I have been taken aback on many occasions when, in the midst of a conference session, it suddenly dawned on me that the just-introduced keynote speaker was in fact the sweaty guy on my left at the food shelter who handed me canned foods for 4 hours. Or the president of some international company sitting at my table was that nice lady who kept filling up the soap bucket for me as we blasted grime from a kid's merry-go-round earlier in the day. Nobody threw their job titles around, nobody tried to be the dominant force in a conversation, nobody sought personal attention…everyone at that moment was equal. It's always an awesome feeling when that conference moment sneaks up on you.

Today, the only annual conferences I attend for my own growth and development are ones that include some type of philanthropic cause or community activity. Industry associations like The Council of Hotel and Restaurant Trainers (CHART) and People Report—early adopters of adding in some type of philanthropic mission to their event models—are now my "go to" events. As important as the content offered and the networking opportunities available are, these particular business events impact me more from a higher purpose standpoint. And for that, they have my loyalty.

Cultures that are purpose-driven have their rewards.

TO SERVE IS TO ROCK

Brands that actively engage in selfless activities to enhance society tend to have a much stronger organizational culture. When philanthropy is prevalent, the culture rocks!

Luckily, this is a part of Hard Rock's DNA; it has been a critical part of the company's value system since its inception. By slapping the mottos up on the walls in the early '70s, Isaac Tigrett and Peter Morton put themselves on notice, forcing the employees to keep the Founders and themselves honest in committing to *Love All – Serve All, Take Time to Be Kind* and *Save the Planet*.

This *All is One* mentality around bettering the human race has literally taken over the annual brand calendar for Hard Rock. There aren't many company initiatives for guests that don't have a charity component tied to them. In fact, the brand created an executive level position solely dedicated to its philanthropic activities and working with celebrities to help bring awareness to various causes. How cool would it be to have a Sr. Director of Philanthropy on your team?

Although Hard Rock International does not make a lot of noise about its philanthropic efforts in the public domain, people have figured it out. Many loyal fans know. And every employee definitely knows. Each Hard Rocker is keenly aware of the heritage and importance of philanthropy in the business…and they covet its continued existence. Whether it's through the Ambassador program or a global cause-related campaign, charity is one of the key factors that show up in employee surveys, validating why people have a strong sense of pride and continue to work for the company. Like many others before me, this was a monumental part of the reason I stuck around for decades.

Each of you should leap at the opportunity to implement a philanthropic agenda into your business. Consider the following crucial steps you can take to create an environment swimming in charitable contributions and directed toward improving the world and those living in it:

- Create an internal, employee-led volunteer group to run point on local philanthropic initiatives.
- Add a half-day community service event to the front or back end of your company's conferences.
- Select and support a companywide charitable cause that make sense for your brand.
- Include some type of purpose or philanthropic cause in your company's Values and discuss it regularly.
- Create a reward mechanism that acknowledges employees who donate their time to company charitable causes.
- Look for opportunities to "go green" in your organization's properties and offices.
- Offer and serve products (in your business or at business events) that are fair trade, locally-produced or have a charitable component.

MY PHILANTHROPIC BUSINESS CRUSHES

Brands that are socially conscious and create environments with purpose are the ones that I regularly support. My loyalty for these organizations is unwavering; I pounce on opportunities to talk about them with others when an "open window" presents itself. Let me share a few of my favorites with you.

In the vernacular of my friend Amanda, the following are some of my all-time, purpose-driven "business crushes."

Axum Coffee

Five minutes from my home, a local start-up coffee house called Axum Coffee has tucked itself into the quaint downtown strip that is Winter Garden, Florida. Like something straight out of the Mayberry, USA—complete with cobblestone streets, iron swings, ice cream shops, a bike trail and a water fountain rotunda at the city center—the township still didn't quite seem complete until Axum came to town.

There are a lot of things that would make this coffee shop a perfect hang-out: building location, interior décor, spiritual-orientation, service-oriented staff and product quality of the coffee, to name a few. All of that alone would already make this a great coffee shop to be supported by the locals. Yet, what makes the brand special is that Axum's business model guarantees that 100 percent of all its profits go to charity. That's right, once all of the overhead costs of the building lease, product inventory and employee labor are paid, the remaining profit is given to the same African farmers providing the commodity product used to make Axum's coffee. It really is a throwback approach to sustainability.

Axum Coffee truly is "serving the world, one cup at a time" as its motto suggests.

Pangeo Tea & Coffee

A few years ago, I had the opportunity to go on a "compassion trip" to Ethiopia with some of my closest friends. The trip was through Global Hope Network International (GHNI), a non-profit organization whose core focus is on helping villages transform themselves sustainably and holistically through a unique coaching method that ultimately empowers the community to free itself of a perpetual cycle of poverty.

Our group's goal was to visit two of the poorest villages in the country and be welcomed thought partners in creating solutions around the critical issues of food, water, wellness, income, education…and I jumped at the opportunity to go. It was an awe-inspiring and eye-opening journey. The sheer number of unforgettable moments on the trip are too numerous to mention here; they would fill their own book. Some of these experiences were captured in real time through our daily blogs and pictures that our friends back home followed throughout the journey. If you are interested, you can see these captured moments on our website at www.ChangersofCommerce.com.

Our GHNI Director for the trip was a former preacher named Jeff Power. Jeff is one of the most caring people I know and has since become a good friend. In addition to the great global work that Jeff does with GHNI, he is the founder and owner of Pangeo Tea & Coffee. As you can imagine, with his access to and ongoing knowledge of Africa—specifically the Ethiopian and Kenyan regions—he has learned a thing or two about the coffee trade. As he dabbled in starting a business in the commodity-crowded field of tea and coffee, he knew that the product quality would have to be Herculean. And it is. I would hold Pangeo's quality and taste up against any major or independent brand. Yet that still wasn't enough for Jeff.

In addition to ensuring that his business transparently supports fair trade for the tea leaf and coffee bean farmers from whom he procures his product, Jeff Power donates a percentage of the proceeds from every sale he makes to those same poor villages that he works with at Global Hope Network.

This is now a personal connection for me. It's so fulfilling, knowing that every morning I drink a cup of Pangeo coffee at home I am supporting the hundreds of poor, but proud souls from the exact villages that our Changers of Commerce group previously "adopted."

And individual home sales of the Pangeo product is just the start.

The brand's broader focus is in having restaurants and coffee shops pour Pangeo products and create a direct connection to a specific village that needs support. The world has become really "small" with the advent of technology and travel; many companies that embody a philanthropic mission want to help both local and global neighbors.

Pangeo's connected business model offering for coffee shops and restaurants looks like this:

- Jeff sources first-class tea and coffee from specific regions where GHNI helps villages.
- He supplies those products to foodservice locations that want to pour Pangeo.
- The brand then pairs each restaurant with a specific impoverished village that becomes "its" village, forming a true partnership.
- A high percentage of Pangeo's profits are then funneled into the specific village in need.

- Pangeo updates the restaurant monthly with stories and pictures of its village's journey out of poverty.
- Using a translator, Pangeo facilitates ongoing Skype calls between the business and its village.

Imagine, thousands of restaurants supporting thousands of villages around the globe and making a huge difference in people's lives. Jeff Power's business model truly reflects the overall principles of Connected Capitalism. This part of his life is a for-profit enterprise, yet he, of all people, knows that there is a higher purpose to his brand.

As much of a fan as I am of coffee houses like Starbucks, Intelligentsia and Stumptown, all of whom have their own social responsibility programs, Axum and Pangeo are brands that have a permanent place in my heart and mind because of their philanthropic approaches to business.

Causecast

We all understand that engaged employees are the best brand ambassadors. We also now know that *employee* engagement through community engagement is even bigger with Millennials. This cultural nuance is critical to today's workforce. However, if the company's philanthropic processes are not user-friendly or the technology is outdated, the spirit of philanthropy could become anemic throughout the brand, despite your best intentions. That's where a community impact firm like Causecast can assist.

Founded by entrepreneur and technologist Ryan Scott, Causecast is a business solutions company that helps organizations engage their employees in corporate volunteering and giving through an active, mobile and social technology solution. The organization was built on the belief that when leaders enlist employees in their social missions, they can generate engagement everywhere—within their company, community and customer base. Through its cutting-edge online platform and hands-on concierge service, Causecast helps companies centralize and automate every element related to volunteering and giving in one place—from donation processing to full reporting at the click of a button.

Take a look at the main services this brand delivers to help other organizations with this challenge.

They will...

- **Develop a customized, branded employee volunteering portal**—that's interactive, social and mobile
- **Offer a full suite of transparent functions for employee-driven philanthropy**—that includes searching, signing up and tracking volunteer activities, giving, matching donations, ready-made campaigns and sections for employee posts and interactivity
- **Quickly respond to and implement disaster relief**—with turnkey efficiency
- **Provide a dashboard for administrators**—that offers 360-degree tracking and reporting of all employee volunteer activity in real time
- **Manage existing and new non-profit relationships**
- **Help develop compelling employee volunteer opportunities**—near specific company locations
- **Create and market community impact campaigns to the masses**
- **Establish competitive social fundraising events**—as a fun way to engage the staff in corporate philanthropy

Causecast is an example of a brand formed to eliminate the perceived complexity of starting and managing an employee-driven philanthropic agenda. It enables businesses to operate their volunteer and giving programs with the highest levels of efficiency, participation and impact to unlock passion and commitment—captivating and engaging everyone. I consider Causecast a philanthropic enabler.

Splick.it

Another company that utilizes the power of philanthropy as an additional part of their business is Colorado-based Splick.it. The company's core business offering is its technology platform for multi-location restaurants, hospitality and other large organizations, which powers its client's branded mobile, web and tablet ordering, payment, marketing and loyalty initiatives. The platform makes it easy for restaurateurs to know who their customers are, what they like to eat and when they like to go out. This then allows those businesses the opportunity to thank the guests for their business, reward them with loyalty points, send them offers and make it easy for them to order and pay without having to wait in lines for a great VIP guest experience.

As cool as the product offering is, it's not the reason I'm a fan of Splick.it.

I love the brand and its founders for their heart-centered approach to connecting customers and companies to a cause bigger than themselves—as a seamless part of the usual business-to-consumer transaction.

In addition to their traditional client offerings, Splick.it created a mobile app called *Order Food, End Hunger*, which allows customers at participating restaurants to "round up" a percentage of their transaction to the nearest dollar—the additional amount going directly toward *No Kid Hungry*. Practically every "rounded up" transaction—in a sense, pocket change that you will never miss—will provide a full, healthy meal for a food-deprived kid. I love the simplicity of it. And of course the cause.

This specific app was not designed to generate any revenue for Spilck.it. Rather, the company's explicit goal with this product is to influence the entire restaurant industry to support the application so consumers can order food and beverage—online or on their mobile phones—while at the same time, contributing to the elimination of childhood hunger in the United States. That rocks.

Hassle-free mashups like this, which combine technology and philanthropy, make a huge impression on today's consumers. Millennials and Digital Natives naturally expect these two worlds to co-exist. With its product and service approach, Splick.it prides itself on building a strong relationship between brands and their customers, but I believe their *Order Food, End Hunger* app could be the catalyst to propel them to the top of the charts in an ever-crowded field of mobile technology.

You rock, Splick.it.

Tori Kelly

A philanthropic enabler of a different sort is music performing artist Tori Kelly. Tori first garnered widespread attention when she auditioned for and appeared on Season 9 of the most popular television show at the time, *American Idol*. Although she did not make it to the coveted Top 24 that season, she has continued to build her fan base by performing customized covers of other artists on YouTube—she has more than 60 million views to date.

In February of 2013, Tori released a single called "Fill a Heart," which she wrote for the *Child Hunger Ends Here* campaign by ConAgra Foods and Feeding America. As part of that campaign, she performed at eight different venues across the U.S. in her "Fill a Heart" tour, each time helping out at the city's food banks during the day before performing at night.

C'mon, tell me that's not cool.

Not only is she extremely talented, Tori's personal culture completely rocks my world. Needless to say, I have a philanthropic crush on Tori Kelly.

Wildflower Bread Company

Wildflower Bread Company is an all-natural, 100 percent, made-from-scratch specialty bakery and restaurant brand based in Scottsdale, Arizona. Founder & CEO Louis Basile started the company in 1996 with aspirations of building a unique neighborhood restaurant that would make a positive, lasting impact on peoples' lives. And he has.

Take a look at how inspiring the company's purpose is:

"We change lives, create traditions, build community and feed the soul with passion. Every time, every day."

With a motto like that, this brand affects everyone.

Internally, the employee culture is filled with love and laughter. The company's website even features an employee-created music video—now used as a recruiting tool—called "Super Flour Power," in which employees sing about how "wild they are about the flour." It's an awesome, real-life example of an employee culture that authentically spills over to the customers and the community. As a true testament to the public's affection, Wildflower Bread Company is consistently included on *Fast Company* Magazine's coveted Top 100 Movers and Shakers list, reaching as high as number two.

The product, the people, the passion, the pride, the purpose...all of it is world class, when it comes to this brand.

The spirit of philanthropy was embedded in the company's DNA by Louis, but it is perpetuated by the company's employees, or "Bread Heads," as they are internally referred. The result is the Wildflower Cares Campaign. Through this philanthropic program, employees sell specific and related products in the restaurants and donate a big portion of the proceeds from each item to charities that resonate with Wildflower's business, employee base and loyal customers.

The three official recipients include:

- **Dine Out for No Kid Hungry**—which focuses on providing nutritious meals for kids living in poverty
- **Communities in Schools**—which works to influence students to learn, stay in school and prepare for life
- **Susan G. Komen Breast Cancer Foundation**—which helps fund research programs to eradicate breast cancer

As part of the company's community focus—and in addition to the formalized Wildflower Cares Campaign—the organization provides daily support to local food banks and shelters and contributes time and products to local non-profit organizations. Each night, the brand donates bread and bakery leftovers to shelters and organizations throughout the area. Additionally, Wildflower has partnered with a local middle-school boy's academy to provide free breakfast for the entire school year to these students who show great academic promise but have had limited educational opportunities. These are only a few of the many programs Wildflower engages in as part of its ongoing business culture.

This specialty bakery makes money. It is definitely a for-profit organization, but it behaves like a non-profit. And for that, the company is rewarded with organizational sustainability. Wildflower Bread Company doesn't just support a singular philanthropic cause, rather it has become a totally purpose-driven brand—one which clearly knows how to foster a culture that rocks.

Maybe your brand is not prepared or able to go "all in" like Wildflower... but you could do *something*.

BTC Revolutions

One brand that specifically exists to help other organizations engage in philanthropy is Be The Change Revolutions, a digital brand marketing and advertising agency that specializes in the foodservice industry. Co-founders Amanda Hite and Brandon Hill are both total rock stars in the hospitality realm and the quintessential experts on using "social media for social good." It certainly isn't the only thing they do for businesses, but once a client starts working with BTC and truly understands the power of social media...igniting a movement to positively affect others is an inevitable game-change for that brand.

BTC Revolutions helps hospitality companies in the following ways:

- **Build and manage communities**—within and for the brand
- **Manage social media sites**—like Facebook, Twitter, LinkedIn, etc
- **Develop mobile technology**—like mobile Apps, mobile software and giant touch screens
- **Create and execute marketing campaigns**
- **Ignite purpose-driven movements**—for causes bigger than the brand

I do not know of another marketing agency that has clients falling as madly in love with them as BTC Revolutions, but I do know the client-to-agency love affair starts at the top with the two co-founders and permeates their employee environment. The company's entire consultant consortium screams of Justin Timberlake-cool. Like the iconic pop star, each member of the BTC team is talented, funny, humble and loved by everyone. They're the cool kids. And with business titles like Chief Change Officer, Chief MVMNTS Officer and the Director of Awesome, how could they not be? They are a culture unto themselves. Yet coolness means nothing without the talent to back it up. And they have it.

The agency has serious street cred in delivering financial results for its clients—each one of them a successful business case study. Once BTC becomes an extension of the brand, team members fully dedicate their hearts, minds and actions to dramatically moving the needle on the business' results. As critical as that is, I just happen to love them for being the philanthropic enablers that they are.

Some of the more purpose-driven initiatives BTC has taken on include:

- **Tweet-a-Thons:** a one-day online Twitter campaign to drive millions of people to a specific website, take pledges and donate money
- **Tweet-Ups:** an event in which like-minded Twitter followers meet each other in person to build momentum and excitement and generate funds for a specific cause
- **Service Events:** purpose-driven activities—held during a client event or an association conference—executed and participated in by BTC

These types of activities are powerful, effective and fulfilling. Your company may already be engaged in philanthropic initiatives like this. If it isn't, seek out some assistance from a digital marketing brand that thinks bigger than just generating more profit for the organization—one that clearly understands today's generations and the key drivers that will secure the loyalty of guests and employees alike. Improved financial results will be only one of the many pleasant outcomes.

Be The Change Revolutions gets it. It clearly is a culture that rocks.

RESISTANCE IS FUTILE

Millennials and Digital Natives will eventually permeate our respective businesses. Tapping into this talent-rich labor pool is inevitable. Ignoring and resisting this fact would be a mistake. Think about it: The Millennials are already here and the Digital Natives are coming soon.

Channeling the bone-chilling mantra of The Borg:

"Resistance is Futile"

Let's not resist them. Let's figure out how to engage them to either strengthen or revolutionize our organizational cultures. Failing to truly understand the specific nuances and needs of today's workforce—like having philanthropy as a priority—is a missed opportunity to develop loyalty. This is organizational work that needs to happen now if you have any hope of attracting and retaining today's "rock stars."

I have shared many best practices, process steps and company examples in this chapter that can help get you started. But your brand has to have a sense-of-urgency mindset to get its arms around the key cultural drivers of the present-day, socially conscious generation. Everyone is waiting.

As U2's Bono once said,

"The world is more malleable than you think and it's waiting for you to hammer it into shape."

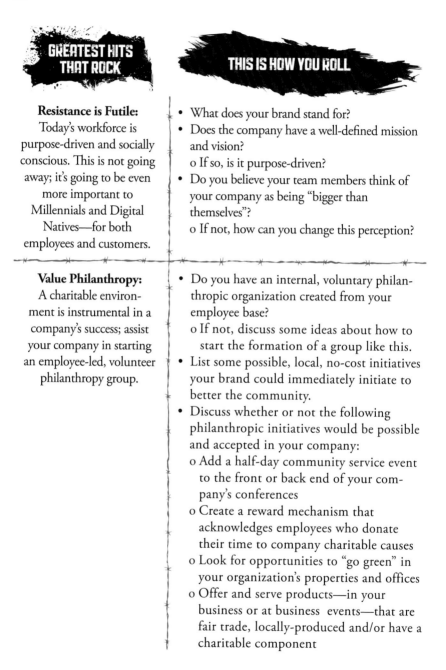

GREATEST HITS THAT ROCK

Resistance is Futile:
Today's workforce is purpose-driven and socially conscious. This is not going away; it's going to be even more important to Millennials and Digital Natives—for both employees and customers.

Value Philanthropy:
A charitable environment is instrumental in a company's success; assist your company in starting an employee-led, volunteer philanthropy group.

THIS IS HOW YOU ROLL

- What does your brand stand for?
- Does the company have a well-defined mission and vision?
  o If so, is it purpose-driven?
- Do you believe your team members think of your company as being "bigger than themselves"?
  o If not, how can you change this perception?

- Do you have an internal, voluntary philanthropic organization created from your employee base?
  o If not, discuss some ideas about how to start the formation of a group like this.
- List some possible, local, no-cost initiatives your brand could immediately initiate to better the community.
- Discuss whether or not the following philanthropic initiatives would be possible and accepted in your company:
  o Add a half-day community service event to the front or back end of your company's conferences
  o Create a reward mechanism that acknowledges employees who donate their time to company charitable causes
  o Look for opportunities to "go green" in your organization's properties and offices
  o Offer and serve products—in your business or at business events—that are fair trade, locally-produced and/or have a charitable component

GREATEST HITS THAT ROCK

THIS IS HOW YOU ROLL

Shift Your Business Model to Connected Capitalism:
Although financial success is the ultimate goal in for-profit organizations, it is not the only goal. Business and society have to be better connected with our communities, government, relevant philanthropic causes and employees' values.

- List the specific ways that your company is already connected to the community you serve.
- Discuss whether your organization is connected with local government to address relevant large-scale problems.
- What would be a relevant charity, directly related to your type of business, that would make the most sense for your brand to support?
- Would the company be open-minded to offering a small portion of sales to a philanthropic cause?
- What obstacles would stand in the way?
- Are your philanthropic efforts tied your employees' values and social causes that resonate with them?
- Can you name a local cause your employees wish to wrap their arms around?
- Does one of your team members have a personal connection to a particular cause?

Seek Out Philanthropic Enablers:
Great resources exist to help organizations get started with and manage purpose-driven initiatives.

- Can you identify some third-party resources that can assist your company in implementing and managing purpose-driven initiatives?
- What would need to happen before you enlist some outside support?

16

COMMUNICATE LIKE CRAZY

"I wanted to be in a band that shared ideas and were in it together."
- Roger Daltrey, The Who

The most successful organizations in the world have a shared mindset.

By following the successes of some Fortune 500 companies, I have discovered that, aside from the fact they make more money and command more market share than their competitors, they communicate like crazy to their internal masses…maintaining a strong sense of transparency and ultimately loyalty. In these high-performing organizations, everyone knows the mission. The lowest line-level employee in any of these companies shares the same view on the purpose of the business as the President or Chief Executive Officer does. Additionally, each person knows how he or she fits into that mission.

Communication is key to ensuring that everyone is on the same song sheet. If it's done well and often, your company's internal messaging will create a collective mindset among the team. And *that* is powerful.

BE LIKE U2

Considered one of the biggest bands on the planet, U2 consists of four members, yet many people do not know the names of the bass guitarist or the drummer. Adam Clayton and Larry Mullen Jr.—the lesser-known musicians in the band—make up the group's critical rhythm section. They certainly don't get the notoriety of the band's other two members, but they are perfectly cool with their roles.

Additionally, Adam and Larry have claimed in interviews that each time they play to a packed arena on tour, they are trying to duplicate *exactly* what they did the night before. The same show, night after night…driven by consistency. They're the steady engines driving the band. Yet, if you listen to discussions with Bono or The Edge—the more well-known, public faces of U2—these two rock stars admit they are trying to do something completely *different* from the night before. They're trying to soar the band to new heights and create something uniquely spectacular with each performance.

With the combination of these two different approaches to performing, all four members of U2 understand both their individual roles and the collective mindset that makes this band one of history's rock treasures. Group members are all on the same page and understand their independent responsibilities while also supporting the ultimate goal of the band: to make some of the greatest music of all time.

It doesn't matter if you're the brand-new technician at the auto repair shop, the dishwasher at the restaurant, the administrative assistant at a technology giant or the toll attendant on a major highway…everybody has a part to play in the band.

SHARED MINDSETS

What's true for a rock group is also true when it comes to an organization and its makeup. Maybe the lead singer or front guy will always get the glory, but every person in a high-performing organization knows that he or she has a crucial part to play in the band's success. This keen awareness—when all team members understand the company's mission, their specific, individual roles and how the company stacks up against the competition—doesn't happen by accident. It occurs when the organization's leadership makes a clear choice to keep the employees as "in the loop" as possible about all things related to their jobs and the brand. That is, those at the top make a conscious decision to over-communicate to employees and ensure they are informed, aware and involved with the inner-workings of the organization and its culture. Individuals may take different paths to create a result, but if the overall result is on par with your mission statement and based on shared mindsets, phenomenal success will be within reach.

Elite companies start the communication at the front end by delivering inspiring and motivating New Hire Orientations, no doubt using well-developed leaders' guides for consistency. They continue the process with industry-leading training initiatives and self-driven development programs. However, these are not the things for which they get recognized. In fact, while most of these rock star companies do a fairly good job with their onboarding processes, it's what they do *after* that initial experience that seals the deal for their employees.

They continue to communicate, communicate, communicate.

Companies that enjoy long-term success seem to have more all-staff meetings, department meetings and one-on-one discussions than others. They don't do this just for the sake of having meetings, but because they clearly understand the power of regular, effective communication as a pathway to empowering the overall workforce.

Abundant and transparent communication ensures that all team members are singing off the same sheet of music.

COMMUNICATION CONDUITS

Consider the following techniques you might use to shift your business to one centered on successful and meaningful communication.

Communicate in the Language in which Employees Dream

Rock historians will probably credit Kurt Cobain for shifting the culture of Rock 'n' Roll in the early '90s. While there may have been other great music produced during that time, it was Nirvana's *Smells Like Teen Spirit* that spoke to an entire generation. That band represented teenage angst like no other at the time. It became the voice of my generation, seemingly speaking directly to us.

Since it was clear early on that the Millennials were going to become the immediate future of our workforce, it was crucial to create a learning culture that would tap directly into that generation's psyche. Therefore, I took a page from the Grunge playlist and focused my energy on trying to echo their voices…or speak their "speake."

I discussed what this type of communication might look like in earlier chapters focused on the Key Cultural Drivers of Today's Workforce. But whether the "speake" is to be in print format or video, written test or verbal validation, performance appraisal or impromptu conversation…employees should feel like we are communicating directly to them, not through a Human Resources filter of big-company legalese.

So when you speak to today's talent, consider communicating with them in the language in which they dream—the way their brains process information as they put their heads down on the pillow at night, close their eyes and drift off to sleep. The way these young people think in their "dream state" is the way our training materials and communication vehicles should be formatted.

Take the time to really think through all the unique ways that today's talent is wired—and let's communicate to them in "language" they understand, appreciate and respond to.

Appraise Often

Another valuable communication opportunity is the performance appraisal. An annual performance discussion is a great way to re-engage team members with their specific job tasks, but it's also a great opportunity to keep employees mindful of the part they play in the brand's mission. This might seem like Business 101, guaranteed to happen at every company, but performance reviews are not necessarily par for the course.

Separating themselves from the competition even more, sustainable brands go beyond the typical performance appraisal for employees. They understand that a one-time-a-year formality is not enough to secure loyalty. Instead they rely on multiple, ongoing performance discussions that ensure clarity, address any outstanding issues and collectively decide on any corrective action. Sure, they have the formal appraisal at "performance review" time, but this is merely process-driven documentation for Human Resources. In these communication-savvy organizations, everyone knows where he or she stands—at all times.

Although performance reviews are supposed to be about the employees' strengths and opportunities, these meetings are also a great vehicle for gauging your own leadership skills. One way I always ended a performance discussion with a team member was by asking, "How am I doing for you?" or "What can I do for you?" Everyone on the team had a specific perception of my leadership style, and asking a question like that gave my direct-reports an opportunity to provide honest feedback about what I could do as a leader to make their world rock. The first few times you ask a question like this, you may get pretty generic answers like, "Everything's great. Nothing needed." However, as you build up trust with a team member over time, he or she will probably provide more specific and valuable feedback with each discussion.

You both win here. You acquire authentic feedback that will enhance your leadership style, and the employee has a sincere invitation to speak his or her mind—another communication conduit that adds to the overall internal environment.

Consider REX Meetings

One format that has been phenomenally successful at solving root cause issues—those elusive *original* causes of problems, versus their apparent but short-term symptoms—is a gathering called a REX Meeting. REX is an acronym for Reality vs. Expectations. The premise of this concept is that people have pre-determined expectations of a brand before they experience it, and they are then either surprised or disappointed by the reality of it, depending on how the experience actually goes. All employees have a "comparison scale" in their mind as to what the company is *supposed* to be, based on reputation or hearsay, versus what it actually is, based on the employee's firsthand observations and experience. Once the mental comparison scale starts to tip toward the stark reality of the way things actually are, the organization will either create rock stars or lip-synchers.

Organizational psychologists and Human Resources professionals have discovered specific turning points in the employee life cycle…when the team member starts to question whether he or she made the right decision in joining the company…when the associate wonders if the company's values match his or her own personal values…even when they might start to consider leaving. If, during one of these crucial moments, an employee feels like things aren't the way they're supposed to or they way they were promised, their loyalty starts to waver. These moments provide the perfect opportunity to isolate the team member and have a conversation about the "state of things."

A REX meeting allows you to have an open dialogue with an employee to better understand his or her expectations or to find out if the company's promises match up to the reality the particular employee is experiencing. It's an overt way in which the organization can identify and potentially close the gap in fulfilling the employee's expectations.

Hard Rock International found this type of meeting to be very useful. Just by having the conversation with an individual, the company was able to address and solve issues early on, before they became big problems for the employee. Perhaps the team member needed clarification about company benefits or a better understanding of the product discount policy. Maybe the progressive discipline process was explained one way in the New Hire Orientation, but in reality, the process managers follow is entirely different. It could be that the team member had visions of easily making a lot of money by just showing up, but now realizes that it takes hard work and strict adherence to company processes to get a favorable schedule, a bigger sales commission or better gratuities.

REX meetings are a great opportunity to keep employees engaged in the overall mission.

Implement Stay Interviews

Close cousins of the REX Meeting, Stay Interviews are deliberate conversations with employees, designed partly to throw a little love and attention their way and remind them that you care, but also to help prevent them—especially the rock stars—from leaving.

While a REX Meeting is traditionally held early in an employee's career with a company to validate whether expectations match up to the business reality, Stay Interviews can be done anytime during a team member's tenure, and they address a broader spectrum of discussion points. If acknowledgement, engagement and reduced turnover are your desired results, then the conversations could and should take on a life of their own. Sure, we can go into the "interview" with a preselected set of topics to discuss, like career development, work safety solutions or feedback on the work environment, but if the conversation takes an employee-generated turn toward family, continuing education or lifelong hopes and fears…let it. Just the act of spending some time with each employee and discussing mutually relevant topics will enhance their affinity for and loyalty to the brand.

Early in his entrepreneurial career, speaker, author and restaurant operator TJ Schier wrote a book called *Send Flowers to the Living* that revolved around this very concept. The implicitly morbid analogy suggests that we should not wait until an employee "departs" before we decide to honor him or her with flowers of respect. Instead we should be doing everything we can now, to get that associate to stick around longer. Schier's approach in the book mirrors that of a Stay Interview: Communicate, develop, reward and recognize employees on a regular basis, *before* they decide to leave. Once an employee decides to bail on the brand, it's too late to try to woo them back. Their disenchantment and disengagement are most likely set in stone.

Stay Interviews are a phenomenal communication vehicle for enhancing engagement and improving retention.

Create Leadership Forums

An open dialogue with the top boss—in which the explicit purpose is to ask questions, seek knowledge and share ideas about making the workplace better—is a spectacular and non-threatening way for employees to have a louder voice. I call these coveted opportunities "Leadership Forums." REX Meetings and Stay Interviews are great communication processes managers can implement with direct reports, but offering staff-level employees direct access to the ultimate leader of the business…that's something special. Most team members I know would leap at the opportunity to have the undivided attention of senior management. This builds trust, mutual collaboration, a sense of ownership…all building blocks for a stronger internal company culture.

Establishing a leadership forum is one of the most effective group communication platforms that an organization can implement. When done right, they can produce substantial results. This is even more true when employee ideas and feedback are recognized and turned into actionable steps…perhaps even as new company standards.

The format of a leadership forum can be formal or informal, depending on the time allotted, space available, number of attendees and the leader's style.

Here are just a few suggestions to get your mental wheels rolling:

- **Breakfast/Lunch with the Boss:** This is certainly easier to pull off in the restaurant industry, but having a conversation with the General Manager over a little food is a real treat; free food and an open ear from the key decision maker in the business goes along way.
- **Brown Bag Lunch:** This is a more informal version of a "Lunch & Learn," in which free education is typically pre-

sented; instead, this is a laid-back format in which attendees bring their own lunch to an open discussion with the top leader, avoiding any wasted work time.

- **Quality Circle Meetings:** This is a more formalized approach in which employees are selected or nominated to attend a discussion with leadership on a more regular basis (Quarterly, bi-annually, etc.); these discussions might be open for anyone to attend and provide feedback or they might be limited to one or two employees representing each department or work group.

As you can see, there is no right or wrong way to structure a leadership forum, as long as the overarching goal is to give frontline employees access to top leadership in a non-threatening forum where they can collectively solve business issues. Beyond that, format is a matter of choice.

Ongoing communication with team members is a key tenet of a strong company culture. Best practices like REX Meetings, Stay Interviews, regular performance discussions and Leadership Forums all go a long way toward solidifying employee loyalty.

Communication is a powerful retention strategy. It's the glue that makes people stick to organizations.

EVEN A BURRITO ASPIRES

A great example of a communication-rich environment is the Boston-based burrito chain, Boloco. The company prides itself on the perfect combination of all brand elements.

- **Product** - the highest quality, premium ingredients, including responsibly-raised meats and organics, served in corn cups and bamboo bowls
- **Atmosphere** - natural and local décor materials that match the community, including old brick, original flooring, decorated columns, detailed ceilings and customized artwork on the walls; Certified Green buildings utilizing recycled materials, LED lighting, low-flow waterheads, and Paperstone tabletops & counters
- **Service** - a guest-obsessed mentality that clearly stands out in the competitive Fast Casual arena, implicitly striving to provide a mix between the unexpected and exactly what the guests want

- **Value** - guests are willing to pay for the premium product, knowing they get an overall premium experience; validated with an unbelievable track record of same store sales increases nearly every year since the brand's inception

In addition to the refreshingly authentic way Boloco is positioned in the public domain—via its hilarious website and heart-warming philanthropic initiatives—founder John Pepper went to great lengths to create one of the most unique internal employee environments you will find in foodservice.

Take a look at some of the anti-industry benefits Boloco provides to create an internal culture that rocks:

- **Highest starting pay for any entry-level employee**—well above any direct competitors and government minimum wages
- **Overtime pay during holidays**—one and a half times an employee's normal rate of pay for being away from their families
- **Monthly transportation budget**—of 50 dollars for each employee to put toward gas or public transportation
- **Free English language classes**—for any English-challenged employee who wishes to attend and learn
- **Relaxation lounges in many locations**—private team member break rooms complete with reclining chairs, flat screen TVs and chalk boards for doodling
- **Four-week sabbaticals for all employees, after 10 years of tenure**—based on the belief that a month of paid time off to retreat and revive will re-engage the person with the brand
- **Company-sponsored holiday parties and family picnics**—many brands in the restaurant industry have stepped away from these expensive and risky internal events, but they are still enjoyed at Boloco

One of the most cherished benefits the brand provides is the inclusion of employees at the company's Leadership Retreats. As part of the regular executive leadership meetings, local Boloco team members are always invited to attend and share their thoughts and recommendations with the company. During the meeting portions attended by employees, the discussions usually have very loose agendas, if any. Team members are encouraged to provide 100 percent honest opinions, positive or negative. Some ideas are guest-focused, while other suggestions focus on employee needs. These Retreats really are a special time, designed to encourage and foster "Bold and Inspired" practices directly tied to Boloco's vision.

Several company initiatives in place today are direct outcomes from team members attending those formal leadership forums. One of the greatest employee-generated ideas that ever came out of a Leadership Retreat is the brand's "Amaze Me" Philosophy.

This concept includes two major tenets that are now part of every new-hire Orientation:

- **Amaze and Delight Each Other**
- **Amaze and Delight the Guests**

From the minds of employees: so simple, yet so powerful.

You can probably imagine the type of results produced in a culture that puts all employees on a quest to amaze everyone around them. It's spectacular.

This "Amaze Me" mentality has ultimately led to the empowerment of *any* team member to comp food—provide it for free—to any guest at any time for any reason…whether it's for service recovery or just to reward a loyal customer. Although the company had to build some financial infrastructure into its budget to support this concept, Boloco employees take this empowerment very seriously and only utilize it to support the culture.

Innovative communication opportunities like the Leadership Retreats are highly coveted at Boloco. And the company's internal metrics prove it. The brand's annual employee turnover averages around 65 percent, versus the industry range of 110 to 130 percent. Sixty-five percent may seem extremely high in most industries and some countries, but it's actually extremely low in the personnel-churning environment of Fast Casual restaurants.

Employee benefits aside, companies like Boloco that have ongoing, authentic and open discussions with their employees keep everyone singing off the same song sheets. Robust communication is a part of a strong culture.

PEOPLE JOIN BRANDS, THEY LEAVE INDIVIDUALS

Gallup Inc., the granddaddy of all survey companies, has worked tirelessly with major businesses and organizations around the world to provide the most comprehensive surveys across a wide spectrum of topics. The company's research and processes are the absolute best. I have seen many people-oriented surveys from Gallup over the years, but none of them floored me more than Marcus Buckingham's 1999 report titled "Gallup's Discoveries about Great Managers and Great Workplaces."

In this unprecedented 25-year study, Gallup surveyed more than two million employees at 700 different companies in a variety of industries worldwide. With that amount of data-point depth, the poll results are about as statistically relevant as any you will ever encounter. What Gallup discovered was a significant relationship between employee satisfaction on one hand and employee retention, customer satisfaction, productivity and profitability on the other. Maybe that seems like old news to you now, but it was a huge affirmation for many organizations at that time. Even more telling was what Gallup discovered as the main crux of an employee's satisfaction with his or her job. It turns out that the immediate supervisor is the single largest influence on an employee's satisfaction and, ultimately, his or her decision to leave a company.

This discovery reminds me of the old saying:

People join brands, but they leave individuals.

In other words, it is usually their boss, their boss's boss, or some high-level executive that causes employees to be dissatisfied to the point of leaving. To avoid conflict or hassle, the team member may say that he or she is quitting because of low pay, scarce benefits or lack of growth, but statistics prove that the real reason is likely the employee's immediate supervisor. Your own internal exit interviews with departing employees may echo these results.

I have been exposed to many hospitality industry statistics, all of which clearly point toward this key reason that people leave their jobs, but Gallup's survey solidified it for me and many others in my line of work. Toxic leadership far outweighs other compelling reasons for leaving a job, including money and career advancement. The way a boss treats employees is vital to the overall happiness of those employees in their current job positions.

LEADERSHIP WITH A HEART

Author, speaker and executive coach Susan Steinbrecher co-wrote a fabulous book with Joel Bennett called *Heart-Centered Leadership: An Invitation to Lead from the Inside Out.* As you might imagine from the crystal-clear title of the book, Steinbrecher and Bennett looked at several aspects of leadership through the lens of certain underlying principles and virtues, ultimately laying out a pathway for any level of leadership to do the right thing. At the core of these principles and virtues was the critical component of communication.

In writing *Heart-Centered Leadership*, the authors meticulously researched, studied and proofed out the scientific facts that would ultimately guide leaders in building their legacies—along with sustainable business results, of course. They made some eye-opening discoveries in the course of their research on employee satisfaction:

- **46** percent of employees claimed to have left a company because they felt underappreciated
- **61** percent of employees said their bosses didn't place much importance on them as people
- **88** percent of employees said they did not receive any acknowledgement for their work

The negativity of these responses seems unusually high and yet I'm really not surprised. After all, I see and hear about these types of employee environments all the time, which validates the book's findings for me. One of the more unbelievable results shared in *Heart-Centered Leadership* is the collective answer to the question, "Why did you leave your last job?" Seven percent of the employees interviewed said they left because their supervisor or manager did not say "good morning" to them.

Seriously? I always thought that was a funny and unrealistic response rate...until I realized that I may have been a part of causing the seven percent to answer this way.

With the teams I was fortunate to lead at Hard Rock, I always felt like I was a pretty good communicator, in the general sense, but I definitely did not engage in enough one-on-one dialogue. Sure, I had monthly team meetings; I always held performance reviews on time; I sent out team-based email instructions...all the usual communication you would find in a big business, but I most certainly did not take the time to make the office rounds to say "good morning" to each person. It wasn't that I didn't like talking with the team—I did. It was really more a matter of my work philosophy that drove me to avoid this type of communication.

As a self-proclaimed workaholic, I constantly strove to do as much work as I could, as quickly as I could, in the daily time allotted—so I could produce the best organizational results and foster the greatest global influence in the industry. Perhaps I was a bit too intense, but my quest to deliver nothing short of excellence in everything our team did drove my work ethic. Unfortunately, that approach did not leave a lot of room for individualized, in-depth conversations, especially during my last few years with the brand. Now I think that was a huge mistake.

Instead of narrowly focusing on the quantity of my own work—the mark of a manager—I should have engaged the team more and supported the quality and quantum productivity of their work…this is what makes a great leader. I now think that those types of influential conversations could have been the best use of my time and resources in terms of my team's impact on the organization. I hope the Hard Rockers that left our department did so for reasons other than my not saying "good morning" to them, but it is very possible that my limited one-on-one communication with them contributed to their decisions. I should have known better.

Ongoing communication with employees in every form, including individualized appreciation and acknowledgement from the boss, goes along way toward employee engagement and ultimately the internal health of any company's culture.

R-E-S-P-E-C-T

If you are in an executive role, you probably realize that you don't achieve any company results on our own. None. All of the results, both good and bad, are generated through the staff—those employees on the front line that create the unique and memorable experiences for guests. These valuable employees do it all. Our job as leaders is to coach them up and provide direction that will ultimately raise them to the next level so they are ready to take on more responsibility. This requires communication, motivation, inspiration, mentorship, patience and, most importantly, respect.

In every leadership study I have ever seen, employees place "respect" high on the list of critical needs in the workplace. Even when we taught "Leadership" as a management course in Hard Rock's corporate university, the competency of respect would consistently make its way to the very top of the desired characteristics for a leader. Employees want to be respected as individuals, as contributors, and as complete human beings with lives outside of work. Where money and position may have been the driving force twenty or thirty years ago—tempered a decade ago with the work-life balance credo—today's generations want even more. In addition to all of the benefits we've already mentioned, employees now want to be treated with unprecedented dignity and respect—a full-time job in and of itself for any employer. This may not suit your company's approach—it may even seem unrealistic—but it is an employee's world these days. In other words, even in an environment of high unemployment, great talent has no problem finding another job.

Rock stars can always get another gig.

Millennials understand that they can easily get another job down the street at a different company if they feel unappreciated or disrespected by upper management. While this may not guarantee that they will then be working for someone who treats them as a valuable resource rather than a number on a

Profit & Loss statement, at least they don't have to stay and deal with "the jerk boss at the other place." Managers never want to be known as "that guy."

For some leaders, the room lights up when they walk into a room.

For others, the room lights up *after* they leave.

In the lightening-speed, hyper-communication environment of business today, the word about a company's management style—or a specific so-called leader—can spread like wildfire, creating an undesirable reputation that can adversely affect the person's career. Once his or her reputation is sullied, the manager will have a hard time maintaining a job in any service-oriented industry.

YOU'RE NOT THE BOSS OF ME

I compare the expectations today's employee has of his or her boss to those of a fan attending a concert of…The Boss. The expectation is that Bruce Springsteen will play a non-stop, high energy, sweat-soaked, three-hour marathon with The E-Street Band—because that's the standard he has set and the reason his fans come to see him perform. To get something less would be a disappointment. Employee expectations of a leader are just as high.

There are several tips and tools I always recommend for ensuring that your company builds the strongest rapport and positive mutual relationship with employees. These include:

- Take Time to Authentically Communicate
- Ask…Don't Tell
- Become a Friend, Instead of a Boss
- Avoid Muscling the Results

Let's take a look at each suggestion to see if these are areas that need addressing in your organization in order to enhance your internal company culture.

Take Time to Authentically Communicate

Authentic communication includes all of the techniques shared in this chapter—everything from REX Meetings to saying "Hello" to each team member. From executing and acting upon employee surveys to establishing open dialogue in a leadership forum. From publically appreciating and acknowledging staff to respecting each person for his or her value and contribution. Each type of communication vehicle you have just adds another layer of cultural health.

Remember, authentic, ongoing communication with employees helps keep everyone singing off the same sheet of music. And that creates organizational productivity.

Ask...Don't Tell

If you are the boss, it's easy to tell people what to do. But if that's all you do, all the time, it can be a never-ending, frustrating journey to a healthy culture. You may never get there with that "cause and effect" approach. You tell people what to do and they do it (or not). That process could go on forever, while you continue to reap the same results.

Nobody wants to be told what to do all the time, but everyone wants to do meaningful work. What helps make the work meaningful is giving the staff a voice in the way the work is done. Enlisting employees in decision-making processes, especially in closing business gaps, produces buy-in and productivity. One of the most effective things a leader can do to empower team members is also the simplest: Ask their opinion about how to resolve an issue, versus telling them what to do. In other words, ask...don't tell.

Your goal as a leader shouldn't be to discover business issues on your own and then solve them by barking out orders to others. Rather, your ultimate goal should be to use the collective power of your workforce to seek out, prevent and solve the root causes of those business issues.

When I was a restaurant manager and noticed that tables had been improperly cleaned during a hectic shift, the quick and easy solution would have been to flag down a busser and send him or her to correctly clean the table. But even if I gave clear instructions on what was wrong with the table, I couldn't be sure that the cleaning process would be done correctly in the future. The team member may have just been responding to my immediate request to "fix" that specific table.

To solve the issue more permanently, I found that it was better to pull the busser aside and collectively discover a solution by asking a series of questions, like:

- Does anything seem out of place with the dining room floor?
- What specifically do you notice about that table?
- Can you tell me what it should look like, based on our training and standards?
- Can we double check that all of the tables are bussed and set up like that in the future?
- Can I ask you to spread the word on this to the other bussers so that we're all consistent?

This is an example of correcting performance, but it can work for just about anything—and the by-product is always a more engaged workforce. Asking front line employees specific questions to seek their approval, solicit ideas, provide feedback, solve problems or help make organizational decisions is a sure-fire way to strengthen the relationship between employees and leadership.

Become a Friend, Instead of a Boss

The relationship between employees and management is a major attractor (or deal-breaker) for current and future generations. To achieve optimal performance, each individual needs to see his or her direct supervisor as a support mechanism and friend, rather than the enforcer of rules. Instead of letting every conversation with staff revolve around work and what employees may be doing wrong, a leader should consider talking with team members about their lives, hopes and dreams, while focusing work discussions on the things employees are doing well. And another thing: Employees of today don't just appreciate being on a first-name basis with every leader in the organization, up to and including the highest-level executive—they practically expect it.

On the surface, this personal approach surely flies in the face of many Human Resource policies designed to prevent lawsuits for favoritism, harassment and discrimination, especially in today's litigious world. But as long as decisions are consistent and based solely on employee performance, there is no reason why a friend-oriented management style couldn't be employed.

Of course there will be times when an employee needs to be coached, counseled or disciplined for breaking a policy or going against the organizational norm, but that's when the relationship shifts into a more stringent employer-employee understanding. And if your brand has a strong work culture, employees are more likely to feel as though they have let a friend down, versus having broken the company's rules.

Avoid Muscling the Results

"My way or the highway" credos no longer work in most industries. The old days of a supervisor getting away with managing people through threats and punishment are long gone. In fact, these type of "throw back" managers stick out like sore thumbs, regardless of the industry. In today's environment, those that try to wield and utilize the power of their positions to get results discover very quickly that those tactics don't work.

These so-called "leaders" soon realize they are outnumbered by caring people who do not respond well to an authoritative management style. It quickly becomes unfashionable, unpopular and ultimately undesirable for fear-inducing managers to stick around, so they eventually leave. Yet, the damage these old-school managers do before they bail can be devastating to a company culture. All of the data produced by exit interviews and surveys support this point. Unfortunately for many brands, employees today are less likely to give this type of manager a chance to improve or leave.

Just like in a rock group, team members quit the band at the first hint of creative differences…because they can.

ALL EMPLOYEES ARE VOLUNTEERS

My favorite piece of advice for shoring up organizational communication isn't just another technique, but rather a mindset that may require a fundamental shift in the management of the business. It revolves around the concept of volunteerism.

Knowing that today's workers hold all of the cards when it comes to hiring and retaining top talent, organizations may have to change the way they communicate with their staff. This specific approach goes above and beyond the old-school authoritative managers just being a little nicer.

To truly understand the behavior shift I am suggesting, consider the following question:

Would you treat your employees differently if all of them were volunteers?

Think about that for a moment.

If every team member no longer depended on you for a paycheck and instead showed up to work each day because they *wanted* to, not because they *had* to…would you act differently with them? With all your heart, you may be thinking "no," and that you already do a great job in the way you communicate with employees. But in your head, the sobering, analytical side of you is saying "yes"…you would *have* to. The human dynamics are completely different when you strip away the hierarchy and promise of money.

People who work in a non-profit environment know this concept well. They realize that in volunteer organizations, there is no power-wielding—because there is no power. The only "muscle" you have is appreciation and truly motivating your volunteers to do things because they want to, not because they will lose their jobs or are offered pay increases. If the only people who support you are ones that are volunteering to do the work, like in a philanthropic organization, then the only valuable exchange a leader can offer are those of authentic words like "Please" and "Thank You.".

Now what if we took that same mentality to a "for-profit" organization as business owners? Of course, our employees would still get paid, but we would treat them as if they were not. In other words, you would want to treat employees so well that they felt as though they were working for the benefit of the company and its cause, not just for the personal paycheck.

Sounds easy, right?

It's not.

Viewing your workforce as a group of volunteers will certainly help generate loyalty to the brand, but creating a true atmosphere of volunteerism comes with a price. You have to cater to your employees' needs…you have to over-communicate with them at every turn…you have to spend more time with each individual…and all of it has to be authentic.

Here are a few thoughts about how to treat your employees as volunteers:

- **Call people working for you "team members" or "associates,"** —versus "staff" or "employees"
- **Say "Please" when making a request**
- **Say "Thank you" for every action…and say it often**
- **Say "Hello" to each employee with whom you come into contact on your way in to work**
- **Say "Goodbye" to each employee with whom you come into contact on your way out**
- **Ask for team member feedback**—and ask for it often, regarding processes, initiatives or issues
- **Ask employees about life outside of the day-to-day business**—like their families, career aspirations, hopes and fears, etc.
- **Seek out opportunities to mentor team members**—help them acquire skills that will take them to the next level
- **Constantly create a welcoming environment**—with positive energy, language, smiles and inspiration

What would happen to the business if this approach were taken by every leader in your organization? I bet it would flourish and employer loyalty would get stronger. In fact, treating team members as though they are volunteers could be the greatest retention strategy you will ever employ.

Perhaps you already have this mindset and personally treat employees the way I am describing here. That is awesome! Your goal then should be to motivate others in your organization to follow suit. If you do it right, you'll change your internal culture—and ultimately the bottom line.

Consider all employees as volunteers…because they are.

LOW-HANGING FRUIT

All of the suggestions and stories I've shared in this chapter are designed to help you enhance the relationship between employers and employees in your organization through the unbelievable power of effective and constant communication. Many of the recommendations will work perfectly, regardless of your industry, while others may not make sense at all for your specific type of business. However, we can all agree that the more information you can share enterprise-wide—and the more communication obstacles you can eliminate, reduce or avoid all together—the closer your company will come to being the place Millennials, and eventually Digital Natives, will want to work.

Ongoing and effective communication helps eliminate many of those issues and bolsters the environment.

Of course, there are many other organizational areas to address when it comes to culture, but if someone were looking for some low-hanging fruit that, if plucked, can result in immediate, positive change, communication is a solid place to start.

Take the time to examine your internal company processes and seek out every opportunity to loop in the entire organization on the critical priorities of the business…and communicate like crazy!

This is how you get everyone singing off the same sheet of music.

GREATEST HITS THAT ROCK	THIS IS HOW YOU ROLL
Over-Communicate: Ongoing communication is the glue that makes people stick to organizations.	• List all the types of communication methods utilized in your organization for both manager and front-line employees. • Debate whether you have enough of the following meetings: o All-staff meetings o Department meetings o Manager meetings o Individual performance discussions • Discuss how it would be possible to perform more than one performance appraisal per year with every employee. • What formats or tools are you missing that could help keep the entire organization in the loop on all brand-related initiatives?
Appeal to Their Dreams: Communicate to people in the language in which they dream.	• Do you feel as though your communication tools and processes fit all learning styles? • Are they inclusive of those to whom English is not native? • Does your organizational language speak the "speake" of your employee base? o If not, what needs to change?
The Volunteer Approach: Treat employees like they are volunteers— because they are.	• Discuss whether or not your company has great employee retention strategies in place. • Debate whether an environment of appreciation exists, in which "please" and "thank you" are common and genuine words used by management.
Be Like U2: To be effective throughout the entire enterprise, leaders need to get everyone singing off the same sheet of music.	• Do all employees clearly know they have a critical part in the business' success? o How can this be enhanced? • Discuss whether all employees feel like they have a voice in decisions.

GREATEST HITS THAT ROCK	THIS IS HOW YOU ROLL
Create Leadership Forums: Implement non-threatening, zero-retaliation opportunities for staff to share ideas with leadership.	• List any type of communication conduits, in which employees can share thoughts and feedback with management, that exist in your organization. o REX (Reality vs. Expectations) Meetings o Stay Interviews • What type of Leadership Forums that makes sense for your culture could be implemented? o Breakfast/Lunch with the Boss o Brown Bag "Lunch & Learn" sessions o Quality Circle Meetings • Discuss how it would be possible to perform more than one performance appraisal per year with every employee. • Discuss the possibility of staff-level employees being invited to attend and participate in leadership meetings, conferences and retreats.
People Join Brands; They Leave Individuals: Most surveys prove that while departing staff will say they're leaving because of a lack of money or growth opportunities, the real number one reason is direct supervisor's poor leadership style.	• Can you think of some leaders in your organization who clearly manage through threats and punishment? • Can you think of a leader in your brand that treats employees as if they were volunteers, not dependent on a paycheck? • Is your company's employee turnover high or low compared to your competitive set? o How is it trending against prior year or the last several years? • What are the specific causes of your brand's employee turnover? o Is this a result of poor leadership? o If yes, how do you know? • Does your company do exit interviews with voluntarily departing employees? o Why or why not? o If so, what are the main findings from the collected data? • Discuss whether the data supports the idea that people are leaving because of an individual. • If there are leadership issues in your business, discuss the initiatives that can be implemented to address the problem.

17

PROFITABLE GROWTH, PROMOTABLE PEOPLE

"I want it all and I want it now."

- Freddie Mercury, Queen

When our training and development team at Hard Rock was but a small and budding department in the mid-90s, we created Rock 101, a trademarked, instructor-led corporate university for managers. During that five-day conference, we taught the gambit of technical managerial skills to all new leaders, regardless of where in the world they worked. We felt it was important to consistently teach the fundamental skills of becoming a great leader. While many companies have some type of week-long training program built into their initial management onboarding, nothing like Rock 101 existed in our industry, at the time. In fact, that training event became bigger than just a conference for most—it became an unforgettable experience. In addition to the technical skills taught, we also spent time on some fun, music-inspired and branded topics a manager would not learn about anywhere else.

One of the more compelling courses for Rock 101 attendees was the "Global Strategy" session, which included a Q&A with the organization's President and Chief Executive Officer. The attendees also had direct face-time with several of the company's key executives, all of whom taught sessions, throughout the week, but this collective block of time with the highest-level person in the organization—the CEO—provided a unique opportunity for participants to learn about the company—and actually ask questions—from the brand's leader.

This was a rare opportunity for a manager running restaurant or hotel shifts on the other side of the world. It was also a much-anticipated experience for the CEO, as the conference afforded *him* one of those rare opportunities to get in front of a captured, concentrated and attentive group of emerging leaders to consistently and directly influence their thinking. Over the decades, every Hard Rock CEO took his turn in the spotlight at Rock 101 and gladly shared his thoughts about the brand. Although the program has morphed over time in name and content, this opportunity for property managers continues to exist.

I *also* looked forward to the "Global Strategy" session and always took away some personal nuggets for bettering my own leadership style from the top executive. In fact, it was in this session, years ago, that former Hard Rock International President, Peter Beaudrault used an analogy to get the participants to engage in understanding, protecting and driving organizational culture. Pete's way of thinking about developing business loyalty—for guests and team members—always resonated with me…to the extent that I continued to use the same analogy and business model at every Rock 101 conference we conducted. And it's also now a key element in my own overarching mindset on enhancing an organization's culture.

The concept initially focuses on *both* parts of the business: the financial and the human.

TWO KINDS OF CAPITAL: FINANCIAL & HUMAN

Most companies are internally broken down into fundamental key result areas, which are then managed and measured. They may have different names in your specific business, but they are generally the same two basic areas: financial results and human capital.

For an organization to reap the rewards of long-term cultural bliss, success must occur in both areas. The company must make money—it's the main reason most businesses exist—but, for sustainability, it must be done with a strong internal employee culture. Exclusively chasing company profits, particularly at the expense of the people actually providing the results, will eventually be disastrous. Conversely, the brand cannot just have a harmonious work environment with a wanton disregard for the company's financial health. That would be just as derelict. If a company's focus is lopsided in favor of either one of the key result areas, eventual failure is inevitable. As business leaders, we need to focus on both people and profits.

To this end, we focused on two aspirational goals during the "Global Strategy" session at Rock 101, each tied directly to the two key result areas all companies seek:

- Profitable Growth
- Promotable People

When performance in both of these areas continuously exceeds our expectations, we create sustainability for the brand. I suggest that business leaders keep these two ultimate outcomes top of mind as they seek to create, enhance or radically alter the culture in their organizations.

Let's dive into both areas.

PROFITABLE GROWTH

Whether it's through an intense day-long onboarding session, a multi-day, instructor-led corporate university or a well-developed e-Learning course, it is vital that, when you introduce new hires to the company, you focus their attention on specific and direct goals. For those of us in for-profit organizations, the business must be able to make money. Plain and simple. In terms of top line sales and revenues, honoring profit commitments to shareholders is goal number one. I'm not talking about a one-year fluke; the true health of the business will be measured by consistent and sustainable financial growth. It's not enough to deliver on the agreed-upon annual budget—you want to far exceed the previous year. The reverse is also true: It many cases, doing better than the prior year is not enough, if the budgeted goal is not reached.

Positive Guest Experiences = Return Visits

Regardless of the industry or the specific metrics a company uses to measure its success, there is one universal truth: For the company to remain healthy, the consumer must keep "going back to the well." They must buy more. In the case of hospitality, guests must regularly return to a business if that business hopes to achieve sustainable financial success. As part of the necessary chain of events, consumers will only return if they have positive experiences with the brand.

These would include (in this order):

- Great Service
- Quality Product
- Comfortable Environment
- Acceptable Price per Value Ratio

There may be some other nuances that are unique to your business or important to you personally, but in my experience, these four sub-sections are the only things consumers really care about. If your customers receive a consistently high-quality product at a fair price, delivered with great service in an environment that is fun, clean and safe, you are almost guaranteed to avoid becoming a "one-hit wonder." This overarching positive guest experience will entice people to come back. And that is your ultimate mission if you hope to achieve sustainable, profitable growth.

This part of the model is visibly displayed below:

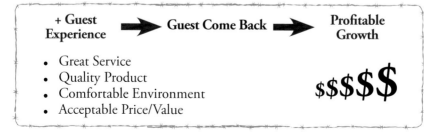

PROMOTABLE PEOPLE

While financial success is crucial to a business, the other, equally crucial piece of this puzzle is the human factor. Most everyone will agree that the people side of the business is the engine that ultimately produces financial results, but I want to elevate this concept to something even more meaningful.

If you're a leader in your organization, you are keenly aware that your front line employees are the ones that do all the work; they get all of the direct results for the company. We can lead the team and manage the processes, but we are totally dependent on others when it comes to making things happen. But we can't just rely on "people." We need *great* people. We must work in a deliberate manner to attract and retain the type of high-potential employees that can help us drive the business forward.

I've used the term "rock star" to identify the unique memory-makers who will produce mind-searing results for a business, but this is just another label for whatever you want to call "top talent." However, when we shift into discussions about creating a sustainable organizational culture, we have to focus on our leadership bench strength. In other words, we need to have back fill— a stable of potential internal leaders that are ready to go when the opportunity arises. I think of these potential leadership candidates as "promotable" people.

A promotable person is ready to move to the next level or shoulder more responsibility. In general, these are what all employers need and most employees want to be.

As we've already established, Millennials want to do meaningful work— and they also want to grow. Regardless of their position in a company's hierarchy, they crave more challenging work, higher salaries and greater influence. Some may not actively seek a promotion; for a variety of reasons, they're thrilled to stay right where they are. Others may never be offered a promotion; they aren't qualified, motivated or deserving. But we would like to think that, within our employee base, these are the exceptions that prove the rule. The majority of our people want to grow and develop.

When we discuss promotable people, keep in mind that it's not just about positions or levels within an organization. Promotable people are the ones that are ready to assume more responsibilities. They have been groomed to respond to the challenge of taking on more and having wider influence and a louder voice. This could be a non-tipped team member working toward becoming a tipped employee because he wants to make more money, a staff-level employee who wants to further her career by taking on a management role, an invisible back-of-the-house employee who wants to become a trainer and take on a leadership role, or even a front line manager aspiring to become the location's General Manager. Whatever the case may be, the objective is to find employees that want to do more, reach higher and grow taller.

"Promotable" is the perfect word to describe individuals who are fully prepared to expand their circle of influence. They're poised to step further into the limelight. It's like when Phil Collins came from behind his drum set and took over lead vocals for Genesis after Peter Gabriel gave up the mantle and left the band in 1975. Collins was promotable. He was ready. And he was the obvious and only choice. There was no need to go to the outside and hire a new leader.

As an employer tasked with training and cultivating a promotable group of employees, you can maximize your efforts with the following initiatives:

- **Seek out opportunities to teach others**—whether in formal, scheduled meetings or impromptu teaching moments
- **Explain the "why" behind the "what" in every decision**—to assist them in the problem-solving and decision-making skills they'll need in the future
- **Build in cross-departmental training**—having an opportunity to step into another business unit's shoes and actually work in that position for a while provides better clarity, ownership and understanding of the business' big picture
- **Create a leadership development program**—including a crystal-clear pathway of objectives (tasks and activities) to complete before being considered for the next organizational level
- **Create a mentorship program**—pair up new employees with veteran leaders to bridge the knowledge gap and ramp up your management bench strength
- **Carve out a budget for educational experiences**—secure some dollars for networking, conferences, seminars and webinars to further develop employees

So, rather than hoarding information, your goal should be to share as much as possible in order to develop promotable people who are ready to step in and drive the business at a moment's notice. This will certainly require more time and patience from you, but the results will be Herculean.

The Army of Giants

The more promotable people you develop and keep on your team, the better prepared your organization will be for the future. This is what "succession planning" is all about—scouting out high-potential employees who have the will to drive organizational success, and then developing them into leadership-ready talent. These willful and highly-skilled individuals take on larger-than-life attitudes and competencies. They become business "giants" in my eyes. Company leaders who truly consider their brands to be learning and development organizations will understand the power of the promotable person—they'll create an army of venerable giants from these high-potential employees.

After all, if you're going into battle against the competition—or your own success metrics—you want to do it surrounded with a fully-trained and motivated army comprised of the best talent you can find and develop…versus finding yourself on the battlefield, slinging a blade alone with little-to-no support.

Great leaders surround themselves with an army of giants, ultimately producing other great leaders.

Jack Welch

Jack Welch, the former Chairman and CEO of General Electric, was a big proponent and practitioner of developing promotable people. Throughout his entire business career, Welch focused on the human talent he surrounded himself with—because he knew that each person was a critical component to his ultimate business success. True, he earned a reputation for being harsh on non-performers, but he was just as generous with his rock stars. Each year, Welch would fire the bottom 10 percent of his management team, regardless of their personal performance. If they were at the bottom, they were dragging down the rest of the company. On the flipside, he lavished huge financial bonuses and stock options on the managers in the top 20 percent. His leadership style may not fit with every organization, but you cannot argue with his results. During Welch's leadership tenure, the company's value rose 4,000 percent.

And here's another part of his legacy: Nearly every senior executive who directly reported to Jack Welch eventually became a President or Chief Executive Officer of a large organization. Although Jeffrey Immelt would ultimately succeed Welch as Chairman & CEO of General Electric, his other direct reports moved immediately into the top executive positions elsewhere. James McNerney became CEO of the manufacturing conglomerate 3M, and later moved to the same position at Boeing, while Robert Nardelli became Chief Executive Officer of Home Depot.

Jack Welch surrounded himself with an army of giants. His deliberate leadership approach of creating "promotable" people influenced cultures far beyond GE's core business and industry.

Harry Bond

Another example of this leadership philosophy comes from my friend Harry Bond, the Chairman and former President of the Illinois-based pizza chain Monical's Pizza. Always a forward thinker when it came to his business, Harry did some pretty innovative things in our industry. He was an early adopter of technology, maintaing a branded business presence in the short-lived online gaming platform Second Life, which he hoped might both create a new revenue stream for the company and help train restaurant managers in compliance-based competencies through virtual simulations. He was also the first in the restaurant industry to connect with Harvard Business School Publishing (HBSP) to develop and provide a series of e-Learning management competency courses—called ManageMentor—for his pizza supervisors. At the completion of these courses, each of these employees received a certificate commemorating their Harvard Business School Publishing "degrees."

Did I mention these were pizza supervisors?

Receiving HBSP-endorsed business certificates?

One of the most innovative and seemingly-risky business practices Harry implemented during his tenure as President was the development and daring transition of his direct reports. Just like Vice Presidents at other restaurant concepts, each of his senior direct reports had an organizational function for which he or she was responsible—Marketing, Human Resources, Information Technology, Operations, Finance. But there were two critical differences in the structure of Monical's Pizza.

First, these company executives were not called Vice Presidents, but rather Team Leaders. And they focused on critical business elements versus organizational departments. One Team Leader would head up "Guest Satisfaction," for example, instead of being Vice President of Marketing. Second, these leadership appointments were temporary. Every two years, Harry would "blow the whistle" and each Team Leader would rotate to take charge of another element of the business.

Whoa. Can you imagine this happening in your brand?

Seriously, think about your own company executives right now and imagine your CEO putting every Vice President on a two-year rotation in a different role or a broad critical business element that touched all areas of the company. Your VP of Finance in charge of Human Resources. Your VP of Ops now running Marketing. Your VP of HR now head of IT.

What would happen?

Chaos, I imagine, for most companies.

But think of the benefits, if it's done right. This collaborative effort would force the elimination of silos and instead engage every Team Leader in every part of the business. Additionally, there is no better way to acquire management skills than by actually using them. After each Monical's Team Leader completed his or her "tour," that leader was basically primed to be a business CEO. These executives became promotable.

In fact, Harry's successor as President of Monical's Pizza, Janelle Reents, followed this exact path. She began her rotation as Team Leader of Guest Satisfaction, then moved to Team Leader of Employee Satisfaction (Operations and HR/Training). Next she took over a key slot on the Franchise Team and then, finally, she became Team Leader of Profitability (Finance, Compliance and Treasury). What was Janelle's background? She started as an hourly employee, but decided to make Monical's her career. Thus began her path to promotability. Harry Bond and his team of pizza company executives were all willing to take a chance like this because they knew the ultimate benefits. Harry surrounded himself with an army of giants. And a rock star emerged.

Harry Bond and Jack Welch are leadership heroes of mine for many reasons, but more so because of their philosophy of developing promotable rock stars.

Positive Employee Experiences = Return to Work

Developing potential leaders is empowering for both the individual and the organization. However, for us to have any hope of developing rock star employees into promotable giants, those same employees have to do one fundamental thing—the same thing we need our guests to do if we expect to sustain financial success—they have to continue to come back. They have to walk through the door every day with a real desire to drive the business toward the target of success. And like our consumers, employees will only return to our businesses if they have consistently positive experiences with the brand.

These experiences might include:

- Money
- Benefits
- Recognition
- Leadership
- Respect
- Growth Opportunities
- Comfortable Environment—fun, clean, safe

If team members are performing meaningful work and receiving fair wages and benefits in an environment where their leaders care enough to motivate, inspire, teach, trust, respect, recognize, reward and continuously develop them...we can practically guarantee they'll return to work each day. This overarching, positive employee experience will warrant people to certainly come back. And that is our ultimate mission on the human capital side of the business—we can't *develop* promotable people if we don't *have* the people.

This second part of the model is visibly displayed below:

The two desired outcomes I've outlined in this chapter—Profitable Growth and Promotable People—are completely attainable, but they do not happen by accident. All of the smaller initiatives (listed and bullet-pointed in the model under each customer or employee experience) represent the elements of the business that require constant attention. These critical initiatives must be developed and nurtured over time. Continuously evaluating processes, validating results and securing employee and customer feedback will help you move at the pace of your stakeholder's needs and make adjustments to the brand.

VALUES + METHODS = BRAND LOYALTY

Values—personal and organizational—are another important element in this cultural business model.

Values are a set of operating guidelines by which we all live our personal lives. These guidelines generally conform to established behavioral rules—based on societal norms, religious doctrine and/or parental upbringing. Every person has values, even if they're not written down, prominently displayed or profoundly broadcasts to the public. Additionally, every person has a *unique* set of values. Someone else's values may resonate with you, while others may seem ludicrous. But we all have them, whether or not we say we do. Even notoriously harsh country dictators have values—they live by a unique belief system. Those beliefs may seem warped to you and me, but they still constitute as values.

Just like individuals, organizations have values. Each business has a set of principle beliefs upon which it operates…even if they are not overtly displayed. An organization's value set may not ever be acknowledged, shared or written down, but people will quickly figure them out based on the company's actual actions. But the really great brands do indeed proudly display their values for all to see—employees and consumers alike—increasing the likelihood that they will actually follow through on their published promises.

Here is where I may throw you for a loop.

Even though every company has them, I believe that organizational "values" are just words…until action is applied against them.

In this context, values are what we *say* we believe or what we are *going* to do. Organizationally, these are displayed in a variety of formats: posters, employee manuals, videos, wallet cards, etc. They are carefully crafted and methodically designed to communicate the company principles and intentions—to employees or external customers or both. At this point, however, they are only words on a wall, a PowerPoint slide or a piece of paper. Saying them out loud does not make them so. It takes hard work and conscious dedication to make the words jump off of the page and into reality.

Methods, on the other hand, are something entirely different than values. Methods are our actual behaviors: the physical actions that people see or hear.

What if I were to ask a group of people, "Do you pay more attention to what people say or what they do?" I'm convinced the group would unanimously answer "It's what you actually do." This has been my experience every time I have asked this question in the past. Actions matter. Our observable behavior matters—a lot more than words. Yes, every company has values, but *believing* in something and actually *acting* upon those beliefs are two very different things. The old adage "actions speak louder than words" is all too true when it comes to how an organization diplays its culture to the world.

Defining "values" and "methods" in these specific ways makes understanding this part of the cultural business model easier. Published values are what we *say* we're going to do. Methods are what we actually *do*. If there is a disconnect between the two, the organization will experience both internal and external problems.

For example, if we verbally and publically announce—through commercials, billboards, websites, a customer "bill-of-rights," etc.—that our customers will get "a consistent, quality product at a fair price, delivered with great service in an environment that is fun, clean and safe," then we must keep that promise—or relinquish all brand credibility. These published values are just words until we deliver on them. If we do not fulfill that contract—if we say one thing and then do another—we create an undesirable culture of confusion for consumers…and the business suffers. If people lose trust in a basic product or service offering because the company makes promises that it does not keep…game over.

The same can be said for the commitments we make to our employees. If we promise—in our employee handbooks, training classes, posters, videos, etc.—that our employees will do "meaningful work and receive fair wages and benefits in an environment where they are motivated, inspired, taught, trusted, respected, recognized, rewarded and continuously developed," then we have to follow through with these pledges. If we break that contract, associates are more likely to quit the brand. At the very least, when we ignore or contradict the brand's promises to employees, we will surely confuse the team. And when confusion sets in, people will act in their own best interests, based on *their* opinions about how things should be done. This confusion alone can be disastrous for a brand that relies on everyone singing from the same song sheets in order to attain positive, enterprise-wide desired results.

For all of the reasons mentioned above, if we're going to scream at the top of our lungs, "Look at all the things that we promise you, customers and employees!" then we'd better deliver exactly what we've guaranteed. Saying one thing and doing something else can be catastrophic for a business.

However, if the organization's desired values and methods actually mirror one another, then the business creates "Brand Loyalty"—the company's positive impression on others is so great that it screams of allegiance to the brand. This is how organizational trust and credibility are ultimately developed in the public eye.

Consider the concept in this diagram:

$$\begin{array}{rl} & \textbf{VALUES } \text{(what we say)} \\ + & \textbf{METHODS } \text{(what we do)} \\ \hline = & \textbf{BRAND LOYALTY} \end{array}$$

When stacked and presented this way, the model showcases that when the values we say we believe in are followed up with methods that we actually use, it creates a self-fulfilling prophecy…the exact type of outward-facing organizational culture that the public can believe in.

The result: Brand loyalty is created.

We have all heard that "doing the things you say you're going to do" is the simplest definition of integrity. The same concept applies to creating, maintaining or changing peoples' perception of your organization. Making and keeping realistic commitments, and then aggressively acting on those promises, is the fastest way to make that kind of impact.

Following are some of my favorite businesses, which I believe exemplify this concept and, as a result, have created universal brand loyalty among both staff members and guests.

Zingerman's Community of Businesses

A few years ago, I delivered a speech to a training association at a community college in Ann Arbor, Michigan. I had never been to this cool college town before and, like I always do just before a speaking engagement, I posted on Facebook my plans for the trip and my excitement to be delivering my "culture" presentation. Although I didn't solicit suggestions about what to do or where to go in the city, many of my friends began emphatically insisting that I must eat at Zingerman's Deli. This was not just one comment from a random friend who lived in the state, but rather several people from across the country who knew about and gushed over this brand. I was intrigued.

I had never heard of Zingerman's before and assumed this was just another deli with some unusually great product. Sure, I love a great sandwich from time to time, but not enough to really go out of my way if it's not already part of my travel plan. However, this would have to be an exception. Too many of my friends had piqued my interest and/or guilted me into seeking out the deli. Even though I'm not a "foodie," I am always on the hunt for a great local meal that's different than the usual chain establishments. People who know my background and the business I'm in tend to keep an eye out for unique, culturally-relevant experiences to share with me.

So I did a little online investigating to discover what the big hubbub was with this brand.

What I found, as my friend Scott Stratten would say, was "a whole lot of awesome."

Co-founded by Ari Weinzweig and Paul Saginaw, Zingerman's Delicatessen was a labor of love for two young lads that wanted nothing more than to serve great made-to-order sandwiches and the most authentic traditional Jewish dishes possible. They opened their Deli in a historic building, on a corner near the Farmer's Market in downtown Ann Arbor, Michigan—and established immediate credibility and instantaneous success. The quality of the food, the care taken in its preparation and the authentic service with which it was delivered practically guaranteed the restaurant's initial success.

Unbeknownst to me before I arrived to facilitate my session, my friend Renee Malone, who was influential in hiring me for the training association speech, personally knew the owners of Zingerman's. She had previously done some learning events with them and, in fact, already planned to take me to dinner at one of their locations to show me the unique experience. It was a nice surprise. I rarely have an opportunity to spend any time "'taking in" the local culture when I'm on the road for a client, so I jumped at the opportunity to be chauffeured to this place I had recently heard so much about.

On the way to our first stop, Zingerman's Delicatessen, Renee gave me the abridged version of the brand, filling in the holes to the story I had previously discovered online. And with each part of the story came another layer of re-spect…for owners who understood the undeniable power of company culture and the results it produces.

Everyone makes his or her first trip to Zingerman's solely for the food. It's the hook that gets people in the door. The bread itself is worth the trip into downtown. Authentic, fresh baked, premium quality loaves of every imagin-able type of bread, each one amazing. For the bread connoisseur, the Deli is a sandwich heaven.

No doubt, the figurative "price of admission" to the Deli is the product. Yet what I noticed during my visit was the fantastic human interaction:

- The infectious passion on every employee's face, mirrored by each customer
- The way the employees interacted and treated each other with respect and fun
- The ever-present attentiveness of the staff—each one taking the time to showcase a product, explain a process or even escort guests to a specific area of the deli for a free sample or demonstration

I could tell this was a culture that rocks.

The next stop on our experiential journey was Zingerman's Roadhouse, the company's full service restaurant specializing in American fare with a unique twist. Based on my fresh observations of the Deli, I was already anticipating that the Roadhouse would yield a convergence of stellar food, good-feel ambi-ance, customized service and an overall differentiated experience.

It was better than I imagined.

As we entered the restaurant and were soaking up the vibe, Ari Weinz-weig, iconic restaurateur and owner of the Roadhouse, was sitting by himself at the bar, pecking away on his laptop—working on his next book—while overseeing the restaurant's operations. It was another awesome bout of fate. Once some introductions were made and after I had professed my newfound love for the brand, Ari unexpectedly joined us for a one-of-a-kind dinner.

Completely unplanned, we spent the next few hours talking about business nuances, organizational cultures and life events, all while noshing on some spectacular Roadhouse favorites. Between the decadent Fried Chicken Mac & Cheese and Donut Sundae, we talked openly about everything from meticulously combining and baking rye flour, cornmeal and wheat into the world-famous Roadhouse Bread to teaching Open Book Finance to managers. From comic book training materials to the time and care it takes to smoke and hand-pull the restaurant's pulled pork. From facilitating corporate universities to writing business books. From crafting brand vision statements to how bacon makes life so much better. We ran the gambit of topics.

Can you tell that it was a memorable night for me?

During our time together, I learned about Ari and Paul's staunch refusal to expand outside of the Ann Arbor area. As successful as they are with each of their current businesses, they have no plans or desire to grow beyond that market. As you can imagine, they have been approached hundreds of times with offers and suggestions for franchising and expanding throughout the U.S., yet they have chosen a different path. Versus trying to duplicate a specific restaurant concept and go down the rabbit hole of the chain restaurant world, their approach was to commit to the community and revolutionize the way food and beverage products are prepared, sold and delivered.

Based on their love for the local community, combined with a crystal clear vision of the company's strengths and a refusal to allow quality control to slip through their fingers, the co-founders chose to develop their organization throughout their beloved city...by creating new businesses and experiences rather than replicating or mass-producing a singular concept. In fact, the brand locations I visited that day were only two of the distinct businesses within what Ari calls the ZCoB—Zingerman's Community of Businesses.

Today, the ZCoB consists of multiple, interconnected Zingerman's-branded businesses, which include:

- **Delicatessen**—offering flavorful, traditionally made sandwiches and specialty foods in an entertaining, educational and service-oriented setting
- **Roadhouse**—featuring a menu of American regional cooking
- **Bakehouse**—producing baked breads and pastries for the Deli and other customers
- **Creamery**—producing handcrafted fresh cheeses, gelato and other dairy products from local milk for the Deli and other customers; also featuring live cheese-making classes

- **Coffee Company**—roasting the brand's authentic coffee for all of the ZCoB businesses as well as other cafes, restaurants and offices around the country
- **Candy Manufactory**—a wholesale candy maker, creating old-fashioned American sweets by hand; items include peanut brittle, marshmallows and the famous Zzang! bars
- **Catering & Events**—providing unique, customized experiences and food for small parties and large events; serving everything from corned beef to caviar, party platters to wedding cakes
- **Mail Order**—an online shop for various food and gifts; shipping breads, cheese, coffee, olive oils and gifts around the world
- **ZingTrain**—sharing the brand's expertise in training, service, merchandising, specialty foods, open book finance and staff management with the public through seminars and customized workshops

Although my love affair with Zingerman's had just begun, I was immediately hooked and wanted to dive further into the secrets of its success. That night, I bought all of Ari Weinzweig's books, which were sold at the restaurant, so that I could continue my cultural education on how the brand delivered memorable experiences to thousands of locals and out-of-town fans each day.

Between the night's conversation, my recent personal observations during two fantastic experiences and the little discoveries I gleaned from the books, here are some of Zingerman's business practices that we can *all* model to enhance our companies' cultures:

- **Visioning:** Not to be confused with an annual strategic plan, this is a published, actively-shared, forward-thinking brand Vision which details what a specific point in the future will look like for the organization; it lists the collective desires of the employees around food, service, financial health, community involvement, fun and learning.
- **Mission & Values:** These are collectively developed by the staff and written down to create organizational commitment, facilitate daily discussions and serve as guidelines when the brand falls short.
- **Collective Decision-Making:** A consensus model is used in all company decision-making at the partner level.

- **Open Meetings:** All company meetings (with very few exceptions) are completely open to everyone in the organization.
- **Servant Leadership:** The bottom-up management approach is taught to all leaders, based on the belief that leaders are in place to serve the organization and treat employees as if *they* were customers.
- **Training and Education:** The company provides constant and readily-available information—for staff members who utilize its extensive internal training materials, and for fans throughout the world who buy Ari's books, enroll in ZingTrain seminars, attend BAKE (the brand's school for home baking) or experience food classes offered to the public.
- **Commitment to Hiring:** They ensure the perfect combination of knowledge, skills and attitude in each employee, because they know their employees are the conduit to emotional connections with the guests.
- **Unique Brand Identity:** Consistent fonts, logos, language and iconic cartoon drawings are used in all communication (internal and external), such as menus, newsletters and posters.
- **Constant Communication:** Detailed and regular information is provided on all business concepts and areas through event calendars, newsletters, posted memos and customized seasonal menus.
- **Positive Energy:** The company advocates fun on a professional level; leaders create workplaces in which employees are encouraged to think positively, be themselves and go for greatness in all they do, with a huge focus on what they are capable of—instead of on what they do wrong.
- **Regular Appreciation:** Public acknowledgment and recognition are staples at the end of every meeting.
- **Open Book Management:** Everyone in the company is involved in running the business; financial information is openly taught and reviewed.
- **Company-paid Healthcare:** It's available for all employees.
- **Community Focus:** The company donates 10 percent of the previous year's profits to the community.

This is a long list, and yet it probably doesn't even come close to covering all of the techniques this company uses to keep its culture strong. Zingerman's is one of those brands that employs all of the major components discussed throughout this book to truly embody a culture that rocks.

Suzy's Swirl

One of my favorite people in the world is business guru Kathleen Wood, who has become a great friend and personal mentor to me. Her accolades in the restaurant industry are vast. Kathleen is a nationally recognized growth strategist, motivational speaker, author and a proven leader in both business and non-profits. She blends her corporate sensibility and rigor with entrepreneurial vigor and innovation to deliver sustainable solutions. In all the years I've known her—and well before that—she has successfully crushed everything she has touched.

Kathleen has been a consultant and strategist for several Fortune 500 leaders and well-known industry brands such as Raising Cane's Chicken Fingers, Buffalo Wild Wings, Famous Dave's, McAlister's Deli, Checker's/Rally's, Interim HealthCare, People Matter, Last In Concepts and Marie Callender's. She also sits on the Boards of several industry associations, such as TDn2K, People Matter and Women's Foodservice Forum, and she is a past President of the Council of Hotel and Restaurant Trainers.

Needless to say…she is a total rock star leader among my tribe. And she has helped others make millions of dollars in their businesses.

Deciding to put all of her leadership advice and consulting expertise into a business of her own, Kathleen joined forces with her brother-in-law, Joe Tierno, to open up a new restaurant concept. Unexpectedly and sadly, Joe passed away during the business' creation, but the loss for the family only served to intensify Kathleen's mission to make their dream a reality. She partnered with her sister, Sue Tierno, and her niece, Jen, to continue the concept's development, and together they opened up a frozen yogurt and dessert concept outside of Chicago called Suzy's Swirl. It would be an understatement to say the 'fro-yo' market is an extremely crowded and competitive business, yet the deliberate internal and external culture created by the founders has pushed Suzy's Swirl to the very front of my mind when I think frozen desserts.

It all starts with a leadership mindset, followed by resounding consensus and buy-in from every employee. The collective mission of the business is to provide:

- **Swirling Goodness** for their Customers—high quality products, extraordinary sevice and exceptional cleanliness with every cup
- **Swirling Greatness** for their Crew—positive work environments that create jobs, careers and franchise opportunities for success and financial reward

- **Swirling Gratitude** for the Community—proclaiming to be not just one restaurant in the community, but *the* community's restaurant by becoming an extension of family and friends and a collaborative partner with society

I would label Suzy's Swirl as a fun, quirky and clever frozen dessert brand dedicated to making a positive difference in peoples' lives. And that positivity is crystal clear; I observed it in the faces of both fans and crew members.

Here are just a few of the customer-facing initiatives the company employs, which may spark some easy-to-implement ideas for your own organization:

- **Chalk Wall**—completely covering an entire wall, kids and adults alike are encouraged to take a few moments to doodle and add to the day's positive energy
- **Social Media Surprises**—whether it's Cyber Monday (Buy One/Get One gift card purchase) or a random "Kids 6 Years & Under Eat Free This Afternoon" post on the company's Facebook page, the loyal locals love to be surprised
- **Special Events**—refusing to be relegated to simply serving cups of yogurt within the four walls, Suzy's holds successful and memorable events in the community, including:
  - The Big Joe Challenge: Named in honor of Joe Tiero, this media-covered challenge consists of an individual consuming 64 ounces of frozen yogurt with 8 ounces of toppings in less than 20 minutes…without leaving the table and while "keeping it all down"; winners get a t-shirt and their picture on the wall of fame, while losers donate $20 to the American Heart Association.
  - Suzypalooza: Designed as a "Start of Summer" appreciation day for loyal customers and the community, the company provides music, games with prizes and local celebrities for a day-long party.
- **Costumed Mascot**—making an appearance at special events, a fully-costumed brand sidekick named, Swirlz brings smiles to everyone
- **Monthly Philanthropy**—each month, the employees collectively choose a charity and establish a financial giving goal; everyone wins here: the recipient charity, the community and the staff

Customer brand loyalty thrives in environments like this. There is a reason why this single Suzy's Swirl location in Gurnee, Illinois has over 9,000 "likes" on its Facebook page. This doesn't happen by accident—or because of the product alone. Loyalty develops because of leadership's laser-like focus on internal culture. So, let's take a peek inward.

If you are looking for a specific roadmap to strengthening your company's internal culture, check out the employee infrastructure Suzy's Swirl implemented on Day One:

- **Professional Principles**: This gets unbelievable attention on the front end, especially for a self-serve frozen yogurt brand; the single-location concept has a well-developed Mission Statement, Vision, Guiding Principles, Values and Non-Negotiables that are detailed and reinforced with each crew member.
- **Robust Training**: Another sign of the company's focused, inside-out approach, employees receive two Orientation days, six days of training and two days of Train-the-Trainer for those who want to make the leap to becoming a trainer.
- **Ongoing Education**: Even after their initial training, team members are taught financial management, marketing and leadership skills.
- **Adult Treatment**: Founders Kathleen, Sue and Jen treat crew members as adults and part of the leadership team; this feels pretty good to the employees, many of whom are in their first job.
- **Constant Communication**: Several different forums are provided for two-way discussions between leadership and employees:
  - Monthly All-Crew Meetings—topics include education, profit discussions, staff recognition, industry guest speakers, philanthropic charity selection, collective ideas on contests and competitions, etc.
  - Communication Boards—up-to-date information posted in staff member areas
- **Customized Rewards**: Of course all crew members get the usual employee discounts and schedule flexibility that come with working in the foodservice industry, but longer-term employees and top performers get additional incentives:
  - Colored Nike Shoes—customized and given to all employees who reach 6-months of employment, are in

good standing and work an average of 20 hours per week
- Engraved Crystal Snowflake—awarded to all employees who reach 36 months of employment, are in good standing and have performed at an exceptionally high level

- **Holiday Party**: Each year, the collective voice of the crew decides what to do for the annual get-together, ensuring both fun and buy-in.
- **Product Tastings**: Employees participate in flavor tastings and provide feedback on all new proposed products; involvement in decisions plus free food is a powerful combination.
- **Career Support**: On several occasions, the founders have been character references and provided written letters of support for crew members' college admissions applications.
- **Life Skills**: Knowing that a first job and adult mentorship can influence young lives, the leadership team uses an authentic combination of organic and deliberate training and discussions on life, helping employees to develop a strong sense of confidence and self-worth; parents have often told the founders that their kids' tenure at Suzy's has improved their lives and attitudes.

Just a reminder here, so you can understand my love for this brand and its leaders: This is a single store operation, in an extremely competitive segment of the hospitality industry, populated with Millennials and Digital Natives—many of them in their very first job. Yet the specific culture and correlating business results at Suzy's Swirl absolutely rock my world.

Just thinking about this brand makes me smile.

Suzy's Swirl and Zingerman's are two fantastic examples of what can happen when brand leaders have their Values and their Methods aligned. Culture catalysts Kathleen Wood and Ari Weinzweig actually do the things they say they will do. And that creates powerful Brand Loyalty—for customers and employees.

Two completely different businesses, both with rock star cultures.

GREATEST HITS THAT ROCK	THIS IS HOW YOU ROLL
Consumers - Keep 'Em Coming Back: To have any hope of creating Profitable Growth, customers have to keep coming back.	• List the initiatives your company has in place to influence consumers to both regularly return and tell others about the brand…ensuring long-term growth.
Employees – Keep 'Em Coming Back: To have any hope of creating Promotable People, employees have to keep coming back.	• Discuss the developmental initiatives in place to keep employees coming back with the hope they can take on more responsibilities.
Build Your Army: Surround yourself with committed, passionate people—create an Army of Giants.	• Discuss whether each business unit has a solid percentage of "giants" who can step in and lead when called upon. • Do you personally have any/enough smart, competent people working for you that are ready to take on more responsibility? • Name the leaders in your company that are known for having "bench strength" on their teams. • Would others in your business call you a developer of people? • List specific examples that would lead them to think of you that way. • What initiatives can you implement—short and long term—to start building an Army of Giants around you?
Do What You Say You Will Do: Values (what you say) + Methods (what you do) = Brand Loyalty If you say one thing, but do something else, you will create confusion.	• What are others' perceptions of your integrity—do they think you'll do the things you say you will do? • Does your brand have an issue with not following through on its stated commitments? o Name a few examples of when this has happened. • Name the obstacles that are keeping you from having your Values and Methods match up. • Is this a concept that your executive team could get behind and address? • Discuss how to share this concept with company executives.

ENCORE

CULTURAL NIRVANA

As a speaker, author, consultant and starving consumer of experience-obsessed organizations, I am on the hunt for Nirvana: the cultural promised land. One side of me just wants to be around companies that are interested in creating memorable experiences that rock, while the other side of me wants to scream about them at the top of my lungs for everyone to hear.

I crave for the different. I crave for the spectacular. I crave being surprised. I want this from big brands and small businesses alike. And I am not alone. People today want to experience great cultures—both as consumers and employees.

What I have tried to deliver throughout the course of the book is *this* undeniable truth:

Culture is everything to the ultimate sustainability of a company.

As this realization becomes more widespread in business today, smart leaders seek out ways to ensure their culture's well-developed existence and immortality. With *Culture That Rocks*, I believe I have provided a holistic blueprint—for the naysayer executive, the legacy employee or the would-be catalyst. Perhaps not every chapter resulted in an epiphany for you, but each one was replete with personal stories, correlating brand examples, bullet point recommendations and chapter wrap-ups that can be shared, discussed and implemented. And we covered a lot of ground together.

Let's reflect on the key take-aways.

In the course of this book, I've…

- **Defined organizational culture**—as a collection of individual behaviors; distinctly different from Heritage (the past)
- **Outlined the analogous correlation between rock bands and business brands**—that as people join or leave, the culture changes
- **Identified "personal culture shifts"**—the defining moments in a person's life that contribute to the development of his or her personality, behaviors and expectations
- **Encouraged you to be the catalyst for change in your company**—starting with a mindset, then evolving into specific actions within your circle of influence

- **Laid the groundwork to prepare you for your impending culture change**—by encouraging you to focus only on those things within your direct circle of impact…knowing your influence will grow
- **Pointed out how leadership can dramatically affect organizational culture**—that these key individuals have the power to light up or extinguish the cultural flame of a company
- **Touted "service" as the biggest cultural opportunity**—for companies that sell a product or provide a service
- **Demonstrated the importance of differentiated service delivery**—knowing that today's public craves service that is customized and personalized for them
  - Showcased many examples of companies that do this well—iconic service veterans as well as lesser-known culture warriors
  - Highlighted that phenomenal service trumps product, price, theme and convenience, regardless of the business or industry
- **Pushed for the avoidance of "acceptable mediocrity" and its associated four-letter words (fine, good, okay)**—and offered techniques to keep you from getting into a sea of sameness with the rest of your competitors
  - Shared case studies of great service-oriented companies, in some unlikely industries (Healthcare, Death Care and Automotive Service Repair), that are taking cues from Hospitality
  - Demonstrated the benefits of providing irreverence and unpredictability as part of your service delivery
- **Emphasized the importance of hiring "right fit" employees**—knowing that they are the amplifiers that ultimately create unique experiences
  - Identified the three "C"s of potential rock star employees (Competence, Character, Cultural Fit)
  - Highlighted the diverse make-up of those individuals coming to work for us when we aspire to hire rock stars rather than lip-synchers
  - Provided some thoughts about where to find and how to recruit top talent
- **Covered in detail the key cultural drivers of today's workforce**:
  - Experience-obsessed

- Identity-oriented
- Visual learners with short attention spans
- Technology-dependent
- Purpose-driven/socially conscious
- **Stressed the importance of understanding and addressing those high-priority needs**—if there is to be any real hope of attracting and retaining the right brand ambassadors in the future
- **Highlighted the need for well-developed communication throughout the organization**—to keep everyone singing off the same song sheets
- **Provided an organizational business philosophy for developing brand loyalty**—having your Values (what you say) match up to your Methods (what you do)
  - The by-products produced will be Profitable Growth and Promotable People

I sincerely hope that the information I've shared here will be valuable to you in your quest to enhance your company's culture. I encourage you to use this book as a workbook as you and your team map out the steps you can take to immediately improve your company's cultural makeup and eventually meet long-term strategic goals. Go back over the "Greatest Hits That Rock" section at the end of each chapter to keep those key points fresh in your mind. Even better, go over each question or discussion prompt in the "This is How You Roll" section with your team, and see how you stack up to those cultural metrics. This work might be the exact spark you need to really address and improve your company's current cultural framework.

Again, I realize that you may just be trying to hold onto a great organizational environment that already exists—or perhaps you've embarked on a journey to get back the "good ole days" of a culture long gone. Regardless, you can absolutely change things for the better. The process won't always be easy—it might even be unpopular at times—but keep in mind that "revolutions are started by a single person with a great idea."

You can be that person. You now have the resources and guidance to begin a cultural shift.

I have been involved in all stages of organizational culture change throughout my life, but never more so than during my illustrious career at Hard Rock. I can assure you that I am not the same person I was before I joined that brand. It changed me. The spirit of Rock 'n' Roll—combined with the unique people that worked there—changed me. But during my 21 years with the company, I also had a part in maintaining, tweaking and re-directing the Hard Rock culture. The brand is not the same because of me. I know…that's a bold statement. But I have to believe it's true. Luckily, I had supportive bosses and an army of giants around me to help continue the heritage born of an earlier generation. But I also worked hard to make a difference and enhance the brand's culture.

This can be true for you. You can help create a "culture that rocks."

In many ways, I envy you and the path that you may be taking—mostly because I personally love evolving with and changing the rules. I love challenging the status quo in the hopes of making things better. I appreciate what these shared concepts might ultimately do for your company's culture. I know the value and power these resources have, because I have been fortunate enough to see and experience them firsthand. It's downright exciting. I only wish I could be there to watch the cultural progression occur for you.

Even as I type these final words for you to consider, I find myself channeling my inner Steve Perry by imagining Journey's "Don't Stop Believin'" blaring in the background. And you shouldn't stop believing. You can do this. You can be the catalyst. I have faith.

Now take a deep breath and collect your thoughts before you share your ideas with the team.

Then start the revolution.

BAND & BRAND REFERENCES

A

AC/DC 10, 126
Adam Clayton 209
Alan Schaefer 152
Alice 104
Amanda Hite 197, 203
Amazon 26
American Idol 201
American Nurses Credentialing Center 90
Amy Winehouse 57
Apple 26, 46, 47, 95, 107, 117, 128, 133, 180
Applebee's 1
Ari Weinzweig 240, 241, 242, 243, 248
Ashlee Simpson 102
A Slice of the Pie 35
AutoTune 102
Axum Coffee 197, 199

B

Banding People Together 152
Barry Manilow 153
Bavaria Hotel Management School 87
Best Buy 48
Be The Change Revolutions 203, 204
Billy Corgan 101
Blue Cross Blue Shield 96
Bob Dylan 21, 136
Boeing 234
Boloco 215, 216, 217
Bono 147, 151, 175, 205, 209
Brad Paisley 117
Brandon Hill 149, 203
Bruce Springsteen 221
Buffalo Wild Wings 245

C

Capital One 96
Caring Capitalism 189
Carol Burnett 103
Carol Shipley 77, 78

Cartoon Network 75
Causecast 199, 200
Certified Green 215
Changers of Commerce 190, 198
Checker's/Rally's 245
Cher 187
Chick-fil-A 26, 111, 112, 113
Child Hunger Ends Here 201
Chili's 188
Cinnabon 26, 32, 33, 189
Circuit City 48
CNN 190
CNN Money 117
Coca-Cola 26, 38, 95, 189
Collaborative Harmony Index (CHI) 152
Colleen Barrett 23
Columbia Asia Hospitals 87, 88
Communities in Schools 202
ConAgra Foods 201
Connected Capitalism 189, 190, 199, 207
Conscious Capitalism 189
Cornerstone 125
Council of Hotel and Restaurant Trainers 195, 245
Creative Capitalism 189
Cultural Self-Awareness Survey 28

D

David Bowie 79, 157
David Holmes 132, 133
Detroit Institute of Arts 87
Devina Sengupta 88
Dine Out for No Kid Hungry 202
DiSC 151
Don't Stop Believin' 254
Doritos 73

E

Earth Day 191
Eddie Van Halen 3
Elvis Presley 160
Entertainment Weekly 94

F

Facebook 109, 176, 177, 203, 240, 246, 247
Famous Dave's 2, 245
Farm Aid 151
Fast Company Magazine 169, 171, 202
FedEx 26
Feeding America 201
Fergie 24
Fill a Heart 201
First, Break All the Rules 153
First Watch 26
FISH! 49
Fish Morgan 71, 72, 107
Five Guys Burgers 38, 117
Flo (Alice) 104
Florida Keys 77
Fortune 100 134
Fortune 500 26, 209, 245
Fortune Magazine 23, 93
Fortune Management 117
Four Seasons 96
Freddie Mercury 229

G

Gallup Inc./Organization 74, 217, 218
Geek Squad 26
General Electric 234
Gene Simmons 24
Genesis 233
Global Hope Network International 197, 198
Google 24, 26, 47, 123, 177
Graham Cohen 183
Green Day 151
Green Mountain 94
Greg Coomer 171
Guides to Greatness 166, 171

H

Half-Life 169
Hard Rock International 1-254
Harley-Davidson 26, 85, 107, 133, 154
Harry Bond 235, 236

Harvard Business School Publishing (HBSP) 235
Hayley Williams 83
Health Care Design Magazine 88
Heart-Centered Leadership 218, 219
Henry Ford Health System 87
Home Depot 26, 234
Hooters 32
Hospital Consumer Assessment of Healthcare Providers and Systems 89
HotSchedules 179
Howard Schultz 27, 69
Hummer 86

I

Icee 86, 91
IKEA 26, 167, 173
Inc. Magazine 35
Independence Airlines 73, 74, 75, 91
In-N-Out Burger 26, 37
Intelligentsia 199
Interim HealthCare 245
Isaac Tigrett 31, 51, 52, 103, 106, 196
Island Bay Resort 77, 78

J

Jack Welch 234, 236
James Carville 74
James McNerney 234
Janelle Reents 236
Jeff Power 198, 199
Jeffrey Immelt 234
Jellyfish 72
Jen Tierno 245
Jessica Watson 87
Jiffy Lube 96, 97
Jimi Hendrix 187
Jimmy Buffet 22
Joel Bennett 218
Joe Tierno 245
John Pepper 216
Journey 254
Justin Timberlake 204

K

Kanye West 83
Kat Cole 32, 33, 36, 189
Kate Podmore 76
Kathleen Wood 245, 248
Keith Richards 67
Ken Blanchard 23, 61
KISS 24, 107
Kuerig 94
Kurt Cobain 141, 211

L

Lady Gaga 106, 154
Lancaster General Hospital 88, 90
Larry Mullen Jr. 209
Last In Concepts 245
Led Zeppelin 3
LEGO 26, 37, 95
Liam Gallagher 38
Linked-In 203
Loews Hotel 75
Louis Basile 202
Lucille Ball 103

M

Macy's 181
Madonna 79
Magnet Recognition Program 90
ManageMentor 235
Marcus Buckingham 153, 217
Marie Callender's 245
Market Metrix 74
Mary Matalin 74
Mayberry, USA 197
McAlister's Deli 245
McDonald's 1, 96, 112
Mel's Diner 104
Member of the British Empire 105
Michael Kneidinger 58, 131
Michael Rawls 70
Michelangelo 148
Mickey Mouse 68
Mick Jagger 67
Microsoft 128
Mike Shipley 16, 77, 78

Milli Vanilli 102
Monical's Pizza 235, 236
Muzak 121
Myers-Briggs Type Indicator (MBTI) 151

N

NASA 134
National Restaurant Association 2
NBC Nightly News 35
NBC's The Today Show 78
Neil Peart 24
Neil Young 151
Neville Isdell 189
Nick Sarillo 33, 34, 35, 36
Nick's Pizza & Pub 33, 35, 36
Nike 24, 26, 247
Nintendo 136
Nirvana 141, 211
Noel Gallagher 38
No Kid Hungry 190, 191, 201, 202
Nordstrom 38, 67, 68, 69, 70
NOW Church 78

O

Oasis 38, 39
Open Book Finance 242
OpenStack 134
Oprah Winfrey 26
Oreos 73

P

Panera Bread 188
Pangeo Tea & Coffee 94, 197, 198, 199
Paramore 83
Partners in Leadership 39
Paul McCartney 131
Paul Saginaw 240
People Magazine 95
People Matter 245
People Report 121
Peter Beaudrault 229, 230
Peter Drucker 5
Peter Gabriel 233
Peter Morton 51, 52, 103, 105, 106, 196
Peter Pan 112

Peter Parker 38
Pete Townshend 24
Phil Collins 233
Phil Knight 27
Pike Place Fish Market 49, 123
Pixar 26
Pleasantville 60
polleverywhere.com 177
Portal 169
Portofino Hotel 75
Publix Supermarkets 26
Punta Cana Hard Rock Hotel & Casino 76

Q

Queen 229

R

Rackspace 134, 135
Raising Cane's Chicken Fingers 245
Raving Fans 61
Red Bull 26
Renee Malone 240
Richard Branson 18, 27, 133
Richard Perinchief 78
Rihanna 123
Rita Gilligan 104, 105, 106
Ritz-Carlton 26, 87
Robert Nardelli 234
Rock 101 229, 230
Roger Daltrey 209
Rolling Stone Magazine 95
Ronnie James Dio 67
Rudolf the Red-Nosed Reindeer 131
Rush 24
Ryan Scott 199

S

Scott Stratten 240
Second Life 235
Send Flowers to the Living 214
Service-Profit Chain 50, 159
Seth Godin 37
Shannon Kraus 88

Share Our Strength 190
Shreya Biswas 88
Skype 199
Slipknot 149
Smashing Pumpkins 101
Smells Like Teen Spirit 211
Southwest Airlines 23, 26, 73, 74, 125, 131, 132, 133
Spider-Man 38
Splick.it 200, 201
Starbucks 26, 68, 69, 70, 86, 94, 98, 107, 124, 125, 133, 199
Star Trek 137
Stephen Covey 29
Steve Jobs 27, 46, 47, 117, 118, 180
Steve Perry 254
StrengthsFinder 151
Stumptown 199
Sue Tierno 245
Super Flour Power 202
Susan G. Komen Breast Cancer Foundation 202
Susan Steinbrecher 218
Suzy's Swirl 245, 246, 247, 248
Sven Gierlinger 87

T

3M 234
Take 5 183
talentminded.com 35
Taylor Swift 45, 83
TDn2K 2, 245
TGI Friday's 1
The Beatles 39
The Borg 137, 205
The Container Store 26, 91, 92, 93, 117
The Dave Matthews Band 22
The Economic Times 87, 88
The Edge 209
The E-Street Band 221
The Experience Economy 95
The Grateful Dead 21, 126
The Oberoi Group 88
The Oz Principle 39
The Rolling Stones 67
The Seven Habits of Highly Effective People 29

The Times They Are A-Changin' 136
The Who 24, 209
Tim Horton's 97, 98
Titanic 45
TJ Schier 214
Tom Perez 72
TOMS 188
Tony Hsieh 169
Tori Amos 5
Tori Kelly 201
Training Magazine 4, 96
Training Top 125 96
TripAdvisor.com 77, 78
True Colors 151
Tufan Ghosh 88
Tupac Shakur 11
Twitter 110, 175, 177, 203, 204

U

U2 147, 175, 205, 209, 227
Undercover Boss 33
Universal Studios' Citywalk 75
University of Florida 87
USA Today 46, 70, 94

V

Valve Software 169, 170, 171
Victoria Secret 26
Virgin Airlines 18, 24, 26, 38, 133

W

Walt Disney 68
Walt Disney World 26, 37, 68, 69, 70, 91
Wawa 141, 142, 143
Wells Fargo 96
Whole Foods 26, 37, 117, 188
Wikipedia 177
Wildflower Bread Company 202, 203
Willie Nelson 151
Women's Foodservice Forum 245

Y

Yellow Dog Eats 71, 72
YouTube 150, 177, 201

Z

Zappos 95, 133, 135, 169, 170
Zappos.com 26, 123, 168
Zingerman's Community of Businesses
240, 241, 242, 243, 244, 248
Ziploc 76
Zzang! bar 243